Bernini's portrait bust of Cardinal Scipio Caffarelli Borghese, the nephew of Paul V (1605–21).

astonishment the austerity and asceticism of Paul IV (1555–9) or the zealous devotion to the purifying of morals of Pius V (1566–72). Humanists and poets, along with the artists, disappeared from Rome. Under Pius V the papal court became a model of decorum, and the numerous prostitutes, who for long had held a position of prominence in Roman society, were banished from the city or restricted to special quarters. Moral reclamation, not the adornment of the city or the building or restoration of churches, was the feature of the anti-aesthetic period of the Counter-Reformation.

As the conviction grew that the tide had been rolled back, and that the victory lay with the Catholic Church in the struggle against the Northern reformers, a change came with the pontificate of Sixtus V (1585–90), who has left his personal imprint on modern Rome. Sixtus anticipated later town-planners by designing straight streets (such as the 'Strada Felice', part of which, the Via Sistina, commemorates his name) and enlarging squares (the Piazza del Popolo – completed by Valadier in the early nineteenth

century – and the Piazza S. Maria Maggiore), which he adorned with obelisks and fountains, thus initiating those scenographic vistas that are so much a feature of Rome. Religious leaders arose to meet the times: St Ignatius of Loyola, St Teresa, St Charles Borromeo and St Philip Neri. St Ignatius' *Spiritual Exercises* had been approved as early as 1548, and in 1568 Vignola began Il Gesù, as the church of the Society of Jesus which had been formed in 1540. In 1575 Pope Gregory XIII formally recognized St Philip Neri's Oratory, with its church of S. Maria in Vallicella (also known as the Chiesa Nuova).

This new age in Roman art and architecture, expressing the Church Triumphant, came to maturity with the pontificate of the Borghese Pope Paul V (1605–21), and was continued under his successors, notably Urban VIII, Innocent X and Alexander VII. It was during this period that so much that is distinctive of Roman church architecture was built. As in the days of Bramante, Raphael and Michelangelo, Rome became again the focus of artistic creativity, the centre to which artists of all nations made their way, and it remained the aesthetic capital of the West until it was superseded by the Paris and Versailles of Louis XIV.

The conscious aim of Sixtus V and his successors was to express the glorious victory of the Church over the heretics by the beautifying of Rome. Their aim was to make it a city worthy of the capital of Christendom – by the laying out of streets and piazzas, the rebuilding of churches, the construction of palaces and villas, and by their decoration with precious marbles, statuary, stucco-work, frescoes, paintings and gilding of a lavishness and richness hitherto unseen. A new spirit pervaded the age, when even religious ecstasy could be expressed by Bernini in terms of a physical sensuousness scarcely distinguishable from sexuality. The beauty of the naked female form adorned the monumental tombs of popes, later to be clothed out of respect for the prejudices of a less spontaneous age. The uncertainties, hesitations and experiments of Mannerism, which had succeeded the first Renaissance, gave way to the self-conscious certainty of High Baroque, which may be looked on, if only on account of the volume of artistic creativity associated with it, as a second Renaissance.

If all this magnificence (unparalleled since the Imperial age) could be attributed *ad maiorem gloriam Dei et Ecclesiae*, this was not the motive that was uppermost in the minds of many of its chief patrons. Often a genuine connoisseurship, a love of art for art's sake (quite contrary to the admonitions of the Council of Trent), was backed by the more questionable desire to glorify the patron's name among his contemporaries and to perpetuate it for posterity. Outstanding among such patrons was the favourite nephew of Pope Paul V, Cardinal

Scipio Caffarelli Borghese. He shared in the post-Tridentine euphoria of his age; in fact, he appears as the living embodiment of its *joie de vivre*. His conversation was sparkling, his banquets were famous, his aesthetic taste was both discriminating and catholic, his expenditure as patron of artists unrivalled in its prodigality. His well-known bust by Bernini, whose precocious genius he was the first to recognize and patronize, stands today in the gallery of the Villa Borghese, which he had built for him on the Pincio by his favourite architect, Flaminio Ponzio. (It was completed on the latter's death in 1613 by the Dutchman known to Italians as Vasanzio.) Bernini represents the Cardinal in all his full-blooded vitality, his head poised in self-assurance, his eyes alert, his lips slightly open, as if caught in animated conversation. He built the Villa Borghese (one among several country villas and town palaces) to house his art collections, which contained, besides much antique and modern sculpture, works by such artists as Raphael, Titian, Veronese, Dossi, Domenichino, Lanfranco, Guercino and Guido Reni. This aristocratic connoisseur also encouraged Caravaggio, whose works he bought at a time when this revolutionary artist was not yet accepted by conventional taste. It was perhaps as a salve to his priestly conscience that the Cardinal rebuilt many churches, among them S. Sebastiano fuori le Mura (by Ponzio, completed by Vasan-

zio), the façade of S. Maria della Vittoria (by G. B. Soria), the façade and forecourt of S. Gregorio Magno (Soria's masterpiece) and S. Crisogono in Trastevere (also by Soria). Though the last is dedicated to S. Crisogono, on the lintel of each and every doorway, carved in finely formed Roman lettering, appears the Cardinal's name, SCIPIO BURGHESIUS. The glory, its recognition, was to be his alone.

If Rome is seen today as a city predominantly Mannerist and Baroque in its architecture – with, nevertheless, some outstanding examples of the times of the Renaissance – this view, unless qualified, can be profoundly misleading. The magnificence that first meets the eye is certainly there on the surface. Yet the visitor, if he pauses to look beyond the external, will find a different Rome, a Rome that is unexpectedly discreet and reserved, at once intimate and reticent. There is a Rome unobserved as well as a Rome observed. And the truth of this is no better exemplified than in the city's churches. In the centre of the city, in the Corso itself, next to the Palazzo Doria, stands the church of S. Maria in Via Lata, with its splendidly bold Baroque façade by Pietro da Cortona, an interplay of surface light and recessed shadow. Tradition has it that this was built over the house in which St Paul lived and in which he wrote his Epistle to the Hebrews. In support of this tradition are pieces

PAGE 13 In the ancient Benedictine cemetery beside S. Gregorio Magno three chapels (*c.* 1607) by Flaminio Ponzio recall the lives of St Gregory the Great and his mother St Sylvia. In the centre the Chapel of St Andrew, with its portico of ancient columns, is built over the Oratory of St Gregory.

PAGE 14 The twelfth-century portico of S. Giorgio in Velabro is raised on four antique columns of the Ionic order, flanked by sturdy angular pilasters in brick, which are capped by marble, with a finely-cut decorative design of squares on the diagonal. On the left are the ruins of the Arch of the Moneylenders, erected in AD 204 in honour of the Emperor Septimius Severus.

PAGE 15 One of the finest examples of Roman Romanesque is the twelfth-century campanile of S. Maria in Cosmedin, the church of the Greek community, framed here by the fluted columns of what was formerly known as the Temple of Vesta but is in fact a temple dedicated to the Conquering Hercules dating from the end of the second century BC.

Introduction:
The Eternal City

Rome, more than any other comparable metropolis, is a city of churches. If this is a commonplace, yet the aspect of Rome that first strikes the visitor, especially if he is a northerner or of a puritanical turn of mind, is the apparent lack, at least on the surface, of those qualities that could be vaguely termed spiritual. He is struck by the worldliness of all this grandeur, this opulent display in the capital of Christendom. In the palaces, the squares with their fountains and obelisks, the lofty columns surmounted by haloed figures, the flamboyant façades of churches, he finds little at first to suggest that the source from which all these derive is the teaching of Christ. The debris of centuries and the accretions of stone and stucco have seemingly obliterated all traces of the footsteps of the Galilean Fisherman. If, charitably, he allows that this magnificence could have been raised to the greater glory of God, more realistically he might confess that it was designed more for the very human glory of the della Rovere, the Borghese, the Barberini. If the Papacy was built on the blood of martyrs, papal Rome was paid for with Peter's pence, the offerings of the nameless faithful.

The face that Rome presents today is predominantly that which it received under the impulse of the Counter-Reformation. The preponderant style of architecture is what was known until recently by the generic term Baroque, almost

universally condemned by the Victorians as a tasteless and undisciplined exuberance of forms, a falling-away from the purity of style of the essentially Tuscan and Umbrian Renaissance or from the warm simplicity of Lombard Romanesque. Tastes, with the times, have changed. Since the end of the last century, when Heinrich Wölfflin first published his researches into the stylistic developments that led architects away from the Renaissance principles of Alberti and Bramante to what he called the 'Baroque' style of the seventeenth century, art historians have clarified and defined the stages of that transition by the use of the term Mannerist. This covers the period between the architectural innovations of Michelangelo (who died in 1564) and his successors, and the fully developed High Baroque of three seventeenth-century masters: Bernini, Borromini and Pietro da Cortona. The Rome that greets the eye of the visitor today is pre-eminently Mannerist and Baroque, with a few examples of later 'classicizing' Rococo. Of Romanesque and even Renaissance building (particularly of churches) there remains comparatively little.

This gap has sometimes been thought attributable to the Sack of Rome by the troops of the Emperor Charles v in 1527, when they stabled their horses in St Peter's and the Vatican and gave the city over to arson and indiscriminate pillage. Nothing that was moveable remained. Some churches suffered structurally, notably S. Spirito in Sassia, which was almost entirely destroyed; but what Rome chiefly lost were treasures of art — precious objects of gold, silver and enamels, tapestries, statues, paintings and books. The main destroyers of Rome, however, have always been the Romans themselves – far more destructive than Goths, Lombards, Saracens, Normans, Lutheran *landsknechts* or Revolutionary-inspired French. In the Middle Ages they burnt for lime the marble which the Roman emperors had used for columns or with which they had faced the temples and public buildings. On the ending of the Babylonian Captivity in Avignon and of the Great Schism, with the return to Rome of the Colonna Pope Martin V on 30 September 1420, a series of popes set about repairing the ruins brought about by the corroding passage of time, the devastation wrought by factional warfare, and the neglect caused by the lack of capital resulting from the long absence of the Papacy – which had been the chief, indeed the sole, source (since there was little or no industry or commerce) of the revenue of the Romans.

It was in Central and Northern Italy – in the cities of Tuscany and Umbria, or at such princely courts as those of the Visconti, della Scala, Gonzaga and d'Este – that from the fourteenth century there occurred a stirring of men's minds and imaginations which heralded the revival of letters and the decisive development in the arts of sculpture, painting and architecture which characterize the Renaissance. In this movement the lead was soon taken by Florence, a city rich by reason of its industry, trade and financial interests. At the unofficial court of the banker Cosmo de' Medici (1389–1464), encouragement was given to artists and scholars, and to the recovery of lost classical *codices*; Florence became the cradle of the humanists. In 1447 the humanists made a successful take-over bid for the Papacy with the election of the scholarly Tommaso Parentucelli, who took the name of Nicholas V. With him, as Gregorovius remarked, 'the Christian Renaissance ascended the papal throne'. From the time of his pontificate Rome, rather than Medicean Florence, was the centre of the Renaissance world, and it was to the popes that architects, painters, sculptors and humanists looked for patronage. Nicholas V 'inaugurated the Maecenetian era of the Papacy'. With the help of the Florentine Alberti (one of the characteristic all-round men of the Renaissance – at once athlete, scholar, painter, mathematician, architect, man of the world and much else besides), Nicholas V drew up comprehensive plans for the reconstruction of the Leonine City, which included the Vatican and St Peter's. This period was not so much remarkable for the attention given to church-building – though notable exception must be made for, among others, Sixtus IV's S. Maria del Popolo, Cardinal Riario's S. Lorenzo in Damaso (by Bramante), Leo X's S. Giovanni dei Fiorentini and S. Maria in Domnica, Bramante's Tempietto of S. Pietro in Montorio, and, of course, the rebuilding of St Peter's, begun by Nicholas V. It was rather for the splendour of its church decoration, to execute which the popes summoned the finest

An engraving of Sixtus V (1585–90) illustrating also some of the major works undertaken in Rome during his pontificate.

artists of the day, almost all of whom were non-Roman. Much of this art perished in the Sack of Rome, but much also from the will of individual popes. The imperious Julius II caused Raphael and Michelangelo to destroy paintings by their predecessors (some by such a master as Piero della Francesca), to make way for their own masterpieces in the Vatican Stanze and the Sistine Chapel.

The torture, rape and murder, the destruction and sacrilege witnessed by Romans during the Sack were a traumatic shock (some religious-minded saw in these events the mark of divine retribution) which compelled thinking men, after their first bewilderment, to consider church reform, to take place universally 'in head and members'. Most artists who had escaped left Rome. The period which followed, from 1527 until the final session of the Council of Trent in December 1563, was a hiatus which allowed the Church to take stock of its position, a time of soul searching and reinvigoration in the religious sense. Men who had lived through the golden age of Leo X (1513–21) would have regarded with incredulous

Contents

OVERLEAF The veneration of the faithful:
votive candles burning before a
Byzantine-inspired icon of the *Madonna
and Child* in S. Maria in Cosmedin.

Acknowledgements

We wish to express our thanks to all those people, both
ecclesiastical and lay, to whom we are indebted for the help
which they so readily gave us, among them His Excellency the
Most Reverend Archbishop Bruno Heim, the Apostolic
Delegate in Great Britain; Monsignor G. B. Re of the Secretariat
of State at the Vatican; Monsignor Dr Charles Burns
of the Vatican Library; Marjorie Weeke of the Pontifical
Commission for Social Communications; and Signor
Paolo Boffa.

Roloff Beny particularly wishes to thank Joseph Natanson
who, with his intimate and discriminating knowledge of Rome's
churches and their art treasures, dedicated so much of his
valuable time in the course of the photography. Further, he
acknowledges with gratitude the assistance given by Antonella
Carini, who supervised the archiving of his Rome studio, and
by Aileen Armellini and David Garstang, who uncovered with
him special aspects of this rich field

Our warmest thanks are due to Elizabeth Kilham Roberts,
who placed her extensive acquaintance with Rome and love for
all things Roman unreservedly at our disposal. Her painstaking
research, and time-consuming task of securing permissions and
entry to not always easily accessible churches and convents, have
smoothed the way over many difficulties. The map of Rome, the
ground-plans of churches and the provision of early photographs
and engravings are largely her work: we are deeply aware of how
much we owe her.

ROLOFF BENY
PETER GUNN

THE CHURCHES OF
ROME

ROLOFF BENY
& PETER GUNN

Weidenfeld and Nicolson · London

Editorial director: Mark Boxer

George Weidenfeld and Nicolson Limited
91 Clapham High Street   London SW4

ISBN 0 297 77903 6

Filmset and printed in Great Britain by
BAS Printers Limited, Over Wallop, Hampshire

THE CHURCHES OF
ROME

OVERLEAF Two of the thirteen huge
figures representing *The Redeemer, St John
the Baptist* and *The Twelve Apostles*
(except St Peter) which crown the
balustrade of Carlo Maderno's façade
(1607–14) of St Peter's.

of masonry of the first centuries AD, which have been found deep beneath the church, on the level with the Roman Via Lata, the original name of the Corso. An oratory, which can be visited, was built where the church now stands. Here we are close, in something more than the imagination, to the apostolic age.

Not only in the catacombs is Rome a subterranean city. From the fourth century and even earlier, but more especially from the time of Constantine the Great, Roman builders, when erecting new buildings, converted parts of existing structures or simply filled them in with rubble and raised their dwellings and churches above. The result is that the Rome of the Caesars lies in places some twenty-three to thirty-three feet below the present surface. Ecclesiastical archaeologists, excavating under some of the older churches, have penetrated layer below layer, to reveal what is truly a palimpsest of earlier churches. In the beautiful basilica of S. Clemente, ablaze with the richness of twelfth-century mosaics, frescoes and Cosmati work, the visitor can enter three successive places of Christian worship, built one on top of the other from the first to the twelfth centuries. The original Roman house, in a room of which the faithful first gathered, apparently belonged to one Clement, possibly a relative of the consul-martyr Titus Flavius Clemens. Next door to his house was a *Mithraeum*, which too can be visited; here a contemporary fresco depicts

Mithras plunging his knife into the bull, the bloody sacrifice that was central to this widely spread cult, the powerful rival to nascent Christianity. The victory of the Church was signalled by building a Christian church over the now deserted *Mithraeum*.

But it is not only below ground that one can come upon this more unobtrusive, even austere, Rome. When Baroque accretions have been stripped away by restorers, the early church stands revealed in the simplicity and purity of a different age of faith. It demands a width of aesthetic sensibility, a catholicity of taste, to pass from the almost domestic intimacy of S. Maria in Cosmedin and S. Giorgio in Velabro, from the tranquil beauty of S. Sabina on the Aventine or the tenebrous gravity of S. Lorenzo fuori le Mura, to the Baroque splendours of Il Gesù or the *trompe l'œil* in chromatic perspective of S. Ignazio – or, indeed, to the daunting, ceremonious magnificence of papal St Peter's. It also requires an historic sense, since much of Rome's history can be read in the fabric and decoration of its churches. Yet the reasons for the stylistic changes in ecclesiastical architecture are not all to be looked for in particular historical events – in the successive sackings, the Babylonian Captivity, the reconsolidation of the States of the Church, still less in the reunification of Italy. Some changes are to be found in purely internal developments within the Church itself – such as in

PAGE 17 The Colosseum under snow. A simple wooden cross symbolizes the cause in which so many early Christians suffered martyrdom here, in what was then known as the Flavian amphitheatre.

PAGE 18 One of the ten *Angels holding Symbols of the Passion* designed for Clement IX by Bernini and executed by his pupils, on the Ponte S. Angelo. The angels carved by Bernini himself are now in S. Andrea delle Fratte. The dome of St Peter's can be seen in the background.

PAGE 19 A little known but characteristically beautiful Baroque fountain in a courtyard near SS. Bonifacio e Alessio.

doctrinal requirements, and in the needs of new Orders. Others are more personal: the characters of popes and cardinals, or the presence of creatively original architects – Bramante, Bernini, Borromini. There is, however, an underlying conservatism in Roman church-building, so that one can talk meaningfully of a 'Roman style'. How much of this is a legacy of the city's Imperial past is perhaps impossible to gauge.

Nevertheless, the Church's claim to catholicity, its appeal to all kinds and conditions of men, may seem to be upheld in the multiform variety of its churches. Somewhere deep in the nature of the city itself, in its history, there lies a profound dichotomy that arose when the grandeur that was Rome was first challenged by the spiritual ideal represented by the Christian Church. To Europeans of all periods the name 'Rome' has signified something other and more than just a city. It has connoted qualities that are difficult to define, perhaps impossible to express, and it has meant different things to different men at the same time, and at different times. To St Paul and the early Christians Rome represented Babylon – 'the whore of Babylon'. To Charlemagne it stood for the resuscitation of the Imperial idea, the merging of temporalities with spiritualities. To St Catherine of Siena Rome was the spiritual centre of Christendom, and the return there of the popes from the fleshpots of Avignon was essential to its religious mission. But the hedonistic threat persisted. If the perhaps apocryphal remark of Leo x is to be accepted, Rome and the Papacy were granted to him by God for his enjoyment. Cardinal Scipio Borghese's sense of enjoyment was infinite; he welcomed Rome with open arms and a generous hand. Despite the Church, to Cavour and Garibaldi Rome was a political goal; for them it was the symbol of a reunited Italy.

Beneath this complexity of individual response there lies an ambivalence that arises from the opposition of the material to the spiritual – of the this-worldly to the other-worldly. The aesthetic and the ascetic, like the lion and the lamb, are uneasy bedfellows; yet with the Romans the beauty of this world, and its grandeur, will keep breaking through, part of their Hellenistic, Mediterranean heritage. An inborn hedonism has seldom been far below the surface. A visitor to Rome today finds it is only a short step, although a far cry, from the crowded, fashionable cafés of the Via Vittorio Veneto down the street to the Capuchin church of S. Maria della Concezione. Here, in a subterranean chamber, the confectioner's art is displayed in the decorative pattern of human skulls and bones in the monks' ossuary. It is so brief a passage from the world of *la dolce vita* to that of *memento mori*. To Romans it has always been so. In this respect, too, Rome remains *Roma aeterna*, the eternal city.

PAGE 20 The unfinished Romanesque-Gothic brick façade of S. Maria d'Aracoeli (thirteenth century), seen from Michelangelo's Piazza del Campidoglio, where stand two giant figures from the Imperial Age – Castor and Pollux. In the background rises the colossal nineteenth-century monument to Victor Emmanuel II.

PAGE 21 S. Rocco, the church of the Confraternity of Innkeepers and Boatmen of Rome's riverside port, the Ripetta, was founded in 1499 by Alexander VI (Borgia). Rebuilt to plans of G. A. De Rossi in 1657, its nineteenth-century façade was erected in 1834 to the designs of G. Valadier, who had been influenced clearly by Palladio.

PAGE 22 The splendid interior of S. Maria d'Aracoeli. Above the high altar is a venerated tenth-century painting of the *Madonna*. The paving is thirteenth-century Cosmatesque. On the left a mosaic-inlaid pillar is part of one of the two Cosmati pulpits remade from the single *ambo* of Lorenzo di Cosma and his son Giacomo (signed, *c.* 1200).

ABOVE The façade (1599) of S. Nicola in Carcere is by G. Della Porta. The church was built in and from the remains of the Temple of Juno and two smaller temples, columns from which can be seen in the external wall on the left. The campanile (restored) was adapted from one of the fortified towers with which Rome bristled in the Middle Ages.

PAGE 25 In the Piazza della Minerva, in front of the Renaissance doorway (1453) of S. Maria sopra Minerva, stands Bernini's charming little elephant, supporting with stoical passivity an ancient Egyptian obelisk (sixth century BC). The elephant was carved by Ercole Ferrata (1667).

PAGES 26–7 View of the skyline of Rome from the Palazzo Senatorio, overlooking Michelangelo's Piazza del Campidoglio. On the right the unfinished façade of S. Maria d'Aracoeli faces the dome and apsidal end of Il Gesù. In the centre the bizarre corkscrew lantern of S. Ivo alla Sapienza rises to the right of the dome of S. Agnese in Agone. On the left is the dome of S. Andrea della Valle, second only in its dimensions to that of St Peter's.

1
The Roman Church in the Age of Persecution ·

The unique position of the Roman Church owes much to the political position of Rome as the capital of the Empire, but more particularly to the well-established tradition of the presence and deaths there of St Peter, the accepted Chief among the Apostles, and St Paul, the Apostle to the Gentiles, whose authority was from the first not merely local but widely acknowledged. Although there is no historical evidence to support the claim, tradition has it that St Peter was in Rome at the time of Claudius (or that of Caligula, *c*. 39). For St Paul's presence in the city there are firmer grounds.

In his Epistle to the Romans, written in 58, Paul mentions by name no fewer than twenty-four of the faithful, attesting to an already flourishing Christian community in the Empire's capital: 'My greetings to Priscilla and Aquila. ... My greetings to Tryphaena and Tryphosa, who have worked for the Lord so well; and dear Persis, too; she has been long in the Lord's service.' The protracted judicial proceedings against Paul in Palestine meant deferring his proposed missionary journey to Spain, but in 61 his appeal to Caesar brought him to Rome. He landed at Pozzuoli, and the Christians went out from Rome to meet him some miles along the Appian Way. During his two-year sojourn in the city, which ended in his acquittal, he continued his proselytizing among both Jews and Gentiles.

In the summer of 64 a conflagration, begun by accident or, as many people believed, at the instigation of the Emperor Nero himself, destroyed much of Rome. Nero cast the blame on the Christians; many were seized, summarily condemned and put to death. This was the first major persecution of the Roman Church. The historian Tacitus speaks of the great multitude who suffered at this time. The Emperor, to entertain his guests at a supper party at his villa on the Vatican Hill, gave orders that the Christians, 'the enemies of the human race', be dipped in pitch and set alight, illuminating the avenues and fountains of his gardens – flaming human torches against the dark green of the cypresses and holm-oaks. The courage with which men, women and children of all classes suffered martyrdom (for neither sex nor age was respected) was not lost on many Romans.

It was during the Neronian persecutions that St Peter and St Paul met their deaths as martyrs for their faith – AD 64 or 67 being the dates usually assigned to that of St Peter. He was crucified by the obelisk in the middle of Nero's circus (today this obelisk stands in the centre of the Piazza of St Peter's), and was buried in the catacomb of the matron Livia, now part of the crypt of St Peter's. St Paul was beheaded at a spot not far from the Ostian Road, known then as Ad Aquas Silvias, today as the Abbey of Le Tre Fontane, which is in the possession of the Trappist Fathers. Here, among the eucalyptus trees near the modern suburb of EUR (Esposizione Universale di Roma) is a group of three small churches: SS. Vincenzo ed Anastasio alle Tre Fontane (founded

RIGHT The Temple of Antoninus and Faustina, erected in the Forum in the mid-second century AD, was transformed in the eleventh century into the church of S. Lorenzo in Miranda. Demolished to reveal the Roman building in 1536, it was rebuilt in 1602 by Orazio Torriani.

by Honorius I in 625, rebuilt in 1221 and restored at the end of the last century), S. Maria Scala Coeli (built in 1583, commemorating St Bernard's vision of a stairway leading up to heaven) and S. Paolo alle Tre Fontane (fifth century, rebuilt in 1599). This last marks the place of the Apostle's execution. His body, wrapped in linen and spices, was recovered by the Roman matron Lucina and buried in her own vineyard in a lane off the Ostian Road, where today stands the basilica of S. Paolo fuori le Mura. Oratories were early built over the graves of both Apostles, and these venerable spots were visited by the growing Christian community of Rome and, increasingly with the passage of time, by pilgrims from farther afield.

It is usually held that Christianity first appealed to the underprivileged and uneducated, the poorest or servile classes. Two considerations, however, may qualify a too-ready acceptance that Christianity did not have early converts among the higher classes in Rome: the conversions among the senatorial order (and in the ruling Flavian family itself), and the social position of Roman matrons. All Roman citizens, whatever their status, were obliged to acknowledge the official religion, that of Rome and Augustus, by making sacrifices or offering incense on the altars of the temples which were built and dedicated to these deities throughout the Empire: a refusal to do this was accounted a treasonable offence, punishable with death. Both Titus Flavius Clemens, who in 95 was consul with the Emperor Domitian, and his wife Flavia Domitilla were Christians and suffered martyrdom for their faith on the orders of his relative, the Emperor. Their niece, another Flavia Domitilla, owned the cemetery and catacomb on the Via Appia, which today is known by her name, and here were buried many of the Christian Flavii. By an enlightened development of Roman law, Roman matrons could own and dispose of their property in their own right, and these virtually free women – matrons such as Livia, Lucina, Priscilla, Marcella or Proba, known to St Paul and tradition – were of immense service to the earliest Roman Church. Such women used – one might almost say, exploited – the privileged status of the Roman matron in furtherance of the Christian cause. The faithful met in their houses in Rome or in their villas in the nearby countryside, and it was they who were active in burying the martyrs during the persecutions under Nero and his successors, particularly Decius, Valerian and, in the closing years of his reign, Diocletian.

A house, or part of a house, set aside for Christian worship was first known as a 'church-house', and was named after the owner or donor as a 'title' – for example, the Titulus Ceciliae (S. Cecilia in Trastevere) or the Titulus Lucinae (S. Lorenzo in Lucina). St Paul wrote saluting Priscilla and Aquila, 'My greetings to the congregation that meets in their house.' Later these first churches were known as the 'house of God' (*Domus Dei*, or simply *Dominicum*, a name which survives today in S. Maria in Domnica). The Greek work *ecclesia* – 'church' – which eventually superseded the word *domus*, originally signified the Christian faithful, not the buildings in which they gathered. At the time of the persecutions there were twenty-five of these titles in Rome. In the church-houses and in the catacombs, the Christians met, prayed and waited during the darkest days. Some of the architectural complexities which these primitive churches exhibit arise from the fact that existing buildings were adapted for the use of the Christian congregation. The Roman villa, both within and outside the city limits, lent itself to such use, the catechumens being restricted to the *atrium*, while the officiating clergy and the initiated celebrated the Eucharist in one of the inner rooms. The bishop's house, the centre of ecclesiastical administration, seems at first to have been outside the city, possibly on the Via Salaria; later it appears to have been on the Via Appia, when, on the Peace of the Church, the Emperor Constantine removed what amounted to an administrative focus of the Church to the Lateran. Often, the bishop and his flock were driven to take shelter in the catacombs, and there, in more relaxed times, they gathered to share the *agapai* (love-feasts) or celebrated the Eucharist at the tombs of the martyrs. Eventually, these hallowed spots became places of pious pilgrimage.

Among the most ancient churches of Rome three are particularly associated with these earliest days, when the Christian faithful heroically faced the brutality of their persecutors, and by their perseverance in the face of death secured the eventual triumph of their faith: S. Pudenziana and S. Prassede (both on the rising ground of the Esquiline Hill, near the great basilica of S. Maria Maggiore), and S. Prisca (on the Aventine Hill).

Pudentiana and Praxedes are traditionally held to have been the daughters of the Senator Quintus Cornelius Pudens, at whose house St Peter may have been a frequent guest; further, it is said that they and their brother Novatus were the Apostle's first Roman converts. During the Neronian persecution, young and socially well-placed though they were, the sisters took it upon themselves to collect the charred or bloody remains of martyrs and to give them reverent burial. In the second century a thermal establishment, the Baths of Novatus, was built, incorporating the house of Pudens, and at the end of the fourth or early in the fifth century a basilica was raised over part of this (replacing an even earlier oratory) and dedicated to S. Pudenziana. There is a tradition that a church on this site was the oldest in Rome. Today the church stands well below the level of the Via Urbana and is approached by a double flight of steps, built in 1870 concurrently with the restoration of the façade, by Cardinal Luciano Bonaparte, grand-nephew to the Emperor Napoleon I and titular of S. Pudenziana. The mural on the façade, depicting St Peter, with Pudens and Pope Pius I on his right and Pudentiana and Pope Gregory VII on his left, was executed by Antonio Manno during work in the nineteenth-century restoration, when some of the fine earlier stonework was retained. The graceful campanile is of the early thirteenth century.

The interior, although the classical columns have survived, breathes the air of the late sixteenth century, when Cardinal Caetani commissioned Francesco da Volterra to strengthen and redecorate the ancient fabric. The latter (followed, after his death in 1601, by Carlo Maderno) built the Caetani Chapel on the left of the church, which, however, is out of keeping with the spirit of the place, with its over-rich adornment of polychrome marbles and stucco. Excavations have revealed sections of the second-century brickwork and paving, part of the *nymphaeum*, with its mosaic floor, of the Baths of Novatus, and, possibly, portions of the house of Senator Pudens. Outside the entrance to the Caetani Chapel is a well-head in which tradition has it that Pudentiana and her sister placed the remains of the martyrs. The Chapel of St Peter, at the far end of the left aisle, appears to correspond with an ancient oratory. In it is a good example of the sculpture of Giacomo Della Porta, the *Deliverance of the Keys* (1594). Behind the apse the Oratorio Mariano contains some interesting, though much faded, eleventh-century frescoes, which include *Madonna with SS. Pudenziana and Prassede* and *SS. Valerian, Tibertius and Urban*, the latter representing the three saints who were intimately connected with the martyrdom of St Cecilia.

But the glory of S. Pudenziana is its apse mosaics. These date from the end of the fourth century, and are thus stylistically in the classical tradition. They are among the most beautiful mosaics in Rome; some critics, indeed, consider them the finest. By an extraordinary act of vandalism Cardinal Caetani's restorer cut away a substantial part, depriving us of two of the marvellous mythological beasts which symbolize the Four Evangelists, two of the Twelve Apostles and the entire lower portion. The scene represents Jerusalem the Golden, with the church of the Holy Sepulchre. On a summer's morning the sunlight reveals the exquisite shades of the subdued colours, and, catching the ridges of the roof tiles of the church of the Holy Sepulchre, seems to set them aflame, so that they glow with a burnished ruddy gold. At the time when the mosaics were executed the belief that St Helena, mother of the Emperor Constantine, had discovered the True

Cross on Mount Calvary was fresh in men's minds, and it is shown here – with a symbolic prominence, richly studded with jewels – on the heights of Golgotha. Below it, seated on a throne, is the majestic figure of Christ, holding in his hand a book on which are inscribed the words, 'The Lord is the preserver of Pudentiana's church'. On either side of the Saviour stand the two Apostles, each highly individualized in appearance, and behind them the two sister saints present triumphal wreaths to St Peter and St Paul, shown as they are usually represented iconographically: St Peter with a full beard and head of thick white hair; St Paul swarthy, with aquiline nose, dark beard, eyebrows meeting above his nose and hair receding from his forehead. Above the buildings of the Heavenly Jerusalem the blue of the sky is disturbed by luminous, flame-like clouds, among which hover strange winged creatures, the lion of St Mark and the most realistic ox of St Luke. The Hellenistic naturalism is attained not only by fine modelling, but also by the subtlety and extraordinary delicacy of the colouring, which is perhaps unsurpassed among Roman mosaics. Here the Church Triumphant has adopted for its own service the art of pagan, classical Rome.

S. Pudenziana is buried in the church dedicated to her sister, S. Prassede. Today one enters S. Prassede from the narrow Via di S. Prassede, through a doorway leading into the right aisle. But it is worth while first to continue along the street and turn right into the Via S. Martino ai Monti. There one sees the main entrance portal, which is formed of two antique columns of granite, supporting the gable characteristic of these mediaeval Roman doorways, as we see them at S. Clemente, S. Maria in Cosmedin and S. Cosimato in Trastevere. On the site of the church of S. Prassede (where, by tradition, the house of Praxedes had stood) an oratory was built at an early date, to be superseded by a church, which was known in the fifth century as the Titulus Praxedis. The present church was erected by Pope Paschal I in 822, at the height of the iconoclastic controversy. The Roman Church was firmly opposed both to the destruction of images and to the neglect of the saints and martyrs, and Paschal, to do honour to S. Prassede and her sister S. Pudenziana, had their bodies brought here from their grandmother Priscilla's catacomb on the Via Salaria and enclosed in one of the beautiful palaeo-Christian sarcophagi which repose in the *confessio*, by the small altar which in the thirteenth century was exquisitely decorated in mosaic by the Cosmati. Paschal went further: he collected from the catacombs the remains of some thousands of martyrs and buried them in the crypts under S. Prassede and in the Chapel of S. Zeno there. An inscription on the wall of the church records this. And he showed his defiance of the iconoclastic decrees of Emperor

Leo the Isaurian and his successors on the throne of Constantinople and his desire to honour Christ, the Virgin and the Saints by commissioning the magnificent mosaics that dignify S. Prassede.

The original basilican character of the church, when sixteen antique pillars of granite separated the nave from the aisles, was later lost when piers were constructed to support the transverse arches needed for strengthening the thousand-year-old-building. The sixteenth-century restorations carried out by St Charles Borromeo, the titular of S. Prassede, were unfortunate. In the Olgiati Chapel – the third on the left – are the saint's chair and the table from where he daily fed the poor of his parish. He said Mass each day in the Chapel of the Flagellation, standing by the column of oriental jasper at which Christ is said to have been scourged, and he spent entire nights in prayer in the crypt. In the chapel to the right of the entrance from the Via di S. Prassede is the very fine tomb to Cardinal Anchero (d. 1286), attributed to Arnolfo di Cambio. Against the pier of the same aisle is a tomb with the bust of Bishop Santoni, sculpted by Bernini as a boy (c. 1610?). Besides S. Prassede's tomb, her church contains two other reminders of her life: in the centre of the nave a disc of porphyry covers the well in which she and her sister were supposed to have buried Christian martyrs; and at the foot of the left aisle, let into the wall, is the granite slab on which she is said to have slept.

But, as in her sister's church, so in S. Prassede it is the mosaics on the triumphal and tribune arches, in the apse and in the Chapel of S. Zeno that have pride of place. What is immediately apparent in these ninth-century mosaics is the loss of the power or desire to represent the sense of depth – the soft modelling of the Roman-inspired figures of S. Pudenziana has been replaced by flat, hierophantic, abstract forms; human beings have become highly stylized patterns of men and women. The Roman sisters have been metamorphosed into eastern empresses. In a word, the work reveals its Byzantine origin.

The two arches – the triumphal arch and that of the tribune – have the Apocalypse as their theme: 'And he carried me off in a trance to a great mountain, high up, and there showed me the holy city Jerusalem. . . . The light that shone over it was bright as any precious stone, as the jasper when it is most like crystal. . . .' On the triumphal arch Christ stands between two angels in the Heavenly Jerusalem,

S. Prassede and S. Pudenziana at his feet. The Apostles approach him, with John the Baptist and the Virgin Mary. To the left and right are Moses and Elijah with an angel, while two angels stand at the gates of the Heavenly City to welcome the Elect of the Lord. In the centre, above, is the monogram 'Paschal'. Two steps of *rosso antico* marble ascend to the tribune. (Napoleon had a mind to carry off this precious stone to form the basis of his throne.) In the centre of the tribune arch is the Lamb of God, flanked by the Seven Candlesticks representing the Seven Churches of Asia, the Four Archangels and the symbols of the Four Evangelists. Beneath, clothed in white, the Twenty-four Elders of the Apocalypse present their crowns.

The mosaics of the apse are modelled meticulously on the sixth-century ones in the church of SS. Cosma e Damiano, overlooking the Forum, but, whereas the latter retain much of Roman naturalism, those of S. Prassede bear all the marks of the Byzantine tradition. The clouds of the earlier mosaic have become wavy lines on which Christ steps down from Heaven to welcome S. Prassede and S. Pudenziana, who are introduced by St Peter and St Paul, each with a hand affectionately placed on one sister's shoulder. On the right stands S. Zeno; on the left, Pope Paschal, with a square halo to indicate that he was still living at the time the mosaic was made. In his hands he offers a model of his new church. A palm tree rises on either side, the one on the left carrying a phoenix, symbol of the Resurrection. This glorious company stands by the River Jordan. Below can be seen a frieze of symbolic sheep proceeding to the raised Mystic Lamb, and, at the extremities, the cities of Bethlehem and Jerusalem. Despite their Byzantine conventionality, however, these mosaics are most effective – moving in their naive directness and sincerity.

Living in the Dark Ages, Pope Paschal had a nostalgic affection for the greatness of Rome's classical past; but he could only copy, and could hardly hope to create anything new. He built his churches in the basilican form and he acquired beautiful objects to adorn them: the stone Roman ship, the *Navicella*, which Leo x replaced in front of his church of S. Maria in Domnica; the splendid antique vase which acts as a *cantharus* in the court of S. Cecilia in Trastevere; and, here in S. Prassede, the antique urn which Paschal put above the doorway (itself made from classical fragments) to the Chapel of S. Zeno (p. 68). And in this chapel Paschal's artists did create something new: a mosaic so beautiful that Romans ever since have called it the Garden of Paradise (*Orto del Paradiso*). The Pope intended the chapel as a resting-place for S. Zeno and other martyrs and as a mausoleum for his mother Theodora. Being dark, the chapel was lit by candle-light, and the *tesserae* of which the mosaic is composed were raised slightly from their bed, so that the pale

LEFT The third-century *Mithraeum* beneath the lower church of S. Clemente. The temple, built to simulate a cave, has seats cut in the rock for the worshippers and contains a sacrificial altar on which is represented the god in the act of slaying a bull, the sacrifice central to the Mithraic ritual.

ABOVE The stone mask in the portico of S. Maria in Cosmedin
was possibly an antique drain cover depicting a river god. Long
known as the *Bocca della Verità*, popular tradition has it that the
mouth will close on the hand of the person who, placing it there,
swears a false oath.

RIGHT The ancient bronze doors from the Curia in the Forum,
where the Roman Senate met, were placed in S. Giovanni in
Laterano during the seventeenth-century reconstruction of the
church by Borromini.

figures would shimmer against their background of glittering gold. The surfaces are covered with mosaic, outside as well as inside. Within, angels, standing on azure orbs, curve upwards from the four corners, with the groining of the vault, supporting with their raised hands a medallion, a corona of triumph enclosing the half-figure of Christ. St Peter and St Paul point to the empty shrine – an allusion to the Second Coming. Among the figures of saints appear the busts of four women: the Virgin Mary, SS. Prassede and Pudenziana, and Theodora, Paschal's mother. Both the Virgin and Theodora are veiled, Theodora having the square nimbus of the living – the only case in Rome of a women being thus honoured. Furthermore, the lettering beside her describes her as *Episcopa*, a bishop. The charm of this miraculous little chapel cannot be described; it is as if here the Byzantine artists unbent, softened by the grace and beauty of their own creation.

Traditions attached to the very ancient church of S. Prisca on the Aventine attribute its origin to apostolic times, linking it with the presence of both St Peter and St Paul in Rome. Archaeological research appears to confirm this, and to connect S. Prisca with S. Pudenziana and S. Prassede. Prisca, a Roman girl whose patrician family lived on the Aventine, is said to have been baptized by St Peter, and was exposed as a Christian in the amphitheatre at the age of thirteen during the reign of Claudius (41–54). When the lions refused to touch her, but instead licked her feet, Prisca was beheaded. She was buried with Praxedes and Pudenziana in the Catacomb of Priscilla, from where, in the third century, her body was removed to the church now named after her. During the Middle Ages Prisca became confused with Priscilla, a Jewish tentmaker whom St Paul had met in Corinth, where she and her friend Aquila were exiled by Claudius, and whom he mentions several times in his Acts and Epistles. On their return from exile, Priscilla and Aquila lived on the Aventine, part of their dwelling constituting a 'church-house', and tradition has it that St Paul, also a tent-maker, stayed with them, as did St Peter, who conducted much of his Roman mission from their house. As a result of the confusion between Prisca and Priscilla, the Titulus Priscae was dedicated in the Middle Ages to 'the Blessed Aquila and Prisca'.

In 1933 excavations beneath S. Prisca opened up a Roman house of the first century, and in 1940 a well-preserved *Mithraeum* was discovered. Earlier excavations in the immediate vicinity had revealed an oratory, possibly of the apostolic period, and also another Roman house, which appears to have belonged in 222 to one Caius Marius Pudens Cornelianus. Whether or not the church of S. Prisca is built over her parents' house or over that of Aquila and Priscilla,

this whole locality of the Aventine is full of reminiscences of the ministries in Rome of both St Peter and St Paul. Moreover, there is a link between the Pudens who lived on the Aventine and the earlier Pudens who lived on the Esquiline (St Peter's convert, whose mother Priscilla owned the catacomb and who was the father of SS. Pudenziana and Prassede). We seem very close here to the world of ancient Rome, when it first heard and heeded the Christian message.

Damaged or destroyed by Robert Guiscard's Normans, S. Prisca was restored several times, chiefly in 1660 when the present façade was built and the fourteen antique columns of the interior were incorporated in pilasters. Architecturally and decoratively the church is disappointing; its interest lies in its history. In the right-hand aisle the modern baptistery contains a large Doric capital, possibly of the time of the Antonines, which was adapted in the thirteenth century as a baptismal font, although popular belief holds it to be that in which St Peter baptized S. Prisca. Nearby a door leads down into a court which gives access to the *antiquarium*, or museum, arranged in the second-century *nymphaeum* of the Roman house. From there one may visit the ninth-century crypt, where an urn contains the relics of S. Prisca. The *Mithraeum*, of the second or third century, is remarkable for its con-temporary frescoes, one of which depicts a Mithraic initiation ceremony and another a procession of believers.

The faith that sustained these early Christians is perhaps best understood today by a visit to the catacombs – among the more important being those of S. Callisto, S. Sebastiano and S. Domitilla, on or near the Via Appia Antica, just without the city walls; that of S. Agnese on the Via Nomentana; and that of S. Priscilla on the Via Salaria. By ancient law all places of burial were outside the city walls and were inviolable, and the early Christian community took advan-tage of this by establishing its cemeteries in private ground which was first provided by donors (often matrons), and subsequently became the communal property of individual city churches. Just as in popular phraseology the blood of its martyrs has been called the seed of the Church, so have the catacombs been seen as its cradle. Here, in these places of death, everything is expressive of hope – a profound, unshakeable faith. St Jerome described the Christian attitude to death: 'Among Christians death is not death, but a taking of rest, a sleep.' All is redolent of a resolute belief, a joyousness in the certainty of resurrection, as is attested in the epitaphs: 'Sabbatia has passed away in the sleep of peace,' 'Laurina, more sweet than honey, repose in peace.'

Until the middle of the third century the inscriptions were often in Greek, though the words might be Latin. Jesus Christ is seldom mentioned by name, but usually by the monogram ✗ (the first two letters of the Greek spelling of Jesus Christ), or by the acronym found by the Greek word for 'fish', *Icthus*, which is made up of the initial letters in Greek of 'Jesus Christ Son of God Saviour'. Alternatively, Christ's name may be symbolized simply by the drawing of a fish. Mural decoration frequently represents scenes from the Old Testament or from the Gospels, since these often crude paintings were intended to take the place of books for a community many members of which were illiterate. Nowhere is Christ shown on the Cross. The most favoured representation of him is as the Good Shepherd, young and handsome, among his sheep (the Apostles, or the faithful), or bearing a lamb on his shoulders.

Everyday objects and animals all have their symbolic meanings, known only to the faithful: an anchor (hope), a trident (the Cross), a ship (the Church), a vase or rolls of bread or a basket (refreshment, the Eucharist), a palm branch (victory over death, martyrdom), an olive branch (peace) and fruit and flowers (the celestial garden, paradise). The dove represents the Holy Spirit; the phoenix (as we have seen in S. Prassede) the Resurrection; the pelican, redemption through Christ; the peacock, immortality. The dolphin, taken over from pagan art as friendly to sailors, suggests the Saviour. It was by means of these symbols that those new to Christianity acquired knowledge of the Christian teaching, and the faithful were strengthened in maintaining their faith during the dark days of the persecutions.

If by the time of Diocletian Christianity had spread through the entire fabric of the decaying Empire, it was not only the exemplary character of the Christians' lives in a disintegrating society (their charity, their humility and the almost obsessive rigour of their sexual relations, the high place given by them to chastity both in men and especially in women) that did much to effect the conversion of so many Romans. It was also the steadfastness and the sufferings of their martyrs, chief among whom were the Roman saints Cecilia, Lawrence and Agnes. Legends about the circumstances of their deaths quickly grew, were widely publicized and proliferated in the popular martyrologies. It was largely the saints' social position, but especially the manner of their martyrdom, that did so much to win over many converts among the upper and educated classes.

St Cecilia was a member of the ancient Roman family of the Cecilii. The church of S. Cecilia in Trastevere (see p. 52) is built over her town house, parts of which still exist and may be seen below the present ground level. The martyrdom of so distinguished a person caused a great stir among contemporary Roman society. It took place most probably during the reign of either Marcus Aurelius or Commodus, *c*.

177. Cecilia was buried in the Catacomb of S. Callisto. Later her grave, lost in the destruction caused by the barbarian invasions, was revealed in a vision to Pope Paschal I (817–24), and her body was removed to the church built over her house. In the sixteenth century Cardinal Sfondrati, the titular of the church, opened the coffin, where her embalmed body was found, 'not lying upon the back, like a body in the tomb, but upon the right side, like a virgin in her bed, with her knees modestly drawn together, and offering the appearance of sleep'. The sculptor Stefano Maderno, who was present at the opening of the coffin, carved in white marble the figure of St Cecilia as he saw her then; this carving reposes below the altar of her church in Trastevere.

Outside the immediate circle of the Twelve Apostles and St Paul no person achieved such prominence in the early Roman Church as St Lawrence. Laurentius was the archdeacon of Rome at the time of the persecution of Valerian, and as such was expected to know where the treasury of the Church was kept. When apprehended and asked to account for it, he is reported to have led before the Roman magistrate a band of the poor, saying, 'Behold the treasure of the Church, for I have expended its treasures upon the poor.' Three days before his own death, meeting Pope Sixtus II with his fellow deacons on their way to execution, he is said to have addressed him, 'Father! Where goest thou without thy son? Holy priest! Whither goes thou forth without thy deacon?' 'I do not leave thee, my son, or desert thee,' replied Sixtus, 'but a still greater warfare for the faith of Christ is reserved for thee . . . in three days the levite shall follow the priest.' The horror of his death is well known: the slow roasting on a gridiron. His death on 10 August 258 and his heroism under the barbarous cruelty of his executioners created a profound and lasting impression among Romans. No less than forty-five churches or oratories within the city are dedicated to him, a number exceeded only by those dedicated to the Virgin Mary. The church of S. Lorenzo fuori le Mura stands where the matron Cyriaca buried the saint in ground which she owned. The church of S. Lorenzo in Fonte stands on the site of the fountain in which he baptized his fellow-prisoners. The church of S. Lorenzo in Panisperna was built on the place of his martyrdom; and the chains which are reputed to have bound him, and the gridiron on which he is said to have suffered, are preserved in the church of S. Lorenzo in Lucina. The church of S. Maria in Domnica, where the matron Cyriaca lived and before which St Lawrence distributed alms to the poor, is also closely associated with his life.

Equally profound was the impression produced by the martyrdom of the girl Agnes, who, with St Cecilia and St Lawrence, is much revered for her part in the final conversion

of Rome. She, too, seems to have suffered at the time of the persecution of Valerian, under the Prefect of Rome Aspasius (257–8), though some maintain that she was martyred during the Diocletian persecution. The details of her death were known early throughout the universal Church. So fast did the legends grow around her, embroidered by the fertility of monkish imaginations, that the facts of her death have been obscured. Even her name is not known for certain. She was most probably a member of the noble Aurelian *gens*, but the Christian name attributed to her may merely reflect her attribute of sexual purity – from the Greek *hagné* ('pure'), or from the Latin *agnus* ('lamb'). Two churches in Rome, widely separated in their times of building and both of outstanding interest, are dedicated to her: S. Agnese fuori le Mura, on the Via Nomentana; and S. Agnese in Agone, in the Piazza Navona. The former was erected by Constantia, or Constantina – the daughter, or at least a close relative, of the Emperor Constantine – over her place of burial, and the latter by Rainaldi and Borromini on the site of her martyrdom. The Piazza Navona is built over the Stadium of Domitian, the shape of which it largely retains, and the topography is reinforced by the retention of the name 'in agone', meaning 'the place for public games'.

Agnes, who was thirteen or fourteen, refused the hand of the Prefect's son, who was violently in love with her for her beauty, on the grounds that she had consecrated her life to virginity. Brought before a magistrate, she confessed herself a Christian. She was sentenced to serve as a prostitute.

Ambrose, a monk writing in the sixth century, assures us that 'the angel of the Lord entered with her' into the brothel to which she had been assigned and caused her hair to grow, so that it concealed her nakedness. Persisting in her confession, she was ordered to be publicly burnt, but miraculously a shower from heaven preserved her, and a wind arose which fanned the flames, so that it was her executioners who were burnt. Finally she was put to the sword. Agnes was buried in her parents' property on the Via Nomentana. 'Here a large crowd of Christians soon gathered, but were compelled to flee by the pagans coming out armed against them. . . .' Agnes' foster sister, Emerentiana, defying the mob, was stoned to death, and was buried in the field adjoining her grave. Ambrose tells of a vision witnessed by Agnes' parents during a vigil at her tomb:

> Suddenly in the dead silence of the night a bright light shone forth, and they saw an array of virgins passing, all robed in cloth of gold; and among them they saw the most blessed Agnes, robed like the rest, and at her right stood a lamb whiter than snow. . . . Blessed Agnes spoke to her parents, 'Do not grieve me more as dead; but rejoice and be glad, because I have gained the mansions of light . . . and am united to Him in Heaven whom while on earth I used to love with my whole soul.' She then left them.

In the face of the firmly held faith exhibited by martyrs such as these, the heterogeneous religious beliefs of pagan Rome lacked the conviction and power to survive.

LEFT Columns of a Roman temple built into the wall of S. Nicola in Carcere (see p. 24).

2
The Peace of the Church: the Constantinian Churches

An inscription on the façade of S. Giovanni in Laterano proclaims it 'The Mother and Head of all the Churches in the City and in the World'. Despite the fame and grandeur of St Peter's, it is this church that is the Cathedral of Rome and of the Roman Catholic world; the Lateran chapter today still takes precedence over that of St Peter's. On the morrow of his victory over his rival Maxentius at the Milvian Bridge (28 October 312) the Emperor Constantine ordered Pope Miltiades to summon a Council in the Lateran Palace; in the following year he installed Miltiades' successor, Pope Silvester I, in the Lateran (regarding this as the papal residence) and began building next door, on the site of the destroyed barracks of a regiment of the defeated Maxentius, a church dedicated to the Saviour, the Basilica Salvatoris. For 1,000 years, until the beginning of the so-called Babylonian Captivity of the Popes in Avignon in 1305, the Lateran was the centre of Western Christendom.

Persecution had failed to break the spirit of the Christians. It was Constantine who confirmed the status of the Church, and it was on him that the Christians looked as their liberator, who allowed them to emerge from their church-houses and the catacombs into the light of the Roman day. On Constantine's own admission Christian portents had fore-shadowed his victory at the Milvian Bridge – at the very gates

of Rome. He declared that he, and his whole army with him, saw in the sky a cross of light, with the words, 'In this sign you will conquer.' In a dream which followed, Christ appeared to him, holding the same sign. This – the Constantinian monogram ☧, the Greek letters *chi* and *rho* which formed the abbreviation of the word 'Christ' – he had painted on the legionaries' shields and placed on their standards. As a consequence of the successful issue of the battle, by the Edicts of Milan (312–13) he allowed the freedom of worship to adherents of all religions. And he went further: he ordered that all Christian places of worship and all their property should be restored to the congregations, even going so far as to compensate existing owners from state funds. Yet, if at first he only allowed Christianity a parity with paganism, from the beginning he placed the resources of the state at its disposal for church-building, and he increasingly favoured the Church with the imperial authority. From thenceforth Christianity was to grow in strength and prestige, except for the brief period during the short reign of Julian the Apostate (361–3), until, by the laws passed in 391–2, the Emperor Theodosius proscribed pagan worship and finally closed all pagan temples.

To Constantine and his family we owe the basilican churches that began to rise as Rome's cathedral and above such venerated shrines as the graves of the Apostles St Peter and St Paul and those of the martyrs St Lawrence and St Agnes. Further, he caused to be built in the Sessorian Palace a fitting repository for the relic of the True Cross which later came to be known as S. Croce in Gerusalemme, and another basilica – the Basilica Apostolorum, on the Via Appia, initially dedicated to the two Apostles to Rome but later renamed the church of S. Sebastiano. (There is a tradition that the bodies of St Peter and St Paul, removed from their too well-known shrines during the persecutions, had lain for some time in the ancient catacombs on that site.) These Constantinian churches, together with the church of S. Maria Maggiore, were to become the great pilgrimage churches. Imperial funds were also expended on smaller churches, such as the beautiful little round church of S. Costanza and the very ancient Titulus Equitii, subsequently known as S. Martino ai Monti.

The site of Constantine's first church of S. Giovanni in Laterano (as it is usually known, since to the original title of the Basilica Salvatoris were subsequently added dedications to both St John the Baptist and St John the Evangelist) was next to the palace of the Plautius Laterani; one of these, a senator, had been executed in 67 by the Emperor Nero for alleged complicity in the conspiracy of Piso, and the palace was confiscated, becoming imperial property. As an imperial residence, it was the birthplace of the Emperor Marcus Aurelius. Septimius Severus restored it to descendants of the original owner, and it was later part of the dowry of Fausta, the daughter of Maxentius, on her marriage to Constantine. The church which Constantine raised was basilican in form, with a wide nave separating double aisles and terminating in a rounded apsidal end.

At this point, it is appropriate to say something of the origin of the Early Christian basilica (p. 281), the form which was to be paramount in ecclesiastical architecture for a millennium. The meaning of the word 'basilica' has never been satisfactorily elucidated; it is the feminine of the Greek word for 'kingly', or 'regal'. Architecturally, it has usually been employed to designate a rectangular, covered building, with colonnades separating one or two aisles from the nave, which was lit by a clerestory, the nave itself being terminated in a semicircular apse. It might serve several purposes: as a covered market, a military training hall for use in inclement weather, a reception room in a rich man's house, or, later, as the imperial audience chamber. In Rome, in Republican times, its use was associated with those colonnaded halls in the Forum that were employed as magistrates' courts, of which the earliest known was the Basilica Porcia, built by Cato in 184 BC. One of the most typical of these was Trajan's Basilica Ulpia (AD 114). Except that here the double colonnades formed a complete ambulatory, this, with its apsidal end, might serve as a model for a typical Early Christian basilica. The existence of the *hypogeum* in basilican form at the Porta Maggiore shows that this type of building was employed for cult purposes in the first century AD, but it seems that the Christians, during the time of persecution,

found it safer to meet in rooms in the 'church-house'. Constantine, when he ordered the construction of the Basilica Salvatoris, may have had in mind the shape of the audience halls in the palaces of the Caesars on the Palatine. Writing to the Bishop of Jerusalem of the basilica of the Holy Sepulchre which he was building there, the Emperor used the word in more than its architectural sense: as connoting something worthy of himself – that is, 'regal'. The basilican form lent itself so admirably to liturgical use that it became adopted throughout the Empire.

The history of S. Giovanni in Laterano is one of repeated destruction and rebuilding, so that all outward evidence of the Constantinian building has been effaced. Yet it must have been very magnificent, since the lavishness of Constantine's decoration earned for it the name of the Church of Gold (Basilica Aurea). Excavations carried out between 1936 and 1939 have uncovered, at the depth of some twenty-three feet below the level of the present church, remains of the barrack rooms and parts of pagan and Christian dwellings, some with frescoes and mosaic flooring; also portions of the pavement of the street separating the barracks from the palace, as well as of Constantine's foundations of his original church.

Adjoining his Basilica Salvatoris Constantine erected, perhaps over a *nymphaeum* of the Lateran Palace, the baptistery of S. Giovanni in Fonte, which for long was the only baptistery in Rome and became the model for later Italian baptisteries. The tradition that the Emperor was himself baptized here by Pope Silvester I after being miraculously cured of leprosy is mythical, as is his 'Donation of the Empire of the West' to the popes, which is said to have followed his baptism. However much Constantine did for the early Church – and its debt to him is great – his motives were essentially political. He had many political crimes to repent of when, ultimately, he actually was baptized on his deathbed in Nicomedia in 337; yet, in the East, he has been regarded as a saint.

A hundred years after Constantine's foundation the baptistery was rebuilt by Pope Sixtus III, after it had been plundered by the Goths; since then it has been repeatedly restored, much of its present appearance being due to work carried out in 1637 by Pope Urban VIII. Externally, it is octagonal in form; within, eight columns of red porphyry, with Ionic and Corinthian capitals (said to have been presented by Constantine), support an architrave from an antique building, upon which rise eight smaller columns of white marble, which in turn support a gilded architrave. Above, the octagonal lantern is lit by eight circular windows. The porphyry columns enclose a circular balustraded basin, in the centre of which is a great antique font of green Egyptian basalt – originally intended for total immersion.

On the right of the entrance from the piazza is the Chapel of St John the Baptist, with its famous bronze doors from the Baths of Caracalla, which, when opened slowly, emit a musical note. Opposite the entrance is the original narthex of the baptistery, transformed in 1154 by Pope Anastasius IV into the Chapel of SS. Rufina e Secunda. Here the fifth-century mosaics show the beauty of Hellenistic art adapted to the service of the Church: the Lamb of God, between four doves, stands in an interlacing of green and gold vine tendrils against a background of deep blue. Next to this chapel, but entered from the octagon, is the Chapel of S. Venanzio, erected *c.* 642 by Pope John IV in honour of his compatriot martyrs from Dalmatia. The mosaics here are most important for the stylistic changes they reveal: those of the tribune are suggestive of their Hellenistic ancestry, while those of the arch are Byzantine, more reminiscent of the mosaics in S. Vitale at Ravenna. Christ appears between two angels, lifted up on red clouds in a sky of gold; below is the blue-draped figure of the Virgin (shown in prayer, with her arms outstretched), with, on the left, St Paul, St John the Evangelist, S. Venanzio and Pope John IV, and, on the right, St Peter, St John the Baptist, a Dalmatian saint and Pope Theodore. On the arch are the symbols of the Four Evangelists and of the cities of Bethlehem and Jerusalem; below them, the eight Slavonic soldier-saints.

To the left of the main entrance, behind the bronze doors made in 1196 by Uberto and Pietro from Piacenza, is the Chapel of St John the Evangelist. The beautiful fifth-century mosaics have all the freshness, vivacity and charm of Hellenistic work, reminiscent of the limpid still lifes of the Catacomb of S. Callisto. Again, the Lamb of God, with a cruciform nimbus, is depicted, here among grapes, flowers and laurels, red-legged partridges, ducks and other birds set in a field of gold.

For the great church built over the shrine of St Peter, Constantine adopted a plan which he repeated elsewhere – for example, at S. Paolo fuori le Mura, the church of the Nativity in Bethlehem and the church of the Holy Sepulchre in Jerusalem, but not at S. Giovanni in Laterano: the basilican church is preceded by a colonnaded portico, or *atrium*. This ground-plan became the model for many later churches, including S. Clemente (p. 49). (To gain an impression of what the interior of old St Peter's looked like, as well as that of S. Giovanni in Laterano before the seventeeth-century restoration by Borromini, one can study the paintings of Filippo Gagliardi in the left-hand aisle of S. Martino ai Monti.) At St Peter's, too, at the end of the basilical hall, cutting across the nave and coupled aisles and extending beyond the latter, the Emperor constructed a transept, to form what was known as a *martyrium*. In the centre of this transept, and slightly in front of the semicircular apse, was the shrine enclosing the tomb of the Apostle, which was thus admirably placed to be visible to the crowd of pilgrims. The tomb-shrine was richly adorned and covered with a magnificent canopy, or *baldacchino*. The high altar itself may have stood in the nave. The façade of St Peter's was decorated by the Emperor with brilliant mosaics, and the upper walls of the nave with frescoes. Over the triumphal arch a dedicatory inscription to St Peter in gold mosaic, placed there by Constantine's wish, perhaps throws some light on his policy: 'Because under thy leadership the world has raised itself in triumph to the stars, Constantine the Victorious has dedicated this church to thee.'

Although in their grandeur Constantine's churches maintained the Roman tradition, in their use of timbered roofs his architects seemed unimaginative, even regressive, when one considers the huge Basilica of Maxentius, where the use of concrete made possible the construction of immense vaults which, even today, astonish the visitor to the Forum. The Emperor reserved his architectural innovations chiefly for the creation of his New Rome, which he was to build at Byzantium and to make the capital of the Empire: Constantinople.

In the centre of Constantine's *atrium* at St Peter's, Pope Damasus (366–84) placed a beautiful fountain (known as a *cantharus*), where, beneath a glittering bronze cupola, raised on slender columns of antique porphyry, stood the great gilded bronze pine-cone from the top of the Emperor Hadrian's mausoleum. Through apertures in the pine-cone and from the beaks of gilded peacocks the water gushed, to fall into a shallow basin intended for the ablutions of the faithful entering the basilica. Today the pine-cone is in the Cortile della Pigna in the Vatican. The holy-water stoup at the entrance of churches is the successor of the early Christian *cantharus*.

None of the Constantinian churches could compare in size or grandeur with the Emperor's cathedral, S. Giovanni in Laterano, or St Peter's, not even that built over St Paul's shrine, S. Paolo fuori le Mura. S. Anacletus had raised an oratory at an early date above the tomb of St Paul, where he was buried by the Roman matron Lucina off the Ostian Road. Of the church founded on the site by Constantine in 324 or 326, the *Liber Pontificalis* states, 'He built a basilica to Paul the Apostle, whose body he placed in a chest and closed, in the same way as he did that of St Peter.' It appears that Constantine's church proved too small to accommodate the number of pilgrims who visited it, since as early as 386 the three Emperors Valentinian, Theodosius and Arcadius

ordered the Consul Sallustrius to erect a larger building, more worthy of the Apostle to the Gentiles. This he did, apparently following the design and dimensions of the Ulpian Basilica in Trajan's Forum. Today the visitor to the church, which was rebuilt after the disastrous fire of 1823, can gain an excellent impression of a classical Roman basilica.

It was natural that the politically aware Constantine should wish to recognize the widely popular cults of the Roman martyrs St Lawrence and St Agnes by honouring them in the construction of splendid churches. S. Lorenzo fuori le Mura – which was built above the martyr's grave at the Campo Verano, the great cemetery of Rome – is one of the most fascinating of Roman churches. This, however, and two other churches which the Emperor built, to commemorate the resting-place of the two Apostles to Rome at the Catacomb of S. Sebastiano (church of S. Sebastiano) and the discovery by his mother, the Empress Helena, of part of the True Cross (S. Croce in Gerusalemme), have been so rebuilt or restored as to obliterate the original Constantinian buildings (see Chapter 4). This is not the case with the church which the Emperor dedicated to St Agnes on the Via Nomentana and the beautiful little mausoleum-church of S. Costanza nearby.

It is usually held that in 324 (some believe the year to have been 342) Constantine built the church of S. Agnese fuori le Mura, at the request of his daughter, or niece, Constantia (Costanza). The *Liber Pontificalis*, however, states, 'About this time Constantine built a basilica in honour of the holy martyr Agnes, to comply with the wish of Constantina, his daughter; he also built a baptistery, including the font where she had been received into the Church by Pope Silvester.' According to Marcellinus, Constantina was 'not a woman, but an infernal fury tormented with the insatiate thirst for human blood'. Constantia's reputation, on the other hand, appears irreproachable, and she seems to have had a particular devotion to the girl-martyr Agnes. Constantia (if it was she) wished the altar of the church to be immediately above the martyr's tomb; consequently, today S. Agnese stands well below the level of the Via Nomentana.

The church is approached by a broad marble stairway (1590), which enters to the right of the narthex. Placed on the walls of the flight of stairs are fragments of lapidary inscriptions in Greek and Latin, which come from the catacombs below. On one fragment (on the right hand near the foot of the stairs) are some verses in honour of St Agnes,

LEFT On the high altar of S. Agnese fuori le Mura an antique torso in rare oriental alabaster has had the head, hands and dress added by Nicholas Cordier in gilded bronze (1610) to represent the martyred St Agnes.

written by Pope Damasus, who has left similar verses of his own composition in other catacombs, inscribed in the calligraphy of his friend Furius Dionysius Filocalus. S. Agnese was rebuilt as early as *c.* 625 by Pope Honorius I, and was restored many times subsequently, first in the eighth century by Adrian I and ultimately in the nineteenth by Pio Nono; nevertheless, it presents today the typical form of an Early Christian basilica – much, in fact, as Constantine built it. With its galleries on the entrance and side walls, it preserves the characteristics, according to Vitruvius, of one type of Roman basilica. The nave arcading is supported by strik-ingly beautiful antique Corinthian columns, the four highly polished columns which are nearest the tribune being of rare Portasanta marble, the next two of fluted *pavonazetto*, and the remaining eight of Serravezza *breccia*. Above, and cor-responding to them, are slender, graceful columns which form the galleries. The coffered ceiling (p. 170) of gilded wood dates from 1606; the mural decoration, mostly from the nineteenth century. The *baldacchino* of 1614, raised on four columns of porphyry, covers the altar, under which lie the bodies of St Agnes and her foster-sister St Emerentiana. On the altar a classical torso in oriental alabaster was rather incongruously converted in the seventeenth century, by additions of gilded bronze, into a representation of St Agnes. To the left of the altar stands a fine antique (Roman) candelabrum, and behind the altar an ancient episcopal throne.

The mosaics of the apse (625) date from the time of Honorius I and represent St Agnes in Glory. The young Roman virgin has been transformed by her gorgeous vestment into a Byzantine princess. Above, the hand of God presents her with the Crown of Life; to the right and left are the flames which could not touch her, and beneath her feet a sword, the instrument of her martyrdom. At the side stand the figures of Pope Symmachus, dressed in purple, and Pope Honorius, in white and purple, holding a model of his restored church. This mosaic shows that by the early seventh century Byzantine influence in this art was paramount in Rome.

A short way from the basilica there stands among the olive- and almond-trees a jewel of Early Christian (or rather, late Roman) art: the church – originally the baptistery-mausoleum – of S. Costanza. As with the church of S. Agnese, confusion persists as to the identity of the person for whom Constantine erected this centrally planned building *c.* 320. But there can be no difference of opinion about the extraordinary beauty of this circular temple, built in the style of a Roman mausoleum; Constantia was buried there, together with her sister, the Empress Helena, wife of Julian the Apostate. Constantia's body was placed in a magnificent carved sarcophagus of red porphyry, now in the Museo Pio-

Clementino in the Vatican. Not long afterwards the building was again used as a baptistery; in 1254 it was consecrated as a church and dedicated to S. Costanza by Pope Alexander IV.

The church has a narthex with apsidal ends, and two niches flank the main doorway. On entering, one is struck by the perfection of the building's proportions. The central space, where Constantia's great funeral urn stood, is enclosed by twenty-four Composite columns, coupled by short architraves and separated by semicircular arches, on which rests the drum of the cupola. This was once covered with magnificent mosaics of biblical and allegorical scenes; most of these were destroyed in 1620 in the restoration carried out by Cardinal Veralli, and what still remained was lost in the restoration which took place in the nineteenth century. However, the early fourth-century mosaics of the ambulatory vaulting (p. 40) are some of the earliest of Christian origin in Rome, and are so beautiful that one doubly regrets what has disappeared. One might be forgiven for thinking them purely Roman – with their tracery of vine tendrils, and their scenes from a joyous vintage, in which cupids take grapes from their baskets to fill the bullock waggons which are about to leave for the treading-press. Other sections are equally decorative, some being filled with geometrical figures, others with medallions of dancing *putti*, winged victories and birds, others with human faces and flowers, yet others with branches, fruit, cornucopias and everyday utensils – delightful patterns of variegated colours on a white ground. Perhaps only the symbolic pails of milk and sheep indicate the Christian message conveyed by these mosaics, which otherwise might be regarded as the charming last blooms, the autumnal flowering, of Hellenistic art.

Apart from these Imperial foundations, the Peace of the Church brought an efflorescence of what may be termed parochial church building. The clergy and congregations of the *tituli*, while wishing to preserve buildings hallowed for them by association with their martyrs, were free to erect churches better adapted to liturgical use and large enough to accommodate the greatly increased number of worshippers. Often they incorporated parts of existing buildings in the new structures, in order to preserve sanctified places – even when the form of the later type of church was most frequently basilican. The absence of architectural ornament, the simplicity and plainness of these early Roman basilicas, left the walls free for the imagination of the artist working in mosaic and fresco. Earlier, representational art had been frowned on as savouring of idolatry; it had been expressly forbidden by the Council of Elvira (*c.* 300). But whatever was the usual practice in the East – and the wall-paintings discovered at Dura-Europus in 1922 prove that they existed

there as early as the mid-third century – the Romans looked on mural representation in a different light. By the age of Constantine the apses, and often the façades, of the churches of Rome glowed with the gold and brilliant colours of mosaic and the walls were enlivened with fresco. The decoration with which Roman churches were adorned from the time of Constantine onwards differed in mood from the elegiac or consolatory art of the catacombs. It was rather commemorative, illustrative and didactic; it reminded and taught the gathered faithful. The iconography was known by all, for the members of the early Church were well versed in the Scriptures.

Of singular interest is the church of S. Martino ai Monti which was built on the slopes of the Oppian Hill, on which once stood Nero's Golden House and the Baths of Trajan. Despite lack of agreement among eminent archaeologists on matters of detail, it is certain that Christians worshipped here from the days of Constantine, and almost certain that they did so even earlier, at the time of the persecutions. The first church-house was known as the Titulus Equitii and was contained in an early third-century block of buildings, deep below and to the west of the present church. From the *Liber Pontificalis* it appears that Pope Silvester I (314–35) built a church on the Titulus Equitii, and it was here that the Pope held a synod in 324, preparatory to the Council of Nicaea of the following year. Constantine may have visited the church; he definitely contributed to the furnishing and gave it property in land. Later the terms Titulus Equitii and Silvestri became confused. It is reported that subsequently Pope Symmachus (498–514) built a church dedicated to St Martin of Tours 'next to that of St Silvester'. The existing church of S. Martino dates from the rebuilding of 'the church of Saints Silvester and Martin', begun by Pope Sergius II (844–7). From the high altar two flights of steps lead down to the elaborate Baroque *confessio* of Pietro da Cortona (*c.* 1650), where rest the relics of Pope Silvester and of the deposed Pope Martin I (d. 655), as well as those of others 'known only to God'. From here the visitor descends to the original Roman buildings. René Vieillard's contention that the large early third-century assembly hall (it measures about thirty-six by sixty feet) was the original Titulus Equitii, and that it was most likely built for the use of the Christian community during the persecutions, is disputed by J.B. Ward Perkins. It may have been only later that it was converted to Christian purposes by Pope Silvester and that the earlier church-house was in other rooms of the complex.

RIGHT As in this fresco in the crypt of S. Martino ai Monti, the early Christians adapted pagan mural decorations to their own religious ends by the use of an arcane symbolism.

What is not in doubt is the extreme antiquity of the site as a place of Christian worship.

How confusing the evidence relating to the origins of these early *tituli* can be is illustrated by the ancient church of S. Anastasia (Titulus Anastasiae) in the Via di S. Teodoro. If Monsignor Duchesne conjectured that Anastasia was a sister of Constantine, there is also a tradition that she was a Roman matron, a friend of S. Crisogono, and met her death at about the same time (*c.* 304) as that saint, during Diocletian's persecution. According to this tradition, she was buried alive at Sirmium, in Illyria (now Mitrovica, in Yugoslavia). It is said that her body was brought to Rome and buried by her friend Apollina in her garden by the Circus Maximus, at the foot of the Palatine. However, excavations under the present seventeenth-century church show that it is built over Roman buildings of the Imperial age. The visitor will find there remains of a first-century portico and part of an *insula*, containing shops, which backed on to the Palatine and faced the road which flanked the Circus Maximus. Subterranean passages (referred to in an epitaph in the church) are said to have communicated with the Imperial Palace in the neigh-bourhood of S. Maria Antiqua, on the farther side of the Palatine. A seventh-century document refers to S. Anastasia directly after the basilicas of the Lateran and S. Maria Maggiore. On rather dubious authority the church of S. Anastasia was intimately connected with St Jerome. How-ever, there is good evidence that Pope Leo the Great (440–61) preached here at the Mass of Christmas morning against the heretical Eutyches, and it became the custom for popes to celebrate the second of the three Christmas masses at S. Anastasia.

A church of the Constantinian age has been excavated beneath (and to the side of) S. Crisogono in Trastevere. The visitor descends by a spiral staircase from the sacristy to the earlier church, which is some twenty-six feet below the present ground level. (The effect of descending directly by the stair is to bring vividly home to one how much higher the level of modern Rome is above that of Imperial times.) The original Titulus Chrysogoni was apparently built near the station of the Roman firemen. The church, attributed to Pope Silvester I, is basilican in form, with an exceptionally wide apse, and appears to have been built above the earlier *titulus*, constructed of bricks similar to those used in contemporary domestic or commercial buildings. Parts of the early de-corative motifs remain; there are also frescoes dating from the eighth to the eleventh centuries, which include, on the right-hand side, an eleventh-century series illustrating the lives of St Benedict and St Silvester.

If, however, there is one church built over an ancient *titulus* which no visitor to Rome should miss, it is surely S.

Clemente in the Via S. Giovanni in Laterano, the street which links the Vatican with the Lateran. Today one enters S. Clemente by a side door in this street, where in the Middle Ages the local residents would often have enjoyed the colour and pageantry of papal processions between the two great basilicas. S. Clemente is one of the few of the old basilican churches to retain its *atrium*, which was entered through the twelfth-century portal, now usually closed. The courtyard, which is contemporary with the church (1108), is sur-rounded by an Ionic-capped colonnade; in the centre an eighteenth-century fountain replaces the ancient *cantharus*. The façade, also of the eighteenth century, was restored by Carlo Stefano Fontana, who retained some of the ancient columns.

Many legends have grown up around the person of St Clement; perhaps there were several Clements and the legends have merged. The best-known Clement, the friend of St Peter and St Paul, who became the fourth pope (88–97), has been variously accounted a relative of the Acilii Glabriones, a relative of the consul-martyr Titus Flavius Clemens or a freedman of the latter's family. He seems almost certainly to have been the author of the Clementine *Epistle to the Corinthians*. There is a tradition that he was exiled to the Crimea by the Emperor Trajan, to work with other Christians in the stone quarries. (Trajan, however, only became emperor in 98, the year after Pope Clement's death.) In the Crimea St Clement, it is said, miraculously saved the lives of his fellow-Christians, who were suffering from intolerable thirst, and for this he was thrown into the sea, with an anchor round his neck. Then the miracles began in earnest. As a result of the prayers offered up by the Christians, each year the sea receded, and the saint's body was eventually found, safely reposing in a small temple. One year a mother, who was visiting the shrine, lost her daughter. Returning next year, she found her daughter safe; the girl had been found and taken care of by St Clement. In art he is represented with the anchor; yet, curiously, though he is shown dressed in papal robes, he is without the papal tiara – which does suggest that there has been some confusion of identity.

In 1084 Robert Guiscard and his Normans, coming to the rescue of Pope Gregory VII, set fire to part of Rome, including the buildings on the Coelian Hill, seriously damaging, among other churches, that of S. Clemente. In 1108 Pope Paschal II filled in the partly destroyed building, rescuing some of the most precious of its marble furnishings, and built the present church above it. Together with the beautiful Cosmati work of the *ambones*, the paschal candelab-rum and choir of the present church, there is the exquisite screen. Parts of the marble of the choir and screen bear the monogram 'Johannes', of Pope John II (532–5), and were in

Upper church

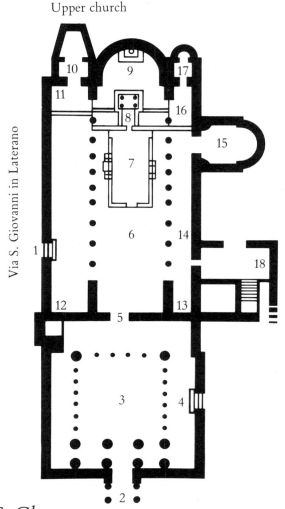

Via S. Giovanni in Laterano

Lower church
Mithraic area

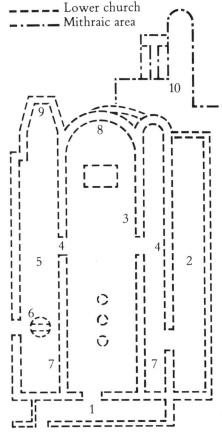

S. Clemente

UPPER CHURCH (1108)
1 Main entrance.
2 Original portico no longer in use.
3 *Atrium*.
4 Entrance to the monastery of the Irish Dominicans.
5 Entrance from the narthex to the church.
6 Nave.
7 Choir (twelfth century), parts of which and the screen (533) come from the original church; two *ambones*.
8 High altar with *baldacchino* (1100).
9 Apse, with episcopal chair and mosaics, *The Triumph of the Cross* (early twelfth century).
10 Chapel of the Holy Sacrament.
11 Monument to Cardinal Antonio Venerio (d. 1479) by a follower of Isaia da Pisa.
12 Chapel of St Catherine of Alexandria with frescoes (*c.* 1431) by Masolino di Panicale.
13 Chapel of St Dominic.

14 Entrance to sacristy.
15 Chapel of SS. Cirillo and Metodio.
16 Monuments to Archbishop Giovanni Brusato by Luigi Capponi (1485) and to Cardinal Roverella (d. 1476) by Giovanni Dalmata.
17 Chapel of St John the Baptist; *John the Baptist* attributed to S. Ghini (fifteenth century) but more probably by a sixteenth-century Mannerist.
18 Sacristy with steps down to the lower church.

LOWER CHURCH (before 385; restored in the eighth and ninth centuries)
1 Narthex.
2 North aisle.
3 Position of the choir before its reconstruction in the upper church.
4 Width of the original nave.
5 South aisle.
6 Circular pit thought to have been used for baptism by immersion.
7 Walls built to support upper church.
8 Apse strengthened to support the apse in the upper church.
9 Staircase to lower area containing *Mithraeum*, associated cult rooms and remains of first-century houses.
10 *Mithraeum*.

An eighteenth-century engraving of S. Maria in Trastevere.

fact taken from the destroyed lower church. The upper church (p. 92) is incomparable in its beauty; even the eighteenth-century restoration (with the decoration in stucco-work and the reshaping of the Ionic capitals to make them uniform) carried out by Fontana serves as a subdued foil to the brilliance of the twelfth-century mosaics of the apse, the fourteenth-century frescoes below, the Cosmatesque inlaid marble of the choir and pulpits, the perfection of the *opus alexandrinum* of the choir paving and the gilded coffering of the *settecento* ceiling. In the Chapel of St Catherine, at the beginning of the left-hand aisle, are the frescoes (*c.* 1431) by Masolino di Panicale which were so much admired by Raphael.

The existence of the buildings below went unsuspected until 1857, when repairs in the adjoining Dominican monastery revealed mural paintings some twenty feet below ground level and the Prior, Father Mullooly, was prompted to investigate further. The result was the discovery of the Constantian basilica beneath – larger than the upper church – and, in subsequent excavations, despite the presence of running water, the uncovering of Roman buildings at a lower level still, some of the Republican period and others of the first or second centuries AD. Here, beside what might have been Clement's original church-house (Titulus Clementis), used by the Christians during the persecutions, stood a *Mithraeum* (p. 32), which has survived in an excellent state of pre-servation, with its sculptured altar still in place.

On the right bank of the Tiber, in the unspoilt quarter whose inhabitants claim to be descendants of the 'original Romans', stand two of the best known and most beloved of Roman churches – S. Maria and S. Cecilia, both designated with the addition 'in Trastevere'. S. Maria in Trastevere is tradi-tionally held to have been one of the first Christian churches

to be publicly open for worship. In the time of Pope Calixtus I (217–22) a dispute arose between the Christian community and the corporation of Trastevere tavern-keepers over the ownership of a hall or assembly rooms, and the case was brought before the Emperor Alexander Severus. Judge-ment was given in favour of the Christians, the Emperor remarking that it was better to have God worshipped, in whatever form, than to allow the place to be used for drunken revelry. Close by was a spot known as the *fons olei*, where it was said that a spring of oil suddenly appeared and flowed away into the Tiber during the course of one day in 37 BC – an event which the Christians afterwards interpreted as a forewarning of the birth of Christ. Shortly before or after the martyrdom of Pope Calixtus (he was executed on the nearby Via Aurelia in 222) an oratory was raised, which was known as the Titulus Callisti. After the Peace of the Church, in 340 Pope Julius I erected a larger building on the site, incorporat-ing both the oratory and the *fons olei*. The present church was entirely rebuilt *c.* 1140 by Innocent II, who retained the traditional Roman basilican form; this at the time when Abbot Suger in Paris was building the church of Saint-Denis, the forerunner of the soaring Gothic churches of the Ile-de-France. To Romans, the Gothic was barbarism.

One of the most familiar sights for the visitor to Rome is the façade of S. Maria in Trastevere – with its mosaics and faded frescoes forming a background to the four *seicento* statues of gesticulating saints above the portico of Carlo Fontana (1702), seen from beyond the same architect's fountain, whose play of water in the dog days brings a welcome freshness to the piazza. To the right is the twelfth-century campanile, with, high up under the summit, a little canopy covering a *Madonna and Child* in mosaic. The façade mosaics, possibly of the mid-twelfth century, were most probably reset by the great Roman painter and mosaicist, Pietro Cavallini. Despite much alteration in later restoration, these figures, with the Virgin Mary in their midst, are usually held to represent the Wise and Foolish Virgins: two to the right of the Madonna can be seen to be without crowns, since, foolishly, they have allowed their lamps to become spent.

Innocent II's rebuilding is most impressive, with a majesty and gravity that are peculiarly Roman. Twenty-one massive antique granite columns of varying thickness, with Ionic and Corinthian capitals (possibly from the Temple of Isis or the Baths of Caracalla), divide the nave from the aisles.

RIGHT As the pastor among his Roman flock, Pope John Paul II officiates in S. Maria in Trastevere. To the right of the apse is the beautiful mosaic, the *Transition of the Virgin* (*c.* 1290) by Pietro Cavallini. The episcopal throne is of the twelfth century; the paschal candelabrum is perhaps a century later.

The effect of this columnar diversity is mitigated by the strong horizontal line of the entablature, the broad architrave supporting a firmly moulded cornice, resting on prominent consoles: much of this, too, was taken from ancient buildings. Of a solemn grandeur are the two great pillars, supporting their finely carved classical capitals and archit-raves, from which springs the triumphal arch, with its nineteenth-century frescoes of the Virgin and Child, angels and the patriarchs Noah and Moses. The sumptuous gilded ceiling was designed by Domenichino in 1617, the painting of the Assumption in the centre being by the same artist (p. 226). The brilliant Cosmatesque pavement was relaid during the nineteenth century. All this magnificence of form and colour is but a prelude to the mosaics of the tribune arch and apse (p. 72).

The mosaics of the arch and half-dome of the apse date from the time of Innocent II, and are thus contemporary with those of S. Clemente and S. Francesca Romana, illustrating the twelfth-century revival of the Roman workshops of mosaicists under the impetus given by Abbot Desiderius of Monte Cassino. On the spandrels of the arches appear the prophets Isaiah and Jeremiah, and above them the symbols of the Four Evangelists, flanking the Cross, and the Greek letters *alpha* and *omega*. Two small birds in cages have some allegorical significance, which has been variously interpreted. In the apse drum, above a frieze depicting the Mystic Lamb and the twelve sheep (Apostles), is represented the Triumph of the Virgin: the grand figures of Christ and the Virgin Mary are shown seated on the same throne, with the arm of the Son encircling the shoulders of his Mother. 'Come, thou whom I have chosen, and I shall place thee on my throne.' 'His left hand will be under my head and his right hand will encircle me.' At the sides appear saints and popes, including Innocent II who bears a model of his church.

Below is the beautiful *Scenes from the Life of the Virgin* (c. 1290) by Cavallini. All the hierophantic stiffness of the earlier mosaics has disappeared, to be replaced by a delightful freshness and directness. The composition of the individual scenes reveals in the rounded forms a grace and tenderness of sentiment that herald a return to a Hellenistic naturalness – the first dawn of the new approach to mosaic and painting that was achieved by Cavallini and his contemporary Giotto. (Giotto was in Rome a few years after the date of these mosaics; in 1298 he completed the *Navicella* mosaic for St

Peter's.) Above the twelfth-century episcopal throne, and over the choir-stalls in the apse, another of Cavallini's mosaics represents the Madonna and Child, with St Peter and St Paul, who present the donor of these works, Bertoldo Stefaneschi. It is most interesting to compare these enchanting mosaics with those of the Augustan age in the sacristy: two most realistic fragments, representing a fishing scene and aquatic birds.

On the right of the altar is a graceful paschal candlestick by the Cosmati, and in front of it on the right of the sanctuary, a spot marked *fons olei* indicates the place where, according to tradition, the spring of oil flowed in 37 BC. Among the artistic treasures of S. Maria in Trastevere are an altar and two tombs in the left transept, attributed to the fifteenth-century Roman sculptor Paolo Romano. The Gothic altar once held a recumbent figure of Cardinal Philippe d'Alençon and a bas-relief of the *Dormition of the Virgin*, both now in the cardinal's tomb on the left. The tomb on the right is of Cardinal Pietro Stefaneschi (p. 96), who, on his mother's side, came from the old Trastevere family of Annibaldi. Also worthy of notice is the sculptured and gilded tabernacle, at the beginning of the right-hand side of the nave, by the fifteenth-century Neapolitan artist Mino del Reame.

The Via Anicia, on which stands the apsidal end of S. Cecilia in Trastevere, recalls by its name that in this locality – where every street has its mediaeval houses, towers, ancient churches and, deep beneath them, imperial and primitive Christian remains – there once dwelt one of the most noble and illustrious of Roman Christian families: the Anicii Probi, whose devotion to the early Church was praised by St Augustine and St Jerome. From the Piazza S. Cecilia one enters under the *settecento* monumental gateway of Ferdinando Fuga into the courtyard before the church, a spot of green tranquillity in this teeming, popular quarter of Trastevere, filled with all the brio of Roman life and colour. Here one may sit quietly in the sunshine, basking in the company of the darting lizards. In the centre of the garden beds and clipped box-trees a shallow square basin of water surrounds the great antique *cantharus* of Paschal I, with its single jet of water, unique in its shapely elegance and in the quality of its white marble. Beneath Fuga's Rococo façade is the twelfth-century portico, with its Ionic columns and Corinthian pilasters of rose granite and African marble – all that remains suggestive of the earlier *atrium*. To the right, in contrast with Fuga's decorative Rococo, rises the red-brown brickwork of the sturdy Romanesque campánile.

To enter the church is something of a disappointment, since S. Cecilia has lost its primitive basilican appearance through repeated restoration, and now reflects the taste of the

LEFT Paschal I (817–24), a fervent admirer of antiquity, placed this Roman *cantharus* in the *atrium* preceding S. Cecilia in Trastevere. To the side of Ferdinand Fuga's *settecento* façade rises the twelfth-century campanile (1113), its red-brown brickwork contrasting with the white of the colonettes.

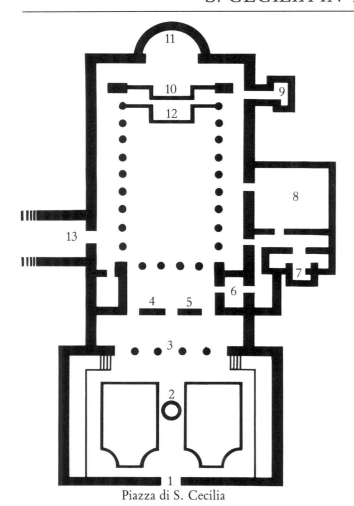

Piazza di S. Cecilia

S. Cecila in Trastevere

1 Gateway (1725) by Ferdinando Fuga.
2 Garden *atrium* with Roman *cantharus*.
3 Portico (twelfth century) with antique columns preceeding Fuga's façade.
4 Tomb of Cardinal Nicolò Forteguerri (d. 1473) by Mino da Fiesole.
5 Tomb of Cardinal Hertford, Administrator of London in 1398, by Paolo Romano.
6 *Crucifixion* (fifteenth-century fresco).
7 *Calidarium* of Roman house, traditionally that of St Cecilia.
8 Ponziani Chapel with frescoes by follower of Pinturicchio (*c.* 1454–1513), and others attributed to Antonio da Viterbo (known 1478–1509).
9 Tomb of Cardinal Mariano Rampolla del Tindaro (1929) by E. Quattrini.
10 *Baldacchino* (1283) by Arnolfo di Cambio.
11 Apse with mosaic of Paschal I: Christ with St Paul, St Cecilia and Paschal I (with the square halo of the living) on the left; St Peter, St Valerian and St Agatha on the right.
12 Statue of *St Cecilia* (1600) by Stefano Maderno.
13 Entrance to enclosed convent of Benedictine nuns containing the *Universal Judgement* (1293) by P. Cavallini.

Settecento, perhaps fittingly represented in the colourful fresco of the nave ceiling: Sebastiano Conca's *Apotheosis of St Cecilia*. According to tradition, the church stands above the palace and church-house (Titulus Ceciliae) which belonged to Cecilia and her husband Valerian and were bequeathed to the Pope at the time of her martyrdom, *c.* 117. A church, or oratory, was built over the original room by Urban I in 230. Rebuilt *c.* 820 by Paschal I – who removed there the body of St Cecilia, which had been revealed to him in a vision – it was restored in 1725 and 1823 by its titular cardinals at those times, Francesco Acquaviva and Giacomo Doria-Pamphilj. Its ancient Roman foundations, however, are visible to the visitor today.

A corridor from the right-hand aisle leads to the *calidarium* (with some of the thermal apparatus of leaden pipes intact) in which St Cecilia is traditionally said to have remained for three days and from which she is said to have emerged unharmed. On the walls are two paintings of the Saint by Guido Reni, *c.* 1603. Roman remains of great interest lie

under the entire church. These can be reached by way of the crypt (over-decorated in a neo-Byzantine manner by G. B. Giovenale, 1899–1901), which contains the sarcophagi of, among others, St Cecilia, St Valerian and St Tibertius, and Pope Urban. Excavations beneath these have revealed remains dating from Republican times to the second century A D: fragments of mosaic paving and of baths, a grain store-house, with containers for the grain, and a chapel for the household gods, with an ancient figure of the goddess Minerva.

Just inside the church are two monumental tombs of more than usual interest: that of the warrior Cardinal Nicolò Forteguerri (d. 1473), by the Florentine Mino da Fiesole, and that of the Cardinal of Hertford (d. 1398), by the Roman Paolo Romano. In the middle of the right-hand aisle the Chapel of the Ponziani (S. Francesca Romana was a member of the Ponziani family) contains frescoes by fifteenth-century artists of the Umbrian school. At the end of the aisle is a twelfth- or thirteenth-century fresco, *Paschal II finds the*

An eighteenth-century engraving of the church and convent of S. Cecilia in Trastevere.

Body of S. Cecilia. Before the high altar the elaborate receptacle in which lies the figure of Stefano Maderno's *S. Cecilia* heightens the pathetic effect of this young woman, shown lying on her side, as she was found when her tomb was opened in 1599. Perhaps it is the delicacy of Maderno's carving and the brilliant whiteness, the purity of the marble, that, while avoiding the sentimental, leave such an impression on the mind. And behind, above the high altar, perfectly in keeping, rises the beautiful Gothic *baldacchino* (1283) of Arnolfo di Cambio.

The canopy is raised on four columns of black and white marble — with ornate capitals and medallions of Cosmatesque mosaic — from which spring almost rounded trifoliated arches. In the spandrels appear crouching figures, and in the gables (whose sloping sides bear pronounced Gothic crockets) angels support rose 'windows'. At the four corners pinnacles lead the eye to the crowning lantern. And below these pinnacles stand the figures of St Cecilia, St Valerian and St Tibertius on horseback, and Pope Urban. In many respects Arnolfo's *baldacchino* at S. Cecilia in Trastevere resembles that of S. Paolo fuori le Mura: both, as distinctively Gothic works, are rarities in Rome.

In his apse mosaics Pope Paschal repeated the theme of those of S. Prassede, but somewhat less happily. It will be remembered that both stem from those of SS. Cosma e Damiano. St Peter and St Paul, presenting Cecilia and Valerian to Christ, no longer touch them with their former affectionate familiar gestures. It is Cecilia who places her hand on the shoulder of the living pope. The figures are stiffer, and the colours less brilliant; one has the general impression that these mosaics are from a different workshop — possibly one of Romans, apprenticed to a Byzantine school or working beside them. Their essential Byzantinism is reinforced by the fact that Christ gives his blessing in the Greek manner — that is, his two first fingers are raised and his thumb crosses to his third finger. In the Roman form of blessing the thumb and first two fingers are raised, the third and fourth turned down. If, artistically, these early ninth-century mosaics must be judged a falling-off, they nonetheless add colour and a distinct charm to the church.

The greatest glory of S. Cecilia in Trastevere can no longer be seen from the main area of the church. The masterpiece of Pietro Cavallini, his *Universal Judgement*, is in the nuns' choir, from which the nuns, members of an enclosed Order, can witness the services in the church, but which can only be entered (with permission) from the adjoining convent. The painting occupies the whole wall and extends below the level of the present floor. Christ (p. 95) stands among the Twelve Apostles, between St Cecilia and St John the Baptist. Beneath him are depicted the instruments of his Passion. Above are angels in green stoles, their wings tipped with grey and pink. The expression of the angels' faces is common to them all; the expressions on the Apostles' faces, by contrast, are highly individualized. Below, angels sound the Last Trump; to the left are shown the saved, while, to the right, the damned descend to everlasting perdition. The work must rank with the most profound of all representations of Christ. By this painting alone, despite restoration, Cavallini shows himself a master worthy to be compared with his great contemporary Giotto.

3
The Byzantine Influence

It has been said that the attraction of Rome's most celebrated churches lies not solely in their beauty, but also in their power to evoke the history of the times through which they have passed. In 330 Constantine removed the administrative capital of the Roman Empire to Constantinople, and thus began the historical process that led to the political division of the Eastern Empire from the Empire of the West, and eventually to the religious separation of the Greek Orthodox Church from the Church of Rome. Henceforth, for nearly 900 years, the East was to assert its influence on the indigenous, or Hellenistic, art of Rome. The origins of the basilican church of SS. Giovanni e Paolo on the Coelian Hill go back to these first years of the absence of the Roman emperors from Rome and of their rule from the Eastern capital.

Today the visitor, as he climbs the narrow lane called the Clivo di Scauro, passes the garden plots near S. Gregorio Magno, with their rows of lettuces and broad beans and the broad-leafed gourds beneath the overhanging vines. As he ascends, he will notice on the left, beyond the buttresses over the lane, the brickwork of a Roman house, its windows and doorways filled in, now forming the left-hand wall of the church of SS. Giovanni e Paolo. Above the wall opposite appear the trees of the Villa Celimontana, the greens of holm-oaks and cypresses. Behind him rises the Palatine, sheltering under its umbrella-pines. Here time has stood still, and any sense of a specific locality is blurred. He might be back in Imperial Rome or on the outskirts of any provincial Italian town, the countryside within easy reach, beyond the walls. From the lane he can see the apsidal end of SS. Giovanni e

Paolo, which is unique in Rome, showing the influence of Lombard Romanesque in the arcading high up below the small-square-blocked cornice, which supports the conical roof of ancient tiles, with their terracotta ridges and furrows of light and shadow. When he reaches the *piazzetta* on which rise the basilica and the adjoining monastery, this transposition of time is sustained, but now it is the Middle Ages that come chiefly to mind.

On his left is the impressive façade of SS. Giovanni e Paolo, with its twelfth-century portico, which replaces the original narthex. This consists of six ancient Ionic columns of African granite, flanked by two columns of the Corinthian order, these being of *lunense* marble. The portico was erected in 1158 by the only Englishman to become pope, Nicholas Breakspeare (Adrian IV). Above the architrave, with its finely lettered dedication, is the 'gallery' (c. 1216), the original openings having been replaced by the present irregularly spaced rectangular windows. The gabled end of the nave contains a beautifully proportioned early fifth-century arcade of five arches, raised on slender marble columns, the width of the central span diminishing in the two arches on either side. The perfection of the architectural symmetry is perhaps lessened by the nineteenth-century cupola to the right. Within the portico can be seen a Byzantine feature: the pulvins, or

RIGHT The round church of S. Teodoro, built in a warm-coloured brick, existed as a deaconate as early as the fifth century. Although many times restored, it retains its appearance of extreme antiquity. The entrance is below the street level, across the pleasing cobbled courtyard (1705) by C. Fontana.

dosserets, above the capitals of the two columns that originally formed the entrance from the narthex to the nave. (Another example of Byzantine influence, operating as late as the twelfth century, is inside the church at the end of the left-hand aisle: a fresco of *Christ Enthroned between Six Apostles*.)

On the right rises the high mediaeval wall of the monastery, and behind it stands the campanile (*c.* 1150), one of the most beautiful in Rome, its upper storeys decorated with Hispano-Arabic polychrome bowls (p. 115). The base of the campanile is formed from remains of the Temple of Claudius, built for her husband by the Empress Agrippina, the mother of Nero – who, failing to drown her, had her stabbed to death at Baiae on the Bay of Naples. In the monastery grounds are remnants of the ancient *vivaria*, where the wild animals were kept for the nearby Flavian amphitheatre of the Colosseum.

SS. Giovanni e Paolo is built on the site of a fourth-century church – the Titulus Bizantis or Pammachi – raised by these two senators over the house in which John and Paul, two Roman officers formerly attached to the household of Constantia, the Emperor Constantine's daughter or niece, were martyred as Christians in 362 on the orders of Julian the Apostate. They were put to death in this, their own house, for fear of the anger of the people; and they were buried here, despite the law forbidding burials within the city. Excavations, begun in 1887 under the supervision of the Passionist Father Germano Stanislaus, were continued (1949–51) at the expense of the late Cardinal Spellman of New York, titular of the church, and led to the discovery of the actual Roman house, on two floors, in which John and Paul lived, died and were buried. More than twenty rooms, belonging to a Roman palace or villa and a Christian dwelling and oratory, have been revealed. In a narrow cell reposed the bodies of the martyred officers; these now lie above, under the high altar, in an ancient porphyry urn. The mural decorations which were also uncovered are of great interest: they range from pagan and Christian paintings of the Imperial age to mediaeval representations of SS. Giovanni e Paolo and of three other martyrs associated with them – S. Crispo, S. Crispiniano and S. Benedetta. In the *triclinium* is a third-century mural, showing two graceful male figures, naked except for their flowing cloaks, joined by swags of fruit and flowers, while a peacock and other birds wander at their feet. Above them, cupids pluck grapes, also amid birds and decorative foliage. Here at SS. Giovanni e Paolo modern archaeology has vindicated mediaeval legends and popular reports surrounding this much venerated spot.

Perhaps nowhere in Rome is the perfection of the Early Christian basilica displayed so clearly, in the purity of its balanced forms, or the spirit that animated its builders felt so intimately present, as in the church of S. Sabina, 'the gem of the Aventine' (p. 60). On entering, one is immediately aware of light. The interior of the church is suffused with light. In this it is like the earliest Roman basilicas and the churches of the East, where, as was not originally the case in Rome, churches were from the first orientated so that they would receive the morning sun through the apse windows. It was the influence of the Counter-Reformation that was to shut out the light from so many Roman churches; the preference then was for a tenebrous twilight, for a 'dim religious light', which was held to be conducive to worship, with the result that clerestory windows were in many cases sealed up. Here at S. Sabina the brilliant illumination comes from both the clerestory and the apse windows (the latter being usual in the East, though rare in Rome – but seen, for example, in S. Giovanni a Porta Latina), where the ninth-century use of selenite in squares, circles and lozenges has been retained in the careful restoration of the church. This was carried out, with the excellent results we see, by A. Muñoz and P. Berthier in 1914–19 and 1936–8.

A priest named Peter of Illyria built the church 422–32 above the site of the Titulus Sabinae, the church-house which had belonged to the noble Roman matron Sabina, who was believed to have undergone martyrdom at the time of Hadrian. A few years earlier, in 410, Alaric the Goth had captured Rome, a cataclysmic foretaste of what the ensuing centuries were to hold. For three days the city was given over to fire and sack, before Alaric, as he had promised, withdrew his troops. The matron Marcella, St Jerome's friend, who lived nearby, sought sanctuary, with many others, at S. Paolo fuori le Mura, but she died shortly afterwards as a result of the treatment she received at the hands of the Goths who tried to make her reveal where she had hidden her treasures. The civilized world was aghast at this profanation of the eternal city. The Aventine, with its patricians' palaces and villas, its temples and gardens, suffered severely. The columns, which are such an architectural feature of S. Sabina, may have come from the ruins of the neighbouring Temple of Juno or Isis, or from one of the more magnificent of the destroyed or abandoned palaces.

In 1218 Pope Honorius III, a member of the Savelli family, whose palace adjoined the church, gave the latter to St Dominic for his newly formed Order, and here the saint

RIGHT The excellence of fifth-century Roman brickwork may be seen in the central drum and the surviving ambulatory (originally there were two) of S. Stefano Rotondo. These round churches, possibly derived from classical mausolea, became the model for the earliest Italian baptisteries.

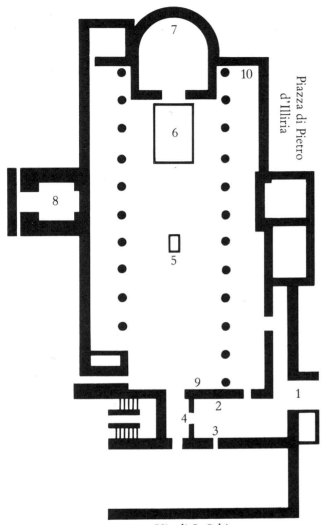

Piazza di Pietro d'Illiria

Via di S. Sabina

S. Sabina

1 Entrance through portico-narthex.
2 Cypress-wood carved doors (fifth century).
3 View into courtyard with orange tree said to have been planted by St Dominic.
4 Entrance to courtyard and monastery.
5 Tombstone of Muñoz de Zamora (d. 1300).
6 Reconstructed Cosmatesque choir.
7 Altar and apse with reconstructed episcopal throne and frescoes (1560) of T. Zuccari.
8 Chapel d'Elci.
9 Mosaic of time of Celestine I (422–32) depicting the Church among the gentiles, '*Ecclesia ex gentibus*', and the Jews, '*ex circumcisione*'.
10 Tomb of Cardinal Auxias di Poggio (d. 1484) by follower of A. Bregno.

lived, between his missionary journeys, until his death in 1221. (It was in the attached monastery which he founded, with its beautiful cloisters, that St Thomas Aquinas taught, and S. Sabina has always remained particularly dear to the Dominicans. In 1370, however, the Senate and people of Rome, in the absence of the papacy, bestowed on the Order, who found S. Sabina too isolated, the more centrally situated church of S. Maria sopra Minerva.)

The approach is through an elegant portico-narthex, formed of antique columns, with fine Corinthian capitals, at the end of which (on the left) an aperture allows one a glimpse, in a courtyard, of the orange tree which is reputed to have been planted by St Dominic. In the beautiful marble framework of the central entrance are cypress-wood doors, carved in low relief, part of them contemporary with the church, and depicting scenes from the Old and New Testaments. This very rare early wood-carving, which has hints of Eastern inspiration, is perhaps the work of two craftsmen working at different periods. On the top of the left-hand panel is one of the earliest (fifth-century) realistic representations of the Crucifixion.

Inside the church, on the wall of the entrance, a mosaic of large gold lettering on a blue ground, which refers to Peter of Illyria and Pope Celestine I (422–32), is flanked by two figures of hierophantic solemnity, also in mosaic, representing the Church among the Jews (*Ecclesia ex circumcisione*) and the Church among the Gentiles (*Ecclesia ex gentibus*). The light streaming in through the twenty-six windows (as in the earliest basilicas, there is a window above each bay) makes one immediately aware that here the right note has been struck: the effect is of a perfectly harmonious relationship of architectural elements. This arises, perhaps above all, from the beauty of the columns supporting the rounded arches of the nave arcading – the first of their kind in Rome, where columns usually support horizontal architraves, as in classical building. The proportions are not accidental, but based securely on the Hellenistic principles enunciated by Vitruvius at the time of Augustus. For example, the height of the columns is nine-and-a-half times their base diameter, and the spacing between columns is five times the diameter – as laid down in the Vitruvian rules on the use of the module. But the height of the Corinthian capitals (the carving being a beautifully crisp rendering of the common acanthus leaf) slightly exceeds the canon, which suggests that their date was

OPPOSITE The beauty of S. Sabina's antique columns (deriving probably from nearby temples or patrician buildings damaged by Alaric the Goth during his sack of Rome in 410), and the close architectural adherence to the Vitruvian rules, have earned the church the title 'the gem of the Aventine'.

closer to the classical age than to that of Constantine, by which time the height of capitals had considerably increased. The columns are of the purest Parian marble, delicately corded for the first third of the shaft, finely fluted for the remaining extent. Around and above the nave arches is a fifth-century frieze of polychrome marbles.

The mosaics of the triumphal arch and apse have perished and have been replaced by frescoes, those of the latter (1560) by Taddeo Zuccari, reproducing the original mosaics. The marble furnishing of the presbytery, including the episcopal throne (a beautiful example of thirteenth-century Cosmati work, its decorative design based on repetitions of circles of porphyry), has been reconstructed, much of it from its original sections, which were recovered piecemeal during the restorations. The simple wooden ceiling was restored to its early form in 1936. In the right-hand aisle is the late fifteenth-century monument to the Spanish cardinal, Auxias di Poggio – possibly by one of the school of Andrea Bregno – of whom the Latin inscription epigramatically states, 'That dying he might live, he lived as one about to die.' In the centre of the nave pavement the tombstone in mosaic of the General of the Order of Preachers, Muñoz de Zamora (d. 1300), is unique in Rome. In its quiet serenity, its austerity tempered by the light that comes flooding in, S. Sabina is perhaps the most perfect example in Rome, in both feeling and form, of the Early Christian basilica.

With the administrative centre of the Roman Empire removed to Constantinople, the political cohesion of the Empire of the West dissolved under successive invasions of Italy by northern barbarians: Visigoths, Vandals, Ostrogoths and, of most lasting importance, Lombards. In 525 – when the Ostrogothic King Theodoric was dying in Ravenna, the capital of his Italic kingdom – the Emperor Justinian determined to regain Italy for the Eastern Empire. The armies which he despatched, under Belisarius and the eunuch Narses, defeated Totila the Goth, and set up the Exarchate at Ravenna, which was the seat of Byzantine governors for nearly 200 years, until, in 728, it fell to the Lombards. The palaces of the Caesars on the Palatine, already beginning to fall into decay, were the residence of Byzantine representatives during this period. (There is a memorial to Belisarius' presence in Rome in the plaque, with its rude lettering, on the wall of the little church of S. Maria

LEFT Detail of the *Triumph of the Cross*, apse mosaic dating from the first half of the twelfth century, in S. Clemente. At the foot of the emaciated figure of the crucified Christ are the grieving Virgin Mary and St John. On the wood of the Cross the Twelve Apostles are represented as doves (see p. 92).

in Trivio, near the Trevi Fountain.) In their distress the Italians increasingly looked to the popes for political as well as spiritual guidance. Pope Gregory the Great (590–604) once confessed that 'he did not know if his office was that of pastor or temporal prince'.

But Byzantine influence was to affect the art of Christian Rome from another and still more immediate source. The rapid advance of the followers of Mahomet threatened the entire Christian world. In 718 the Moslems were repulsed under the very walls of Constantinople by the Emperor Leo III the Isaurian. Christian refugees from Asia Minor, among them artists, found asylum in Rome and Southern Italy. Then, in 726, Leo III, impressed by the rigours of Islamic monotheism, issued an edict forbidding the veneration of images and ordering their destruction in the churches. Many monks and artists fled from the imperial persecutions and sought refuge in Rome, where the iconoclastic decrees were resisted, under the leadership of popes such as Paschal I. A large Greek colony became established in Rome, with their own churches, one being S. Maria in Cosmedin.

Finally the popes, pressed on all sides by the Lombards, and unable, because of the acute political and religious dissensions, to secure assistance from the Eastern emperors, turned to the Franks. Pipin and his son Charles both led armies over the Alps. With the defeat and deposition of the last of the Lombard Kings, Desiderius, in 774, Italy and the papacy were secured. The coronation of Charlemagne as Emperor by Pope Leo III in St Peter's on Christmas Day, 800, marked the resuscitation of the Roman Empire of the West and the inauguration of the Papal States.

It may well have been that the little church of S. Maria Antiqua, tucked away in the Forum, was the chapel of those Byzantine officials who, taking their orders from the Exarch in Ravenna, occupied the former imperial residences on the Palatine. Next door was a monastery, whose members were Greek monks who had fled from the iconoclastic persecutions. S. Maria Antiqua is an eloquent memorial of this period, in its mural adornment a deliberate merging of Eastern and Western hagiology and of Byzantine and Roman art. An enthroned Christ has, on his left, the saints of the Roman Church (among them the great popes – St Clement I, with his anchor, Silvester I, Leo I and Gregory the Great), and, on his right, those of the East (among them the theologians, St John Chrysostom, St Gregory Nazianzen and St Basil). The Virgin Mary is exalted, as are two Eastern saints, Julitta and her son Quiricus, figures little known in the West. In the chapel at the end of the left-hand aisle is a splendid Crucifixion. Beneath the sun and the moon Christ, open-eyed, hangs on the Cross in a long blue Syrian tunic,

An eighteenth-century engraving of S. Maria in Cosmedin.

his feet nailed separately to the wood. Beside him, on the right, looks up a sorrowing Magdalen, and from the left an expressionless (but almost Hellenistic) St John gazes on the scene. In the background, which is full of lively action, appear the centurion Longinus and a soldier, perhaps the one who offered the sponge dipped in gall. In the juxtaposition of artistic styles the Byzantine predominates; but in some figures a Roman hand is detectable. In S. Maria Antiqua is substantiated, at this time of stress, the claim of the popes to the universality of the Church.

The earthquake of 847 destroyed S. Maria Antiqua. In the thirteenth century another church, dedicated to S. Maria Liberatrice, arose above it. It was not until 1902 that this was removed and S. Maria Antiqua was revealed: an invaluable testimony to Rome's stand against Eastern iconoclasm.

The expatriate Greek colony in Rome largely congregated in the low ground between the Circus Maximus and the spot where the ancient drain of the Cloaca Maxima flowed into the Tiber, the bank of which, at this point, was named Ripa Graeca, after them. Today the area centres on the engaging Piazza della Bocca della Verità, with its two remaining Roman temples, which are known (erroneously, it would seem) as the Temple of Virile Fortune (*c.* 100 BC; in 872 it was transformed into a church dedicated to S. Maria Egiziaca) and the Temple of Vesta (a circular building of the second century BC). Here the Greeks had their church of S. Maria in Schola Graeca, or S. Maria in Cosmedin. The latter name is said to have arisen from the beauty of the church's adornment when it was rebuilt by Pope Adrian I in the eighth century: the word *Kosmedin* ('adornment', or 'embellishment'), derives from the same Greek root as the English word 'cosmetic'. The origins of the church are obscure. On this spot temples to Ceres and Proserpine and to

PAGE 65 The Pantheon, erected in 27 BC by Agrippa, the Emperor Augustus' son-in-law, was rebuilt by the Emperor Hadrian (AD 118–25). In 609 Boniface IV dedicated it to the Madonna and all the Martyrs (S. Maria ad Martyres). It contains the tomb of Raphael, as well as tombs of some members of the House of Savoy.

PAGE 66 One of the oldest of Italian round churches, S. Stefano Rotondo was probably built in the fifth century and dedicated by Pope Simplicius (*c.* 470). Although originally consisting of a central drum surrounded by two ambulatories, only the inner ambulatory has survived. In the twelfth century, the timbered roof threatening collapse, Innocent II constructed the transverse supporting wall, the three circular arches being raised on ancient columns of granite.

PAGE 67 The simplicity of architectural form of the Early Christian basilica is revealed in S. Giovanni a Porta Latina, the original church (although subsequently rebuilt) being founded in the fifth century. As occurred so frequently, the builders used materials, in particular columns, taken from classical buildings.

PAGE 68 So rich in glowing colours are the ninth-century Byzantine-inspired mosaics in the Chapel of S. Zeno in S. Prassede that the Romans have long called the chapel the Garden of Paradise. It was built by Paschal I as a mausoleum for his mother Theodora.

MARIA·VIRGO·ASSVPTA E·AD ETHEREV THALAMV INQVO·REX·REGV·STELLATO·SEDET·SOLIO
EXALTATA·EST·SANCTA·DEI·GENITRIX·SVPER·CHOROS·ANGELORVO·AD·CELESTIA·REGNA

the Undefeated Hercules were originally built, and nearby was the establishment of the Prefect of the Grain Distribution. The present crypt was possibly part of a church-house dating from the age of the persecutions. Corinthian columns from the Roman structures have been embodied in successive rebuildings – that which we see today owing much to one Alphanus, chamberlain-architect to Pope Calixtus II in the early twelfth century. Originally Adrian's church, in accordance with the Eastern custom, had galleries for women and triple apses. These apses – so much a feature of Eastern churches, where the central apse had two subsidiary ones, known as *prothesis* and *diaconicon* – have been retained in several other Roman churches which show Byzantine influence, among them S. Giovanni a Porta Latina (fifth century), S. Saba (seventh century) and S. Maria in Domnica (ninth century).

From the piazza, looking beyond Carlo Bizzaccheri's pleasant eighteenth-century fountain, with its genial tritons, one faces the portico (with its central gabled portal, added in the twelfth-century restoration); beside it, on the right, rises the soaring contemporary campanile, with its seven storeys of two- and three-mullioned openings, one of the most graceful of the late Romanesque bell-towers which are so characteristic of mediaeval Rome. Inside the portico, on the right, beyond the monument to the architect-prelate Alphanus, we come to

a great stone disc: the giant's face of the *Bocca della Verità* (possibly from an ancient well, or a drain cover, or the mask of a river god), known to generations of Romans for the legend that the gaping mouth will close and crush the hand of any perjurer who dares to place it there (p. 34). The eleventh-century main doorway, by Johannes de Venetia, is sculpted with motifs from the antique, as if the artist was looking back in order to reach forward.

The restored interior, basilican in form, deeply impresses one by the dignity of its tranquil austerity, the mediaeval frescoes that once covered its walls having almost entirely disappeared. (The apsidal paintings are modern.) The paving here has two beautiful examples of mosaic work: that of the nave (p. 120) is *opus alexandrinum*, and before the high altar is a rare specimen of eighth-century *opus sectile*. The work of the Cosmati here is quite magnificent: the choir, the *ambones*, the paschal candlestick (with the little lion at its base) and the *iconostasis* (an especially Greek feature) – all dating from the eleventh to the thirteenth centuries. Particularly beautiful is the Gothic *baldacchino* (p. 121) over the high altar, the signed work of Deodatus, the third son of Cosmas the Younger; it is dated 1294. The icon of Our Lady above the episcopal throne is said to have been brought from Constantinople by Greeks fleeing from the persecution of Leo the Isaurian. (In the sacristy is a portion of mosaic, part of a destroyed eighth-century *Epiphany* from Old St Peter's.) There is no more revealing memorial to the Greek presence in Rome, and to the Byzantine influence so visible in some of its churches, than the carefully restored S. Maria in Cosmedin.

Just off the Piazza della Bocca della Verità, in the Via del Velabro, stand the ruins of the Arch of Janus Quadrifrons; dating from the Constantinian period. In the Middle Ages they were incorporated in the fortress of the turbulent Frangipane family. Here in classical times was the *velabrum*, the market-place mentioned by Horace in his *Satires*. In the seventh century it was inhabited largely by Greeks, and *c*. 682 Pope Leo II restored for them the already ancient church, which he dedicated to one of their most revered saints, St George of Cappadocia, who, since the time of its Norman kings, has been the patron saint of England.

Placed as it is directly against the ornate Arch of the Moneylenders which was erected in 204 in honour of the Emperor Septimius Severus, the church of S. Giorgio in Velabro is remarkable for its tranquil simplicity both within and without. Flanked on the left by the robust twelfth-century campanile, the façade has a deeply corniced gable-end (pp. 14 & 114). The portico, of the same period, is supported by two broad brick pillars at either end and by four graceful columns of the Ionic order. The wide entablature is topped by a delicate cornice, from which rises the roofing of warm-coloured tiles.

The interior (p. 75) is divided into a nave and two aisles by sixteen free-standing columns, taken from different classical buildings, with Ionic and Corinthian capitals which support the series of arches on which rests the plain wooden ceiling. The austere but pleasing plainness derives from the taste with which its restoration was carried out by A. Muñoz in 1926. The altar, the *confessio* below and the *baldacchino* of three tiers resting on small columns are all the work of the Cosmati. The thirteenth-century frescoes in the apse, which show, on the left, St George with his white charger and crossed banner, have been attributed both to Giotto and to Cavallini, but have been restored beyond recognition.

These two neighbouring churches of S. Maria in Cosmedin and S. Giorgio in Velabro share that particular quality of almost homespun intimacy which a northerner associates with those ancient parish churches to be found in the French or English countryside.

The presence of these exiled Greeks in Rome and the effect of a strong Byzantine influence are reflected in three of the most interesting smaller churches: S. Giovanni a Porta Latina, S. Saba and S. Maria in Domnica.

The setting of S. Giovanni a Porta Latina, off the ancient Via Latina and just within the city side of the Aurelian gateway, is of great charm: a large cedar spreads its branches over the beautiful portico and a carved mediaeval well-head, with its twin columns. On the left, its foundation in the portico, rises an elegant campanile, its six storeys opening in triple-mullioned windows. Since its foundation, perhaps as early as the fifth century, the church of S. Giovanni has had a chequered history – after the French invasion of 1798 it was used as a barracks, a wool store and even a tannery. It has been well restored to its earlier mediaeval appearance. In both the portico and the nave (p. 67) the antique columns are of granite and different marbles, but homogeneity is achieved in their Ionic capitals. The three windows of the central apse reveal the Byzantine influence, and from the outside the apses are seen to be polygonal – another Eastern feature. The church is notable for its cycle of twelfth-century frescoes: in the nave, scenes from the Old and New Testaments; in the apse, the symbols of the Four Evangelists, with the Twenty-four Elders of the Apocalypse.

A short distance from S. Giovanni a Porta Latina, in the Via di Porta Latina, stands what can be best described as a small jewel casket of architecture – the hexagonal Oratory of S. Giovanni in Oleo. This little building is said to mark the spot where St John the Evangelist emerged unscathed from a cauldron of boiling oil, to be banished by the Emperor Domitian to the island of Patmos. The design is reputed to be by Bramante, but its exquisite decoration, both within and without, are by Borromini. The founder, the French prelate Benoît Adam, has placed above the door, together with his armorial bearings, the touching inscription, 'Au plaisir de Dieu'.

During the seventh and eighth centuries Basilian monks, fleeing from the East, were given refuge in Rome, where they built a monastery and church on the Aventine and dedicated them to their patron, S. Saba of Cappadocia. The site which they were granted was much venerated, since on it were the church-house and oratory which had once belonged to St Sylvia, the mother of Pope Gregory the Great; these form the present crypt. Above, they built their church, with its three apses, as required by the Eastern liturgy. Today one enters through the Romanesque gateway into the courtyard in front of the portico to the church (with its beautifully arcaded fifteenth-century loggia and, on the left, the rudimentary bell-

RIGHT The nave of S. Giorgio in Velabro is separated from the aisles by sixteen diverse columns in marble and granite coming from antique buildings. Above the Cosmatesque *baldacchino* the fresco of St George of Cappadocia on a white charger has been attributed both to Cavallini and to Giotto.

tower). The interior of S. Saba is most interesting, with its antique columns and Cosmati work, part of the latter being let into the wall of the right-hand aisle. Particularly noteworthy is the episcopal throne (p. 91). The frescoes, too, are of great interest – especially the seventh-century *The Healing of the Paralytic* and a group of monks (ninth- or tenth-century) from St Sylvia's oratory, also the thirteenth-century *Madonna and Saints* on the left-hand side of the church. Above the triumphal arch is an *Annunciation* of 1463. The apsidal paintings are said to be sixteenth-century copies of the mosaics dating from the time of Adrian I (eighth century). In S. Saba one is conscious of the fruitful mingling of East and West.

That indefatigable opponent of the destructive philistinism of the iconoclasts, Pope Paschal I, built, or rather rebuilt, three Roman churches in honour of the Virgin and the Holy Martyrs, the objects of their attacks: S. Prassede, S. Cecilia in Trastevere and S. Maria in Domnica. S. Maria in Domnica recalls the church-house (*domnicum*) of the early Christians, being, in fact, built over that of the matron Cyriaca on the Coelian Hill, celebrated as the spot where St Lawrence used to distribute food to the poor. The church is also popularly known as S. Maria della Navicella, from the carved stone Roman ship placed in front of the portico, the original being replaced with a replica by Giovanni de' Medici, when he was titular cardinal, before becoming Pope Leo X. Paschal appears to have left the earlier building much as it was – its eighteen ancient columns of granite, with their Corinthian capitals of marble, and the two beautiful Ionic columns of porphyry sustaining the triumphal arch – but he added the subsidiary apses, according to Greek usage. Beneath the ceiling, decorated with symbols from the Litany of the Virgin, runs a frieze, executed by the Renaissance artist Pierino del Vaga to designs by Raphael's pupil, Giulio Romano. When the crystal chandeliers are lit, the church has a ceremonious gaiety that suggests the golden age of Leo. But it is the iconoclastic age of Paschal that is recalled by the apse mosaics of S. Maria in Domnica.

If the Pope rebuilt the church to do honour to the Virgin and to fly directly in the face of the destroyers of images, he made no attempt to disguise the fact in these beautiful mosaics, where, for the first time, it is Mary who occupies the place of honour (pp. 78–9). (The earliest representation of the Madonna is in the Catacomb of S. Priscilla, which dates from the mid-second century.) In S. Maria Domnica she is shown as the Queen of Heaven, with the Christ Child on her

LEFT In the West the popes resisted the iconoclastic decrees of the Eastern emperors. The mosaics in S. Prassede are a testimony to the veneration felt by Paschal I for Christ, his Mother, the saints and martyrs.

knees, in the midst of the angelic host, in white and gold, whose haloes present a cloud-like pattern. Pope Paschal, with the square halo of the living, reverentially kneeling, holds her foot. His monogram appears over her head. Above is a frieze of mosaic, again entirely Byzantine in inspiration: Christ, sitting on a rainbow, is approached from either side by the Twelve Apostles, their forward movement causing their tunics to flare out behind them. These magnificent mosaics are certainly the work of exiled Greeks.

Among the greatest glories of Roman churches are the mosaics which they contain. It was soon appreciated that curved surfaces lent themselves best to the scintillating play of light which brought out most effectively the colours of the *tesserae* of which mosaics are composed – the blues, yellows, whites, greens and ochres, set against the splendour of gold. In Byzantine mosaics two main influences (at times conflicting) are involved: the Hellenistic, with its balance and refinement, ideally naturalistic and employing perspective; and the Semitic, seeking to express an idea, forceful, hierophantic, in which perspective is only schematic and the figures are seen frontally, arranged so as to give emphasis to the idea which the artist seeks to convey.

In the apsidal mosaics of SS. Cosma e Damiano in the Forum we see displayed in all its beauty of form and colour the developing Byzantine manner. This church, dedicated in 527 to the Syrian doctor-martyrs Cosmas and Damian by Pope Felix IV, is built into the remains of Vespasian's Forum of Peace and of the mausoleum erected by the Emperor Maxentius for his dead son, Romulus, which now serves as a circular vestibule. These magnificent mosaics, among the finest in Rome, became the models for those of the ninth century which we have noted in S. Prassede and S. Cecilia in Trastevere, and also for those in S. Marco. Mosaics even as late as those of S. Maria in Trastevere reveal the influence of their prototype in SS. Cosma e Damiano. Here, on a background of deep blue, standing on flame-coloured clouds, rises the majestic bearded figure of Christ, his right hand raised either in blessing or in the course of expounding, his left hand holding a scroll. Below, the Apostles Peter and Paul lead St Cosmas and St Damian, each holding the martyr's crown, to their Saviour; beyond them appear St Theodore (on the right) and (on the left) the still-living Pope Felix IV with the model of his church. The aquatic plants in gold on which they stand symbolize the River Jordan; beneath these, the sheep represent the Twelve Apostles. Although the Hellenistic element is still present, the elaborate folds of the drapery and the elongated faces already herald the full Byzantine style, which was to culminate in Western art in the blaze of colour and attenuated forms of El Greco. These

The Byzantine mosaics in S. Maria in Domnica also bear witness to Paschal I's (817–24) defence of the cult of the Virgin against the decrees of Leo the Isaurian. Beneath his own monogram, the Pope (with the square halo of the living) kneels at the foot of the Virgin, seated with the Christ Child between two bands of angels.

78

mosaics confirm the early presence of Byzantine artists in Rome.

The ancient church of S. Marco (Titulus Pallacinae) was almost totally reconstructed by Pope Gregory IV, whose pontificate (827–44) overlapped with the conclusion of the iconoclastic controversy in favour of the Western, Roman view. Here again the apse mosaics follow the tradition set by SS. Cosma e Damiano, but the falling-off from the original model is apparent; it may be that these mosaics were made in native workshops or by Romans working alongside Greeks. Resplendent as is the gold of Gregory's mosaic in this essentially eighteenth-century interior, the figures of the saints lack any animation, are stiff, hieratic, lack-lustre and, placed as they are on a kind of pedestal, seem too remote from the living. St Mark the Evangelist does place his hand on Pope Gregory's shoulder as he presents him to Christ, but it appears that the force of the original theme and inspiration is wearing thin. These mosaics in S. Marco were the last to be produced in Rome for nearly 300 years. The resuscitation, when it came at the end of the eleventh century, was again Byzantine-inspired, under the influence of Greeks employed by the Abbot Desiderius at Monte Cassino.

As evidence of the powerful effect of Byzantine influence on Roman ecclesiastical architecture and art we may cite its persistence in the fortress-like monastery and church of SS. Quattro Coronati, on the Coelian Hill, rebuilt *c.* 1110, after their destruction by Robert Guiscard, for Pope Paschal II. A watercolour by Franz E. Roesler, painted at the end of the last century, shows SS. Quattro Coronati standing completely isolated, looking more like a baronial castle than a church or a monastery. Today the squat entrance tower and the two keep-like courts, which one crosses before one enters the church, reinforce this impression. Here again are to be found the Greek galleries reserved for women. From the left-hand aisle one passes into the beautiful early twelfth-century cloister, the work of the Cosmati Magister Paulus — one of the most charming of Roman cloisters. Off it is the ancient Chapel of St Barbara, with remains of ninth and thirteenth-century frescoes. But if one has any lingering doubt about the longevity of the Byzantine tradition, a visit to the little Oratory of St Silvester (p. 70) in the adjoining convent, which is entered from the second court, will resolve it. The series of frescoes there, *Scenes from the Lives of the Emperor Constantine and Pope Silvester I* (1246), is convincing proof of the long continuance in Rome of this influence of the East.

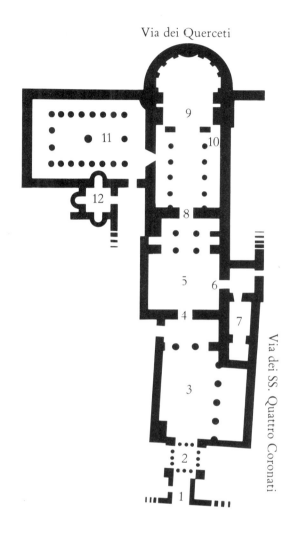

Via dei Querceti

Via dei SS. Quattro Coronati

SS. Quattro Coronati

1 Gateway.
2 Romanesque campanile.
3 First courtyard.
4 Original entrance to the church.
5 Inner courtyard.
6 Entrance to the Oratory of St Silvester.
7 Oratory of St Silvester.
8 Present entrance to the church.
9 Church with the original large apse.
10 *Matronea.*
11 Cloister.
12 Chapel of St Barbara.

The fortress-like structure of the church and monastery of
SS. Quattro Coronati as it appeared at the end of the last
century. During the Middle Ages it served as a bastion in the
defence-works of S. Giovanni in Laterano. Painting by F. E.
Roesler (1852–1907).

S. Marco

1 Renaissance façade and portico by Giuliano da Maiano or
    L. B. Alberti.
2 Stone inscribed to Vannozza Cattanei, mother of Cesare and
    Lucrezia Borgia; moved here at an unknown date from
    her tomb in S. Maria del Popolo.
3 Bas-relief of St Mark in lunette above central doorway by
    Isaia da Pisa (1464).
4 Nave with columns of Sicilian stone, and a coffered and
    gilded ceiling (1466) by G. and M. de' Dolci.
5 *Resurrection* (c. 1600?) by Palma the Younger.
6 Altar dedicated to Pope St Mark with a porphyry urn
    containing his remains (336).
7 Apse with mosaic of time of Gregory IV (828–44), showing
    Christ blessing, with a phoenix at his feet; on his right,
    Pope St Mark, S. Agapito and S. Agnese; on his left, S.
    Felicissimo, St Mark the Evangelist and Gregory IV.
8 Sacristy with remains of a mural by a follower of Cavallini
    (early fourteenth century) and painting, *St Mark*, by
    Melozzo da Forlì (fifteenth century).
9 Entrance to garden courtyard.

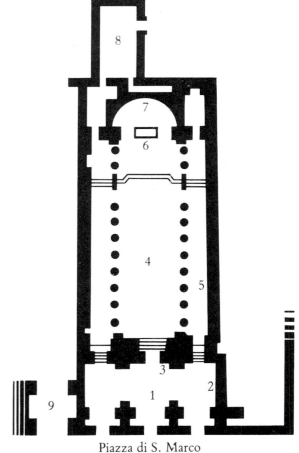

Piazza di S. Marco

4
The Pilgrimage Churches

After the Holy Land itself Rome became the foremost place of pilgrimage. With the evangelization of the North, the work largely of such men as St Martin of Tours, St Augustine of Canterbury and St Boniface ('the apostle to Germany'), by the eighth century the whole of the Western world was looking to Rome as its spiritual centre. Men and women were powerfully drawn to visit in person the shrines of the Apostles Peter and Paul, to see with their own eyes the actual places where St Lawrence and St Sebastian had suffered and to worship at the tombs of such martyrs for the faith as St Cecilia and St Agnes; the lives of all these saints were known to everyone from the popular martyrologies. With the conquering progress of the Moslems in the Middle East and the capture of Jerusalem in 638, Rome became the principal goal for peaceful Western pilgrims, whereas the Holy Land became the scene of the 'armed pilgrimages' of the Crusades.

The fashion for the Palestinian pilgrimage was set as early as the time of Constantine by no less a personage than the Empress-Mother Helena. Other Roman matrons followed her, like Melania or Paula and her daughter, who were accompanied on their tour of the Holy Places, which took place after 385, by St Jerome. The latter was in two minds about the value of pilgrimages: 'Access to the courts of

heaven', he wrote, 'is as easy from Britain as it is from Jerusalem, for the Kingdom of God is within you.' Nevertheless, despite some doubts and admonitions expressed by the early Christian Fathers, pilgrimages soon became established as part of the life of the Roman Church and grew in popularity throughout the Middle Ages, especially after the introduction of Jubilee Years by Pope Boniface VIII in 1300.

In Rome, 'the threshold of the Apostles', the churches of St Peter's and S. Paolo fuori le Mura has always received the especial veneration of the faithful. The other five great pilgrimage churches, according to tradition, are S. Giovanni in Laterano (Rome's cathedral), S. Maria Maggiore, S. Lorenzo fuori le Mura, S. Croce in Gerusalemme (the repository of the Empress Helena's relics) and S. Sebastiano on the Via Appia. In the Middle Ages there grew up around these important churches veritable townships, which catered for the pilgrims who flocked to Rome: monastic buildings of all kinds, hospices, inns, stables, baths, wine-cellars, shops (for the sale of everything from food and clothing to reliquaries and images), churches, shrines, oratories, and cemeteries. Mediaeval drawings show, for example, the great complexes that arose around S. Giovanni in Laterano and St Peter's. The latter, which included colonies of foreign nationals (like the Saxons, with their church and hospital of S. Spirito in Sassia), was enclosed within walls, for protection against the Saracens, by Pope Leo IV c. 850, thus creating within the city another, the Leonine City.

If at first the motive for going on a pilgrimage was primarily devotional, later it may have been undertaken as an

LEFT Arnolfo di Cambio's Oratory of the Crib (c. 1289) was brought to S. Maria Maggiore in the late sixteenth century by Domenico Fontana. Of the figures, Joseph, the three Magi, the ox and the ass are the work of Arnolfo; the Madonna and Child date from the sixteenth century.

act of expiation for some crime or sin, and, later still, in order to gain the indulgences offered to those who performed it and carried out in a contrite spirit certain specified acts – such as, for example, visiting these 'pilgrimage' churches in Rome. Primitive guide-books, like the *Salzburg Itinerary* and *Einsiedeln Itinerary*, helped the pilgrims on their way. Once in the Eternal City, pilgrims during the period from the twelfth to the fifteenth centuries could use as a guide to the ancient monuments and churches the popular (but misleading) *Mirabilia Urbis Romae* (*The Marvels of the City of Rome*).

The pilgrims (each dressed in a grey cowl showing a red cross, with broad-brimmed hat, staff, scrip and gourd) usually travelled in parties, singing songs which are among the most beautiful of the Middle Ages, such as 'O Roma nobilis orbis et domina' (O Rome, noble mistress of the world) and 'In Gottes Namen faren Wir' (In God's name we go forth). The fervour and excitement grew as they approached Rome the Golden, until, from the height of the Triumphal Way, they beheld the walls, high towers, churches and other buildings of the city. One ecstatic Irishman may be quoted as expressing the feelings of the pilgrim at his journey's end: 'O Rome, exceedingly glorified by the triumphs of the Apostles, crowned with the roses of martyrs, all white with the lilies of confessors, adorned with the palms of virgins, strengthened by the merits of all the saints! O city that enshrinest so many of their holy bodies, all hail to thee!'

In *c.* 1450 the Englishman John Capgrave, an Austin Friar from King's Lynn, made the pilgrimage to Rome; he has left us a description, written in English, of the city and its principal churches: *Ye Solace of Pilgrimes*. He lists the seven pilgrimage churches in this order: St Peter's, S. Paolo, S. Sebastiano, S. Giovanni in Laterano, S. Croce, S. Lorenzo, S. Maria Maggiore; and he then goes on to name sixty of the other main churches which he visited. He is careful to note, for every church, the occasions and the terms in years of the indulgences offered. Referring to the steps of St Peter's, he states, 'These greces [steps] be in number *XXIX*, and as often as a man goeth up on these greces because of devotion as often has he for every gre vii year of indulgence granted by Alexander the Pope as we find written in old remembrance.' Some sixty years after Capgrave's pious visit, Tetzel's sale of indulgences was to provoke another Augustinian monk, Martin Luther, to post his ninety-five theses on the church door at Wittenberg.

Above the tomb of St Peter (who was buried by the matron Livia in her own ground, close by his place of execution) an oratory was soon erected by St Anacletus. The basilica raised above this by Constantine was separated from the piazza by an *atrium* – known later as Paradise from the beauty of its mosaics of flowers, ferns and foliage and from Pope Gelasius' gilded *cantharus*, placed in its centre. The piazza itself was the scene of much colour and animation, with the coming and going of pilgrims among the booths and stalls of money-changers and sellers not only of vital necessities but also of holy objects – crosses, amulets, devout pictures and reliquaries. It had all the air and appearance of a popular fair. From this piazza to the *atrium* the pilgrims ascended on their knees the twenty-nine steps counted by Capgrave (others give the number as thirty-five) – even Charlemagne, during his memorable visit of 774, performed this action of devotion and humility. At the top of the steps an emperor, at the time of his coronation, would be received by the pope. At the farther end of the *atrium*, before the narthex, stood a statue of St Peter. Five doorways led into the church; of these, the central doorway (which was called, from the sixth-century silver-work of its doors, the *Porta Argentea*) had been replaced in 1445, on the orders of Pope Eugenius IV, with the bronze ones designed by the Florentine artist Filarete, which were retained when St Peter's was rebuilt (p. 250).

If, externally, the basilica stood in all the splendour of its façade mosaics and of its roof, ablaze with tiles of gilt-bronze – spoils from the temple of Venus and Rome, from the Capitolium and from the Pantheon – this was only a foretaste. Within the sight was overwhelming in the sheer magnificence of all the gold, silver and mosaic, and in the brilliance of the light, part of which came from the 700 candles kept burning night and day before the fifty-two altars, reflected in the white marble floor, which had once served in Nero's circus. The wide nave was separated from the double aisles by rows of ninety-six antique columns of different orders both in their capitals and bases, composed of various marbles or of polished granite. Above the delicately carved architraves – again varying, since they, too, came from ancient buildings – light streamed in through the round-headed windows of the clerestory, beneath the raftered ceiling. Beyond the splendid *confessio* and shrine the nave terminated in the great semi-circular apse, with its episcopal throne and the seats for the clergy. Below the tribune arch (with Constantine's mosaic, showing the Emperor himself being presented to Christ by St Peter, and with his dedicatory inscription) a beam supported a large Cross between two keys; beneath these was the Pharos, a gigantic candelabra capable of holding some 1,300 candles, which were lit only at Christmas and Easter and on the feasts of St Peter and St Paul. Two relics were preserved in chapels: St Peter's chair and 'the Veronica' – the cloth on which was imprinted the likeness of Christ which appeared when Veronica, seeing him on his way to Calvary, gave it to him to wipe the sweat from his brow. To the left of the

The Piazza of St Peter's in the sixteenth century, showing Old
St Peter's and a wing of the Vatican, by Marten van Heemskerck.

basilica was the Chapel of St Petronilla, converted from the
circular mausoleum of the Emperor Honorius by Pope
Stephen II in 752, when, on fulfilment of King Pipin's
promise of aid against the Lombards, he removed the saint's
body from the Catacomb of Domitilla and made her patron
saint of the kings of France. These were some of the sights that
rewarded the eyes of pilgrims to Rome until *c.* 1450, when
Old St Peter's, after a lifetime of some 1,150 years, showed
signs of irreparable decay and Nicholas V arrived at the momentous decision to replace it with a new church (see p.244).

From the Pyramid of Caius Cestius by the Porta Ostiensis
(now Porta S. Paolo) a covered colonnade sheltered the
mediaeval pilgrim from sun and rain as he made his devout
way to the tomb of the Apostle to the Gentiles in the church
of S. Paolo fuori le Mura on the Ostian Road. Constantine's
building, rebuilt and enlarged in 386 on the orders of the
Emperors Valentinian, Theodosius and Arcadius by the
Consul Sallustrius, was completed by the Emperor Honorius, with noteworthy contributions from Galla Placidia,

the daughter of the Emperor Theodosius. S. Paolo has
suffered from earthquakes, pillage by Saracens, neglect (the
whole area was dangerously malarial) and, finally, the fire of
15–16 July 1823. This disaster was caused by a careless
workman who, after his day's work, left a brazier of live coals
under the roof, thus bringing about, in a single night, the
destruction of Rome's greatest surviving early basilica. In the
morning the only remains of the nave to be found among the
smoking ruins were the stumps of calcined columns. The
restoration of the basilica was made possible by worldwide
contributions from Catholics and non-Catholics alike; the
building was reconsecrated in December 1854 by Pope Pius
IX, in the presence of prelates from every part of Christendom.

At S. Paolo, during the Middle Ages, besides the
monasteries, there were also hostels, inns and bath-houses for
the pilgrims, and even public lavatories: an inscription states
that, *c.* 500, 'Symmachus made one for the use of human
necessity.' After the Goths cut the aqueducts, water was
drawn from the Tiber by water-wheels. Refreshed in body,
the mediaeval pilgrim, from the thirteenth century onwards,
would have been greeted by the glorious colour of the façade
mosaics by Pietro Cavallini. He would have entered the
church through the splendid bronze doors, inlaid with silver

niello-work, portraying saints and martyrs, which were wrought in Constantinople in 1070 by Staurakios of Chios, under the supervision of Hildebrand, Abbot of S. Paolo, later the great Pope Gregory VII. Within, eighty magnificent fluted columns of *pavonazzetto* and precious Parian marble divided the nave from the double aisles – a great glade cut through a forest of stone. Of these columns twenty-four, perfectly matched in size, colour and finish, were taken by either Constantine or Valentinian from a single classical building; the remaining fifty-six came from various pagan temples. Ahead, the pilgrim would have seen the huge triumphal arch (which has survived) created by the artists who cut the mosaics for Galla Placidia's mausoleum at Ravenna, supported by two immense Ionic columns of rare marble and glittering with the gold among its coloured mosaics. In the centre, Christ, between two angels, raises his hand in benediction. Above are the symbols of the Four Evangelists; the Twenty-four Elders of the Apocalypse present their crowns; below, against a ground of blue, stand the imposing figures of St Peter and St Paul. Beyond, the mediaeval pilgrim would have seen the Apostle's tomb, covered by the beautiful Gothic *baldacchino* (1285) of Arnolfo di Cambio; behind this, the apse was all aglow with mosaic. On the nave walls the 'portraits' of all the popes, from St Peter onwards, were represented in circular medallions in mosaic. Above them two rows of magnificent frescoes in panels represented scenes, on the left, from the lives of St Peter and St Paul and, on the right, from the Old and New Testaments.

Today, when the visitor enters the modern *atrium* or *quadriportico* (by G. Calderini), he is rebuffed by the hard, unyielding quality of the stonework and by the architectural heavy-handedness. The downright clumsiness of the campanile might have offered a forewarning. Within, he is impressed by the spatial immensity, the highly polished marble of the floor, the monolithic columns of granite from Montorfano, with their Corinthian capitals, and the gilded coffering of the ceiling, which bears the arms of Pope Pius IX. But it is all sadly lacking in the breath of life; for this, it requires the animation, the crowds and the colour of the ceremonial that mark the Saint's feast-days of 25 January and 30 June. Without these, it remains, as one commentator described it, 'a great marble monotony'.

S. Paolo once gloried in its mosaics, its frescoes and a carved wooden crucifix by perhaps the best-known of Roman artists, Pietro Cavallini. A crucifix, which is said to have spoken to St Bridget of Sweden, remains in the chapel to the left of the apse. In the apse are early thirteenth-century mosaics, made by Byzantine workmen who had been engaged on the mosaics of St Mark's, Venice. Lacking capable native Roman craftsmen, Pope Honorius III had to

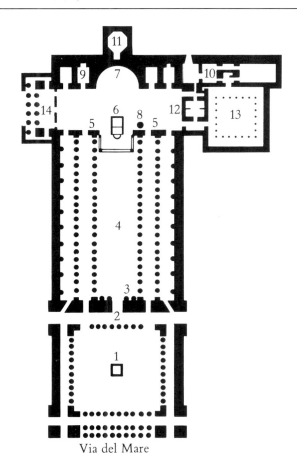

Via del Mare

S. Paolo fuori le Mura

1 *Quadriportico* by G. Calderini (1892–1928).
2 Façade with nineteenth-century mosaics.
3 Original bronze doors (1070) much damaged in the fire of 1823.
4 Nave and double aisles with eighty columns of Montorfano granite.
5 Triumphal arch of Galla Placidia with original fifth-century mosaics.
6 High altar with *baldacchino* (1285) by Arnolfo di Cambio; below, the tomb of St Paul.
7 Apse with restored mosaics dating from the time of Pope Honorius III (*c.* 1220) and other mosaics by P. Cavallini, removed from original façade.
8 Paschal candelabrum (1180) by Nicolò di Angelo and Petrus Vassallettus.
9 Chapel of the Holy Sacrament with the tomb of Pietro Cavallini (d. 1321) and *Crucifix* (fourteenth century) attributed to Tino di Camaino.
10 Sacristy.
11 Campanile.
12 Baptistery.
13 Cloister (completed before 1214) by the Vassalletti.
14 Side entrance with portico.

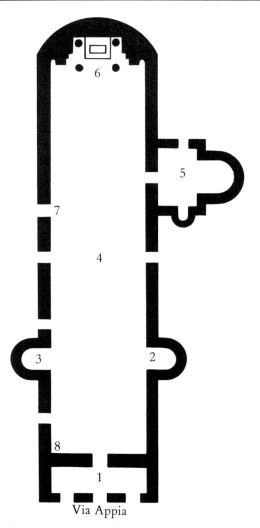

Via Appia

S. Sebastiano

1 Façade and portico by Flaminio Ponzio and G. Vasanzio
  (1612) with coupled granite columns from ancient
  basilica.
2 Chapel of the Relics containing the reputed imprint of the
  foot of Christ when he met St Peter on the Appian Way
  (*Quo Vadis?*) and one of the arrows of St Sebastian's
  martyrdom.
3 Chapel of St Sebastian (above the saint's burial place) with
  his recumbent statue (*c.* 1650?) by A. Giorgetti.
4 Nave with Vasanzio's ceiling showing arms of Cardinal
  Scipio Borghese and Gregory XVI.
5 Albani Chapel.
6 High altar with four antique green marble columns and
  busts of St Peter and St Paul (*c.* 1600?) by Nic. Cordier.
7 Entrance to sacristy.
8 Stone engraved by order of Pope Damasus (366–84) with an
  eulogy on the martyr Eutychius.

request the Doge Pietro Zanni to lend him these artists. Their
coming marks the revival of the Roman school of mosaicists,
which was soon to produce, at the end of the thirteenth
century, such masters as Cavallini and Jacopo Torriti. Some
of the former's work – including his *Madonna enthroned with the
Christ-child*, once on the western façade – has been moved to
the apsidal arch; other mosaics by him, also from the earlier
façade, are on the reverse of the triumphal arch. In the right
transept stands a great twelfth-century paschal candelabrum,
signed by Nicolò di Angelo and Petrus Vassallettus. This has
all the rude force of the Romanesque, with but little hint of the
future of sculpture under the influence of the Pisani – a
powerful example of essentially mediaeval art. From here one
passes to the exquisite contemporary cloister (again, in part
the work of Vassallettus, but so very different), which shares,
with that of S. Giovanni in Laterano (see p. 108), the
distinction of being the most beautiful of all Roman cloisters.

The basilica of S. Sebastiano (originally called S. Sebastiano
ad Catacumbas) – outside the city walls, on the ancient
Appian Way – was placed by Capgrave next after St Peter's
and S. Paolo. It was venerated since early times by pilgrims,
on account of the belief that the Apostles' bodies were moved
here during the era of persecutions. The original oratory – or,
at least, the church built by Constantine – was certainly
named after the Apostles, but the belief that their bodies ever
rested here has been questioned, and it does seem unlikely that
they should have been removed for safety to such a busy
highway, lined with hostelries. However, in the catacombs
beneath the present church (which were so well known that
the word 'catacomb' was first, and for a long time, associated
solely with this spot) can be seen, scratched on the walls, some
seventy *graffiti*, invoking the aid of 'Peter and Paul' or 'Paul
and Peter', in about equal numbers. Much later the church
and the city gate leading to it were renamed after St Sebastian.
In a 1375 edition of the *Mirabilia* the writer remarks:

> At Saint Sebastian is the cemetery of Saint Calixtus at the
> Catacombs. And without is the *campus agonis* [place of
> public games], wherein is an idol, at which Saint
> Sebastian was shot with arrows. And near by is the well,
> wherein Saint Urban baptized . . . and had his hiding-
> place. And in Saint Sebastian is Pope Stephen, and the
> place where he was beheaded. . . . There also in a field,
> over against Saint Sebastian, nigh to his chapel, is a well,
> out of which he christened Saint Cecilia and Tiburtinus
> and Valerian.

The true catacomb of St Calixtus nearby was only discovered
and explored during the last century. The scene of St
Sebastian's martyrdom, so often represented in Renaissance

painting, is usually regarded as having been on the Palatine, the site now occupied by the little church of S. Sebastiano al Palatino.

St Sebastian, a young officer of the Praetorian Guard, was thought to have suffered under Diocletian. Suspected of condoning or actively assisting other Christian soldiers, he was condemned, shot by archers and left for dying. He was rescued, nursed and cured of his wounds by the matron Irene. On his recovery he openly confronted the Emperor; thereupon he was beaten to death and his body was cast into the common sewer. It was recovered by the matron Lucina and buried in her crypt on the Appian Way, not far from the pagan mausoleum of Cecilia Metella — situated on that cypress and sepulchre-lined stretch of the ancient road so familiar to lovers of the picturesque.

The present basilica was built for the connoisseur Cardinal Scipio Borghese by his architect Flaminio Ponzio, and completed at the latter's death in 1613 by the Dutchman G. Vasanzio. Entering through the portico, which was once filled with colour from the early seventeenth-century frescoes of Antonio Carracci, the visitor is struck by the effect of luminosity and by the sense of quiet sobriety and calm resulting from the white walls of the wide nave and by the painted ceiling (which represents St Sebastian and the Borghese and Cappellari arms). In a chapel to the left reposes the body of St Sebastian, removed by the Cardinal from its original resting-place in the crypt directly beneath. The recumbent statue of the saint below the altar is one of the best works of Bernini's pupil, Antonio Giorgetti. Pope Stephen I is buried beneath the high altar.

The church is in the possession of the Franciscan Order. The Catacombs of St Sebastian are among the most frequently visited of these Roman subterranean cemeteries and are notable for the early *graffiti* mentioned above (some of which incorporate the Greek word *icthus* – 'fish'), for some beautiful Roman frescoes of vases of fruit and of birds, and for some very fine stucco-work in a *columbarium* of the Imperial age. These catacombs are typical of the many that occupy a vast area in the region of the Appian Way.

During the Middle Ages, grouped around S. Giovanni in Laterano and the Lateran Palace, there were not only the buildings housing the entire papal administration but also monasteries, church schools, hospices, inns and hospitals for the reception of pilgrims and emissaries to the Holy See — thus constituting, like the Leonine City, a self-contained ecclesiastical township. In the Lateran Palace (or *Patriarchium*) were the council hall and the banqueting-hall, with its tribune and no fewer than six apses covered with a mosaic, which was built by Leo III in honour of Charlemagne and was the brilliant

PAGE 89 Of a grave beauty is the little Romanesque cloister (rare in Rome) at S. Lorenzo fuori le Mura. Off the cloister is the entrance to the catacomb of St Cyriaca, where in 258 the Roman matron Irene buried the charred remains of St Lawrence.

PAGE 90 S. Lorenzo fuori le Mura is formed by the junction of two churches, carried out in the eighth century by Adrian I. The present presbytery is in the edifice founded by the Emperor Constantine (330), employing disparate columns and architraves from classical buildings. The beautiful *baldacchino* (1148) is the first to be signed by the Cosmati.

PAGE 91 Cosmati work in the ancient church of S. Saba, founded in the seventh century: the back of the simple episcopal throne is topped by a marble disc with a cross in brilliant mosaic. Above it is a fourteenth-century fresco of the *Crucifixion*. The other apsidal murals, also by an unknown artist – the *Madonna and Child*, *Christ between St Andrew and St Saba*, *Procession of Sheep and Mystic Lamb* – are of 1575.

PAGE 92 In 1108 Paschal II began the reconstruction of the upper church of S. Clemente after the destruction wrought by Robert Guiscard and his Normans. The pavement, paschal candlestick, *ambo* and *baldacchino* are contemporary work of the Cosmati. The apse mosaic, representing the *Triumph of the Cross*, ranks among the most glorious achievements of the Roman mosaicists of the first half of the twelfth century.

QVI SVA PRO MERITIS RADIANTEM FRON
CARDINEVM TRIBVIT VIRTVS ETIAM VIRTVAV
ASPICE QVM LACRIMIS LECTOR QVO MARMORE C
IMPIA MORS RAPVIT FORMAM NATVR
ANGELICAM DEDERAT SAPIENS ET DOCTV
PRAEFVIT ELOQVIO TITVLVM QVI SERVAT
ANGELA PETRVS ERAT NOMEN SIBI VNE
DE STEPHANESCIS MATERNO CARDINE N
AVI SIMILI HANIBALE NAM LONGI TRAMIT
OSSA IACENT TELLVS ANIMA SIBI GLORIA

+ OBIIT ANNO DNI M CCC XVII MENSIS OCT
VLTIMO MAGISTER PAVLVS FECIT HOC O

scene of the ceremonial feast held after the Emperor's coronation on Christmas Day, 800. (One of these apses has been preserved on a wall facing the Piazza di Porta S. Giovanni, restored in 1743 by Ferdinando Fuga, who used what remained of the original mosaic.) In the piazza stood the equestrian statue of Marcus Aurelius – fortunately preserved owing to its being mistaken for a representation of Constantine the Great and eventually moved to the Piazza of the Capitoline Hill. Here, in S. Giovanni in Laterano and its surrounding buildings, was the hub of the universal church until the beginning of the fourteenth century, when the French Pope Clement V moved the seat of the papacy to the banks of the Rhône.

During the fourteenth century two fires finally destroyed both basilica and palace, and it was the failure of Pope Urban V to rebuild the former that prompted Petrarch's rebuke: 'How can you enjoy the delights of your residence on the flowery banks of the Rhône? How can you enjoy banqueting in halls with ceilings of gold, while the roofless Lateran, almost level with the ground, lies exposed to wind and rain?' At the end of the century, when Gregory XI, responding to the call of St Catherine of Siena, returned to Rome, such was the ruinous state of the Lateran that he took up his residence at the Vatican.

In the late sixteenth century Pope Sixtus V, who elsewhere did so much to adorn Rome, destroyed the ancient papal administrative centre and demolished the remains of the earlier Lateran Palace, replacing it by the present barrack-like structure, the work of his favourite architect, Domenico Fontana. However, he spared the baptistery, the beautiful early thirteenth-century cloister created by the Vassalletti and the papal chapel – a jewel of Cosmati work, known as the Sancta Sanctorum from the relics which it contained. He had Fontana remove the papal staircase to the ancient council hall of the Lateran Palace to serve as an approach to the chapel. This stairway, the Scala Sancta, which is ascended by the devout on their knees, is said to have been the stairs of Pilate's *praetorium*, which Christ mounted at the time of his trial, and to have been brought to Rome from Jerusalem by the Empress Helena.

In 1646, the basilica being in danger of collapse, the work of restoration was entrusted by Innocent X to Francesco Borromini. The interior was completed in time for the Jubilee of 1650; it is a work, therefore, of the period of the High Baroque. Borromini solved the problem of preserving the ancient framework by encasing each pair of consecutive columns in a wide pillar, which he framed with giant pilasters the height of the nave. Against these he placed coved niches, composed of columns of *verde antico* supporting a pediment in the centre of which is the Pamphilj dove,

PAGE 93 The choir screen, altar *paliotto*, framing of the *confessio* and pavement in S. Cesareo are all the work of the Cosmati (thirteenth century). The angels drawing back the curtains come possibly from a Renaissance tomb. The *baldacchino* is from the time of Clement VIII (1592–1605).

PAGE 94 Detail of angels from the *Universal Judgement* (1293) by Pietro Cavallini in the convent attached to S. Cecilia in Trastevere

PAGE 95 The central figure in Cavallini's *Universal Judgement* must be accounted, in its solemn majesty, one of the most moving of all representations of Christ.

PAGE 96 The monumental tomb to Cardinal Pietro Stefaneschi (d. 1417), in the style of the early Renaissance, by the Roman-born sculptor Paolo Romano in S. Maria in Trastevere.

carrying an olive branch in its beak. The niches contain
outsize statues, of a brilliant whiteness, of the Twelve
Apostles. Above are scenes in white stucco (they were
originally intended to be of bronze) by Algardi (1650).
Although the reconstruction of S. Giovanni in Laterano
has its detractors, admirers of the architect will appreciate
the imagination displayed both here and in the ornament
of the oval frames of the clerestory, also in the resettings
for the monuments of popes, cardinals and high dignitaries
in the aisles. In the nave the pervading whiteness contrasts
with the sumptuous gilding of the sixteenth-century ceiling,
with the colour of the arms of popes who have contributed
to it, and with the beautiful Cosmatesque paving, which was
presented by Pope Martin V, a member of the Colonna family
whose device, a column, is included in the design. This
Pope's bronze tomb, by the Florentine Simone di Giovanni
Ghini (*c.* 1443), is before the papal altar, and its inscription
proclaims Martin V to have been the 'Felicity of his Age'. He
certainly did much for Rome's churches. Behind the first
pillar on the right is a fragment of Giotto's fresco of Boniface
VIII proclaiming the Jubilee of 1300. Under the Gothic
baldacchino (1367) of Giovanni di Stefano the high altar (at
which only the Pope may celebrate Mass) is said to contain
the table at which St Peter celebrated Mass in the house of
Pudens, and on the altar is a silver *ciborium*, reputed to contain
the heads of St Peter and St Paul.

In 1884 Pope Leo XIII ordered the architects Vespignani,
father and son, to lengthen the choir and tribune and replace

ABOVE A view of the Lateran in the sixteenth century by
Marten van Heemskerck, showing the equestrian statue of
Marcus Aurelius (now on the Capitol) in its earlier position.

RIGHT In preparation for the Jubilee of 1650, Innocent X had
Borromini strengthen and remodel the interior of S. Giovanni in
Laterano. The architect coupled the ancient columns and
enclosed them within huge pilasters. Statues of the Apostles were
placed in *aedicules* supported by columns of *verde antico*.

the apse mosaics of Jacopo Torriti and Jacopo da Camerino.
Although reset and restored, these mosaics (1284–94) have a
rare beauty all their own. In the centre appears the head of
Christ, surrounded by cherubim, and, above, the Holy Spirit
descends in the form of a dove. Beneath, a gem-studded Cross
rises from the four streams of Paradise, at which the faithful,
represented as deer and lambs, slake their thirst. The figures of
the Virgin, St Peter, St Paul and other saints, and the tiny
figure of Pope Nicholas IV, can be seen beside them. Below
them all flows the River Jordan, dotted with swans and boats.
Between the windows, among palm-trees, one can see a row
of nine Apostles and the two small figures of the artists.
Despite its removal and renovation, the work has freshness
and great charm. (For the beautiful cloister, see p. 111.)

On 8 December 1735 Clement XII laid the foundation
stone of the façade of S. Giovanni in Laterano, the
commission for which had been won in a competition by the
Florentine Alessandro Galilei. Here there was no *settecento*
falling-off in that essentially Roman quality of *gravitas*. With

S. Giovanni in Laterano

1 Façade and portico (1735) by A. Galilei.
2 Fresco of *Boniface VIII proclaiming the Jubilee of 1300* by Giotto.
3 Torlonia Chapel.
4 Massimo Chapel.
5 Cenotaph of Silvester II (d. 1003).
6 Papal altar; above, Gothic *baldacchino* (1367) by Giovanni di Stefano; below, *confessio* (c. 1443) containing the tomb of Martin V by S. Ghini.
7 Tomb of Innocent III (d. 1216) by Gius. Lucchetti (1891).
8 Presbytery.
9 Apse with mosaics (c. 1290) by Jacopo Torriti and Jacopo da Camerino (transferred and reset 1884).
10 Old sacristy.
11 Colonna Chapel.
12 Cloister.
13 Corsini Chapel.

S. Giovanni in Fonte

14 Font.
15 Chapel of St John the Baptist.
16 Chapel of SS. Rufina e Secunda (also called of St Cyprian and St Justin).
17 Chapel of S. Venanzio.
18 Chapel of St John the Evangelist.
19 Courtyard.

Piazza di S. Giovanni in Laterano

Piazza di Porta S. Giovanni

its high plinths and its one gigantic Corinthian order of pilasters and half-columns, it has more than a suggestion of the work of Palladio. The powerful central section, which is crowned with a pediment, contains an arcaded loggia, from which the Pope gives his blessing on Ascension Day. Of the white stone figures of the fourteen saints who, with Christ, surmount the balustrade, it has been said that they appear to be struggling in a high wind. But, seen from a distance, in the bleaching strength of a Roman sun, they are most effective, adding a human note to this most impressive of façades, which is stately rather than austere, as befits Rome's cathedral church.

The intervening space between S. Giovanni in Laterano and S. Croce in Gerusalemme, and the view from the former church, were once interrupted by a hill known as Monte Cipollaro, from the onions and garlic grown there that were eaten, following a pagan custom, on St John's Day, 24 June. This hill was levelled by Benedict XIV in the mid-eighteenth century, when he restored and radically altered the church of S. Croce. The earliest record of a church called Jerusalem was in a fourth-century biography of Pope Silvester I: 'Constantine opened a basilica in the Sessorian Palace, where, in a golden reliquary, are kept pieces of the Holy Cross, and named it Hierusalem.'

Seen from the piazza, the *settecento* façade (p. 237) is arresting, owing to the interplay of concave and convex surfaces and to the deep-shadowed recesses seen between the plain walls of the adjoining Cistercian monastery. But it is arresting not in the manner of the contemporary façade of S. Giovanni in Laterano; rather, it is striking as an example of *settecento bizarrerie*. The reconstruction of S. Croce in 1743 was the joint work of the little-known Domenico Gregorini and Pietro Passalacqua. The visitor proceeds into an oval narthex, which seems to owe something to the influence of Borromini, but without that master's touch. Inside, eight granite columns in the nave are the sole survivors of the earlier church. The *settecento* impression is heightened by the

View of S. Croce in Gerusalemme in the early eighteenth century, showing the church set among vineyards with ruins of Roman aqueducts in the background, by the English artist John Alexander.

S. Croce in Gerusalemme

1 Façade (1743) by Dom. Gregorini and P. Passalacqua.
2 Oval narthex.
3 Enclosed chapel with old crucifix and fourteenth-century fresco.
4 Nave with eight antique columns, eighteenth-century pilasters, Cosmatesque pavement, and Renaissance holy water stoups.
5 Basalt urn containing the remains of S. Cesario and S. Anastasio.
6 High altar and tomb (1536) of Cardinal Francesco Quiñones, confessor to Emperor Charles v, by Jacopo Sansovino.
7 Chapel of St Helena with mosaics attributed to Melozzo da Forlì; the earth under the floor was brought from Calvary, thus giving the church the name of 'in Gerusalemme'.
8 Gregorian Chapel (1523) built by Cardinal Carvajal with *Pietà* by unknown, early seventeenth-century artist.
9 Entrance to the Chapel of the Relics which contains pieces of the True Cross and thorns from Christ's crown.
10 Remains of the Castrensian Amphitheatre built into the Aurelian Wall.

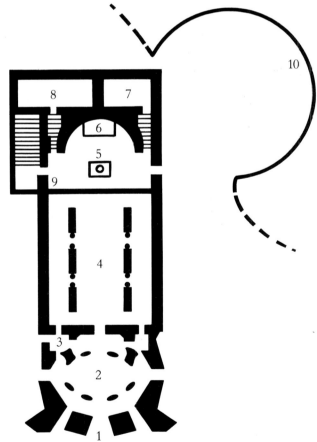

Via S. Croce in Gerusalemme

colourful paintings of Corrado Giaquinto. The murals (*c.* 1492) in the apse, *Christ in the Act of Blessing* and *Scenes from St Helena's Finding the True Cross*, were for long thought to be the work of Pinturicchio, but are now generally attributed to the native Antoniazzo Romano, who acted as assistant, on their Roman visits, to such Renaissance painters as Pinturic chio, Signorelli and Melozzo da Forlì.

From the Middle Ages onwards pilgrims have flocked to S. Croce not for the association of the church with St Helena or Constantine, but rather for the precious relics that the former brought back to Rome from her trips to the Holy Land. Today these are kept in the modern (1930) Chapel of the Relics: pieces of the True Cross and the inscription over it, a nail and two thorns from Christ's crown. The stairway that ascends to the chapel is known as Calvary.

In the subterranean Chapel of St Helena, the only part of the original Sessorian Palace which remains, the pavement is said to rest on soil brought by the Empress from Golgotha. Here, in the vaulting, are some exquisite mosaics, thought originally to have been placed there in the fifth century by the Emperor Valentinian III, but redesigned in the late fifteenth century by Melozzo da Forlì, and perhaps Baldassare Peruzzi, who may have followed closely the Hellenistic originals. The central medallion, with the figure of Christ, is surrounded by ovals framing the Evangelists and by four smaller scenes from the Legend of the Cross. In the niches of the arch are St Silvester I, St Helena, St Peter and St Paul. The ornamentation and the profusion of colour are delightful: each oval is supported by a winged figure rising from a flower, and is flanked by brilliant peacocks on a gold ground, with interven ing decoration of birds, fruits and flowers. There is a cock beside the figure of St Peter. A somewhat incongruous note is introduced by the statue of Helena on the altar; for this, an antique statue of Juno has been adapted, and a seventeenth century head has been added to represent the Empress Mother of Constantine.

Both historically and architecturally, S. Lorenzo fuori le Mura is among the most remarkable and fascinating of Roman churches. Seen from the Piazzale S. Lorenzo, flanked over the wall by the cypresses of Rome's cemetery, the Campo Verano, and with the tall column capped by the bronze figure of the saint in the centre of the Piazzale, S. Lorenzo presents the visitor with an impression of har monious unity. The nave façade is proceded by a portico

OPPOSITE The beautiful decoration in low relief of the Early Christian sarcophagus in the portico of S. Lorenzo fuori le Mura is remarkable for the absence of any specifically Christian symbolism among the vines, grapes and *putti.*

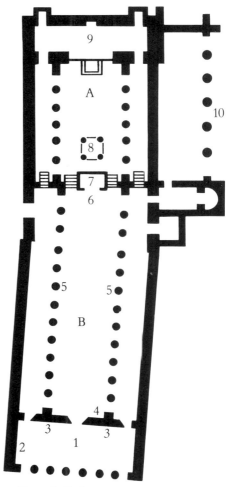

Piazzale S. Lorenzo

S. Lorenzo fuori le Mura

A Early church of S. Lorenzo (330).
B Later church of the Virgin (432–40).

1 Façade and portico (1220) by Vassallettus.
2 Sarcophagus (seventh century?) decorated with scenes of children gathering grapes.
3 Romanesque stone lions.
4 Tomb of Cardinal Guglielmo Fieschi (d. 1256).
5 Pulpits and paschal candelabrum (twelfth–thirteenth centuries) by the Cosmati.
6 Triumphal arch with Byzantine mosaics (sixth century).
7 High altar, with *confessio* containing the remains of St Lawrence and St Stephen.
8 Papal altar with Cosmati *baldacchino* (signed Giovanni, Pietro, Augusto and Sassone, sons of Paolo, 1148).
9 Narthex of early church and entrance to the tomb of Pius IX.
10 Cloister.

(1220) supported by six slender columns of the Ionic order; one of the most perfect porticos in Rome, it is the work of Vassallettus. To the right, set back, rises the Romanesque campanile of a century earlier (p. 270).

S. Lorenzo, however, is formed from the conjunction of two churches, originally orientated in opposite directions and with their apses almost contiguous. St Lawrence was buried by his friend in life, the matron Cyriaca, in her property outside the city walls, on the road to Tivoli. The earlier of the two churches, built over the shrine by Constantine, was completely reconstructed by Pope Pelagius II (578–90). In the meantime the other church, dedicated to the Virgin Mary, was built next to it by Pope Sixtus III. The demolition of the apses and the union of the two churches, begun perhaps in the eighth century by Adrian I, was completed in the early thirteenth century by Honorius III, who engaged Vassallettus to build the portico. This explains the different floor-levels in the church and the unusual disposition of the interior. It was Pio Nono's good taste which caused Virginio Vespignani to remove the Baroque accretion in the middle of the last century and thus restore S. Lorenzo to its earlier beauty – and it is beautiful indeed. Pius' taste cannot be held responsible for the decoration of his own tomb, which is in what was the narthex of the Constantinian, or Pelagian, basilica. But somehow it does convey something of the spirit of his troubled period.

Under the portico two Romanesque lions flank the central doorway. Miniature-like frescoes of the time of Honorius depict scenes from the lives of St Lawrence and St Stephen, who is buried here beside St Lawrence in the crypt of the *confessio*. In the portico are two ancient sarcophagi, one with delightful *putti* in relief, playing among the grape-harvest (p. 103); there is also the monument to the statesman Alcide De Gasperi (d. 1954), the work of one of Italy's foremost modern sculptors, Giacomo Manzù. One enters first the church originally dedicated to the Virgin; the nave is separated from the aisles by twenty-two Ionic-capped columns of granite and *cipollino* marble taken from a classical building. The two *ambones* and the paschal candelabrum are beautiful Cosmati work of the twelfth–thirteenth centuries; the Cosmatesque pavement is also particularly fine, with its arms of the Savelli (Honorius' family) appearing among the interlacing of mosaic. Also by the Cosmati are the magnificent episcopal throne (of porphyry circles surrounded by mosaic) and the screen, one of the most perfect works of this brilliant Roman family of sculptor-mosaicists. Another example of their skill in S. Lorenzo is the tabernacle that contains the splendid Roman sarcophagus which forms the tomb of Cardinal Guglielmo Fieschi. Somewhat strangely, this sarcophagus depicts a wedding ceremony.

Although, in his church, Pope Pelagius employed fluted

classical columns with Corinthian capitals to support the women's galleries, the architraves of delicate Roman carving are strikingly disparate, coming as they do from different pagan buildings. The slender antique columns which raise the rounded arches of the gallery are executed with great delicacy. The rafters of the Renaissance ceiling make a splendid foil to the stonework, picked out as they are in purple and gold. The *baldacchino*, with its three-tiered pyramidical canopy on rows of little columns, is the earliest signed work (1148) of the Cosmati – by one Paolo and his sons. On the triumphal arch, Byzantine mosaics of the sixth century depict Christ with saints. From the sacristy on the right the visitor passes to the charming late twelfth-century cloister, which is distinctly Romanesque in inspiration. In the cloister is the entrance to the Catacomb of St Cyriaca, where, in 258, she brought the charred remains of the martyred St Lawrence.

So closely does S. Maria Maggiore resemble an Imperial second-century basilica in its obedience to the Vitruvian canon, that it was thought to have been precisely this, adapted at an early date for use as a Christian church. It has been known also as the Basilica Liberiana and as S. Maria della Neve – 'Our Lady of the Snow'. This arises from the legend that a Roman patrician named John and his wife, being childless and wishing to leave their wealth to the Virgin, were visited by her in their sleep and told to build a church in her honour in a spot that would be marked by snow. Approaching Pope Liberius to inform him of their intention, they were surprised to learn that he had had an identical dream. This was in August 358 – and Rome is hottest in August – yet, when the Pope accompanied them to their property on the Esquiline Hill, they found there a large patch of snow. Thereupon Liberius, with the couple's money, built the basilica and dedicated it to the Virgin. This Liberian basilica was possibly in the vicinity, but it is not the present S. Maria Maggiore, which is the work of Pope Sixtus III (432–40), who wished to single out for honour the Blessed Virgin, whom the Council of Ephesus (431) had recently declared, in opposition to Nestorius, to be the Mother of God.

Whether seen from the Piazza S. Maria Maggiore, which the basilica faces, or from its apsidal end, with its high flight of steps on the Piazza dell' Esquilino, the exterior of S. Maria Maggiore is equally impressive. Its campanile (1377), the highest in Rome (250 feet), out-tops the column and obelisk

RIGHT In his portico (1220) to S. Lorenzo fuori le Mura Vassallettus retained from the doorway of the earlier church the two splendid Romanesque lions, reminiscent of those in the Romanesque churches of Apulia.

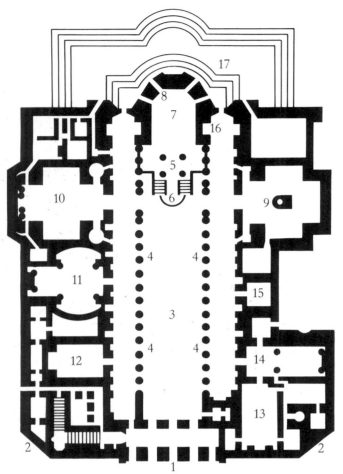

S. Maria Maggiore

1 Façade (1743–50) by F. Fuga.
2 Twin ecclesiastical palaces (left, 1605 and right, *c.* 1743) adjoining the church.
3 Nave with ceiling decorated with the first gold sent from the New World to Alexander VI.
4 Mosaics (fifth century) showing scenes from the Old Testament on either side of the nave.
5 High altar with *baldacchino* by Fuga.
6 *Confessio* with reliquaries of St Matthew and other saints; in front, kneeling statue of Pius IX.
7 Apse with mosaics showing *The Virgin in Glory* (1295) by Jacopo Torriti.
8 Gothic windows.
9 Sistine Chapel (1585) by Dom. Fontana with the tomb of Sixtus V and the Oratory of the Crib (*c.* 1289).
10 Pauline or Borghese Chapel (1611) by Flam. Ponzio with the tomb of Paul V.
11 Sforza Chapel (1564) by G. Della Porta, perhaps on design of Michelangelo.
12 Cesi Chapel (*c.* 1550) by Guidetto Guidetti.
13 Sacristy (1605) by Flam. Ponzio.
14 Baptistery by Flam. Ponzio.
15 Chapel of the Reliquary (1750) by Fuga.
16 Tomb of Bernini and that of Cardinal G. Rodriguez (d. 1299) by Giov. di Cosma.
17 Steps at rear of the apse (1673) by C. Rainaldi.

of the adjacent squares. The apse itself (1673) – Baroque at its scenographic best – is by Carlo Rainaldi; the octagonal cupolas set back on either side are somewhat earlier – that on the left by Domenico Fontana, and that on the right by Flaminio Ponzio. The entrance façade (p. 236), which combines so felicitously with the adjoining palaces, is by the Florentine Ferdinando Fuga, and was begun in 1743. Above the wide steps the portico, with its five openings, is surmounted by an arcaded loggia, the larger central bay (where papal benedictions are given) flanked by two lesser bays, forming an attractive architectural contrast of lit stonework and shadowy recesses. The pediments of the portico produce an undulating, wave-like effect. In the loggia are two series of late thirteenth-century mosaics, which once adorned the earlier façade, by the little-known Filippo Rusuti. The lower series depicts the legendary circumstances attending the founding of the Basilica Liberiana.

On entering the church one is struck by the brilliance, the magnificence of S. Maria Maggiore: one might almost say that it is the epitome of ecclesiastical splendour, and it is not difficult to concur with the widely held view that it is the most beautiful of the great Roman churches. The floor is a shining Cosmati carpet of porphyry and marble, patterned in the circles and swirls of mid-twelfth-century *opus alexandrinum*. The nave is bounded by faultless columns of the Ionic order in Hymettan marble, thirty-six in all, the lines being broken only by the arched entrances to the Pauline Chapel (on the left; built for Paul V) and to the Sistine Chapel (opposite; built for Sixtus V), which are supported by monoliths of polished granite of the same order. Above the architrave and the deep cornice on shallow consoles, fluted Corinthian pilasters reach to the ceiling, which is coffered with unparalleled richness. This was designed *c.* 1498 by Giuliàno Sangallo for Pope Alexander VI; the great rosettes, the decorative motifs and the Borgian bull are all leafed with Peruvian gold, the gift of Ferdinand and Isabella of Spain to their countryman and traditionally held to be the first gold to reach Europe from the New World. The perfection of the shapely columns and of their spacing owes much to the *settecento* architect Fuga, who, deeply versed in Vitruvius, at the time of Benedict XIV boldly transformed the existing heterogeneous collection of columns by paring down those that were too thick, shortening those that were too long, and providing them with identical Ionic capitals and bases. Also by Fuga is the impressive *baldacchino* over the high altar, where four columns of deep red porphyry, laced with palm leaves of golden bronze, support, between two angels at the angles, the papal arms, surmounted by a crown and cross (p. 217).

The magnificence of S. Maria Maggiore is enhanced by the richness of its chapels, particularly the Sistine Chapel (p. 160) and the Pauline (or Borghese) Chapel. The former (in the shape of a Greek cross, with a cupola) was erected for Sixtus V (Peretti) in 1585 by Domenico Fontana; the latter (repeating the shape) for Paul V (Borghese) in 1611 by Flaminio Ponzio. Both are of an extraordinary sumptuousness, with their wealth of rare marbles and precious stones (agate, amethyst and lapis lazuli), their sculpture, their gold and silver-work, and their Mannerist painting. In the Sistine Chapel, and in contrast to its almost overpowering richness, is the Oratory of the Crib, which contains one of the church's most cherished relics: the wooden boards from the 'Holy Crib', enclosed in a silver reliquary. Fontana moved to S. Maria Maggiore the thirteenth-century chapel of Arnolfo di Cambio, with its beautiful Cosmatesque altar-front and pavement; most touching are his figures of the Magi, St Joseph and the ox and ass (p. 82). In the Pauline Chapel is the celebrated Madonna, 'painted by St Luke', Byzantine in type, of uncertain date but possibly of the ninth century. In this chapel a charming ceremony takes place on 5 August each year, when, during a celebration of High Mass, thousands of tiny white flower petals float gently from the little cupola of the chapel, in memory of the traditional founding of the church.

But, as with other Roman churches, it is its mosaics that are the greatest glory of S. Maria Maggiore. The interest here is both aesthetic and theological. The mosaics of the nave walls and the triumphal arch are of the fifth century; they were placed there by Sixtus III, as an inscription on the arch indicates: 'Xystus Bishop to the sacred people of God.' The Pope's intention was to prefigure and justify the unique position of the Virgin Mary, as the Mother of God. The mosaic panels of the nave – placed high, and therefore difficult to see except on the rare occasions when the light is favourable – depict (on the left) scenes from the lives of Abraham, Isaac and Jacob, and (on the right) scenes from the lives of Moses and Joshua. These Old Testament scenes, mystically interpreted, prepare us for those on the triumphal arch. In the centre of this is the Throne of God. On the left, from top to bottom, appear the Annunciation (to Joseph as well as to Mary), the Epiphany, the Massacre of the

Innocents, and the city of Jerusalem; on the right, the Presentation at the Temple, the Flight into Egypt, the Magi before Herod, and the city of Bethlehem. Here for the first time Mary is portrayed in all the rich attire and majesty of a Byzantine empress. But when the Child appears, as he does just below in the Epiphany, it is as a boy, seated alone on a bejewelled divan-throne, a cross on his nimbus, the star in the East between attendant angels behind him, Mary reverently beside the throne, the Magi approaching in Persian dress. Christ from the first takes precedence, but Mary is exalted as Mother of God.

The exquisite apse mosaics (p. 69) by Jacopo Torriti (signed; 1295) are to be interpreted as the culminating act in the glorification and cult of the Virgin Mary. Here the Byzantine joins hands with the Hellenistic; this work has been regarded as the last of the long line of Roman masterpieces in mosaic which stretch back to antiquity. Within a circle, Mother and Son are shown sitting side by side, both glorified: the apotheosis of Mary, when Christ places the crown on his Mother's head. The mosaic will be seen as a decorative whole, where every detail receives its due: Christ and the Virgin are placed in a setting of luxuriant acanthus-leaf scrolls, among which wander peacocks, cranes and partridges; below flows a river, with boats, fishermen, birds, fish and swans – even with river-gods, as if the artist was working from a Hellenistic original. The Byzantine element is tempered with a Hellenistic naturalness, partly through Torriti's delicacy and subtlety of colour: rose, pale pearl and lilac soften the contours and forms, in contrast with the brilliance of the reds, blues and gold, and are modulated by the coolness of the light blues and greens. The composition is most effective: Christ and his Mother, flanked by adoring angels and a line of saints, with the tiny kneeling figures of Pope Nicholas IV and the donor, Cardinal Jacopo Colonna. Below, between the Gothic windows, Torriti has placed other scenes relating to Mary and her Son, centring on a finely designed *Dormition of the Virgin.*

The extraordinary beauty of Torriti's mosaics – marking, with the mosaics of Cavallini, an era in Roman ecclesiastical art – tends to make one overlook the excellence of the Renaissance bas-reliefs of Mino del Reame beneath them; another relief, a *Madonna and Child*, from the *ciborium* ordered by Cardinal d'Estouteville in 1463, is in the sacristy. And perhaps one is inclined to neglect much else in S. Maria Maggiore. But one should not leave by the entrance to the Piazza dell' Esquilino without an appreciative pause before the tomb of Cardinal Rodriguez (p. 110), with its Gothic canopy and mosaic decoration by Giovanni di Cosma. Nor should one ignore the stark stone slab over the tomb of Bernini, who made tombs of surpassing richness for others.

5
The Roman Tradition: the Art of the Cosmati

In Rome during the twelfth and thirteenth centuries there was a renaissance of ecclesiastical art, which some have rather unjustly dismissed as a 'false dawn'. It came to an end at the beginning of the fourteenth century, with the transference of the seat of the popes, its patrons, to Avignon. Alongside the magnificent mosaics of such artists as Cavallini, Torriti and Jacopo da Camerino, whose work was largely figurative and pictorial, there developed another mosaic style which was essentially decorative. The technical skill of these Roman craftsmen in marble, with their workshops and guilds, often ran in families, generation after generation carrying on the profession of architecture, building, sculpture or mosaic. Such families were those of Paulus (*fl.c.* 1100) and his sons and grandsons, the Laurentii, the Rainerii (or Ranucci) and the Vassalletti. Owing to the frequent recurrence of the name Cosmas, these families have been collectively known as the Cosmati, although there was no family with that surname. The outstanding beauty of their work, particularly in the mosaic which has taken its name from them, reserves a special place for the Cosmati in any account of Rome's churches.

Their chief influences were twofold: antiquity, which they saw all about them in Rome and which they carefully

studied; and the Siculo-Campanian schools of Byzantine mosaic-workers in Southern Italy and Palermo, whose work became known to them from examples in Monte Cassino, Ravello, Amalfi and elsewhere. The Cosmati developed their own canons, which were distinctly classical. It was only later that a Gothic trend briefly appeared – possibly through the influence of Cistercian abbeys like Fossanova, and certainly through the presence in Rome, in the second half of the thirteenth century, of the Tuscan sculptor Arnolfo di Cambio, who was closely associated with the celebrated Pisani. So strong was the classical tradition (and, in decoration, the Byzantine) among the Romans that they were able to fend off successfully the challenges of both Romanesque and Gothic. If the Romans were aware of the magnificent cathedrals and churches being built by the Normans in Southern Italy – at Bari, Bitonto and Trani, for example – they were resistant to their Romanesque style. Traces of it may appear in cloisters such as those of S. Cosimato in Trastevere, SS. Quattro Coronati or S. Lorenzo fuori le Mura, and in the arcading (late though this is) in the apse of SS. Giovanni e Paolo. The Gothic influence showed itself, though only rarely, in windows with pointed arches (as in S. Maria Maggiore), in tabernacles (as in S. Clemente), in tombs (again in S. Maria Maggiore, also in S. Maria Aracoeli, S. Maria sopra Minerva and elsewhere), and in a few *baldacchini* – these last chiefly influenced by those of Arnolfo di Cambio in S. Paolo fuori le Mura and S. Cecilia in Trastevere. Only one Roman church shows the Gothic style fully: S. Maria sopra Minerva.

LEFT Classical regard for proportion, formal inventiveness and the beauty of the inlays of porphyry and mosaic make the cloister (1215–32) of S. Giovanni in Laterano (with that of S. Paolo fuori le Mura) one of the Cosmati masterpieces. An inscription here reads: 'Vassallettus, noble and skilled in this art, began this work with his father, which he has finished alone.'

Looking from the Piazza della Minerva, where Bernini's sturdy little elephant, with its endearingly creased posterior, stoically supports an Egyptian obelisk of the sixth century BC (p. 25), the visitor, regarding the church's plain rectangular façade, with its three eye-windows and Renaissance doorways (1453), has no forewarning of the architectural style of the interior, which is restored Gothic. The present church's history began c. 1280, when Pope Nicholas III started to rebuild an earlier church, on the site of a pagan Temple of Minerva, using as his model the beautiful Florentine S. Maria Novella, which is itself an Italian version of French Cistercian architecture. In 1370 the Senate and people of Rome, the Pope being in Avignon, presented the church and the adjoining monastery to the Dominicans of S. Sabina. The Friars Preachers have possessed it ever since. As the 'barbarous' Gothic style never found favour among the Romans, Carlo Maderno and others made extensive alterations in accordance with the taste of their age. The 'restoration' to Gothic took place in the middle of the nineteenth century at the hands of Fra Girolamo Bianchedi, who encased the pillars and half-columns of the nave in marble, and covered arches, ribs and vaults with neo-mediaeval painting. The result is most unfortunate; how much better it would have been if the unadorned architectural members had been allowed to speak in their own authentic Cistercian voice.

The Italian art historian Venturi is specific about the nature of the activities of the Cosmati: 'Sumptuous decorators as they are, the Cosmati are first and foremost builders.' And, he might have added, designers and architects. Their work is to be seen in a number of porticos, portals and cloisters, and in the campanili, although few of these bell-towers can be attributed to individuals or to specific workshops.

In their porticos the Cosmati preferred the use of the classical architrave to that of the arch, a notable exception being the restored arcaded portico of S. Maria in Cosmedin. If the architraved portico by Vassallettus at S. Lorenzo fuori le Mura is highly successful in its classical dignity, hardly less so is that of S. Giorgio in Velabro. Another early portico, of the beginning of the twelfth century, is that of S. Lorenzo in Lucina, just off the Corso. The church over the house of the matron Lucina was rebuilt by Pope Paschal II. (Inside is the reputed gridiron on which St Lawrence suffered martyrdom;

LEFT Giovanni di Cosma's Gothic tomb of Cardinal Gonzalez Rodriguez, Archbishop of Toledo (d. 1299), in S. Maria Maggiore. In the mosaic above the Cardinal is represented kneeling before the Virgin and Child, with St Matthew and St Jerome.

also a monument erected by Chateaubriand in memory of the Roman sojourn of his countryman, the painter Nicholas Poussin.) Like these other porticos, Paschal's is of a severe simplicity, the granite columns of the Ionic order supporting an austerely moulded architrave, all darkened with age. On the right, the campanile is contemporary with the portico; the openings of its three top storeys are of a comparatively rare design, consisting of pairs of mullioned windows.

Early mediaeval covered portals can be seen at S. Clemente, S. Prassede, S. Maria in Cosmedin and S. Cosimato in Trastevere – the last being now deep below the level of the market square in which it stands. On the Coelian Hill, not far from the Piazza della Navicella, stands the little church of S. Tommaso in Formis, once the chapel of the Order of Trinitarians, whose hospital it adjoined, and whose function was to rescue Christian captives from the infidels. The doorway here is set within a semicircular arch, raised on two pilasters in marble. The arch is signed, 'Master Jacobus with his son Cosmatus did this work'; the date is 1218. Above is a tabernacle – again, of a rounded marble arch resting on two columns; within, a circular mosaic depicts Christ enthroned between a black and a white slave, the Order's work of redemption knowing no colour bar. The church, whose main structure is Baroque, stands today within the park of the Villa Celimontana, its entrance being beyond the Arch of Dolabella (AD 10); it is approached by a delightful flower-bordered passage.

Among the most glorious achievements of the Cosmati school were their cloisters. Beautiful as are the marble cloisters of SS. Quattro Coronati – possibly by Paulus, c. 1113, when he seems also to have built the dumpy tower over the entrance to this fortress-like building – or of the brick-built court of S. Cosimato in Trastevere (c. 1200), it is the cloister of S. Giovanni in Laterano and S. Paolo fuori le Mura that remain the Cosmati's masterpieces in this field. The cloister at the Lateran (p. 108) was built in the years 1215–32, during the pontificates of Honorius III and Gregory IX. An inscription reads, 'Vassallettus, noble and skilled in this art, began this work with his father, which he has finished alone.' Pilasters separate arcaded bays of five arches, resting on graceful coupled columns of diverse shapes – twisted like barley sugar, intertwined, fluted and straight, some inlaid and bejewelled with brilliantly coloured mosaic, and all enchanting in the inexhaustible resourcefulness of their design. Within the colonnade, behind each pilaster the vaulting of the bays springs from antique columns with Ionic capitals. Externally, the spandrels between the rounded arches contain delicately carved designs of foliage, human heads and animals. Above, on the entablature, a frieze of mosaic is surmounted by a bold pattern of interlacing rectangles and circles of mosaic, which, even when dimmed with age, can catch the light and delight the eye with their pinpoints of colour. Finely wrought moulding intervenes between these and the corbels which support the cornice: a frieze of mosaic, capped by beautifully chiselled foliage in low relief between powerful lions' heads – these almost in the round. With the admirable proportions and balance of the architectural forms (classical in feeling), the beauty of the carving and the glorious colour of the porphyry and mosaic work, the cloister of the Lateran reveals the perfection of the art of the Cosmati. Notable, too, are the sphinx, copied by Vassallettus from a classical model, the ninth-century well in the centre of the court and fragments of Cosmati work in the cloister, including part of a tomb by Arnolfo di Cambio and of a *ciborium* (1297) by Master Deodatus. The mediaeval canons of the Lateran could enjoy their meditative tranquillity amid surroundings of a rare beauty.

The cloister at S. Paolo fuori le Mura – smaller and perhaps more intimate than that of the Lateran, but comparable in the beauty of its architectural forms and in its use of polychrome marbles and mosaics – was begun in 1205 by Vassallettus for Abbot Peter of Capua and completed under Abbot John *c.* 1214 (some authorities say later, perhaps 1235). It has been conjectured that it was Abbot

Peter who, from his knowledge of the Siculo-Campanian schools of mosaicists, introduced the Byzantine use of porphyry and mosaic into the decoration of Roman cloisters. Structurally and decoratively, the cloister closely resembles that of S. Giovanni in Laterano, except that the arcades here consist of four arches. Vassallettus, however, has introduced human faces of a charming youthfulness into his cornice over the central doorway of the arcades. On three sides an inscription in blue letters on a gold ground relates the story of the beginning, progress and completion of work on the cloister.

The campanili, those square bell-towers of brickwork that are so characteristic not only of Rome but of the towns and villages of Lazio as a whole, share a family likeness. Their origin could have been Lombard, but perhaps they are the direct descendants of that first Roman campanile of Old St Peter's, built (*c.* 754) by Pope Stephen II after the coronation of Pipin the Short. However tall, they rise sheer, straight, uncompromising, their storeys usually equal in height, being separated by string courses, which are sometimes accentuated into a decorative frieze or a cornice resting on tiny blocks or corbels. The lower storeys most frequently have a blind arcading of two or three arches; the upper are most often open (the uppermost, containing the bells, always so), the arches

PAGE 113 The elegant, eight-storied campanile, dating from the twelfth century, of the church of the Greek community, S. Maria in Cosmedin. The fountain by Carlo Bizzaccheri (1715) in front of the church reflects the geniality of the Roman *Settecento*.

PAGE 114 The twelfth-century campanile and portico of S. Giorgio in Velabro demonstrate the excellence of Roman mediaeval brickwork.

PAGE 115 Perhaps the most beautiful of all Rome's campanili is that of SS. Giovanni e Paolo (*c.* 1150), which has been recently restored. In addition to its mullioned windows and rich cornices, its face is decorated with inset porphyry and serpentine, and bowls of Hispano-Arabic origin.

being supported by colonettes (a Romanesque motif) of white marble. These campanili vary in height from the single-storeyed entrance tower of SS. Quattro Coronati, with its four-arched arcade, to the slim elegance of that of S. Maria in Cosmedin, with its eight storeys, or the slender beauty of seven-storeyed SS. Giovanni e Paolo (both dating from the twelfth century, the latter restored in 1951). Among the earliest must be that of S. Maria in Cappella (1090); not much later are those of SS. Rufina e Seconda and the little S. Benedetto in Piscinula, tucked away in Trastevere, with their primitive simplicity; and early, too, are those of S. Lorenzo fuori le Mura and S. Agata dei Goti. An eleventh-century origin has been claimed for the graceful campanile of S. Giovanni a Porta Latina. From the twelfth century also date those of S. Maria and S. Cecilia (both in Trastevere), S. Giorgio in Velabro, S. Pudenziana, S. Silvestro in Capite, S. Marco and (so beautiful in its soaring gracefulness) S. Francesca Romana, whose topmost three storeys show the same unusual feature as at S. Lorenzo in Lucina, having double openings, each sub-divided, in this case by a slender white marble colonnette. An early thirteenth-century exam-ple is the campanile of S. Sisto Vecchio. These Roman campanili owe much of their charm to the colour of their brickwork (often taken from earlier structures) – those warm shades of brown, offset by the whiteness of the colonnettes, turning russet or rose-gold from the rays of the sun as it sinks over the Campagna.

But despite Venturi's claim for the Cosmati to be recognized primarily as builders, it is above all as decorators that they make the most vivid impression on the visitor to Rome's churches. The brilliance of the purely decorative patterned mosaic employed by the Cosmati in the church furniture which they themselves designed – the paschal candlesticks, episcopal thrones, *ambones*, altar-frontals, pulpits, screens (whether for the sanctuary or in the choir) and funerary monuments – derives directly from the materials which they used. These consisted chiefly of clear or opaque coloured glass (blue, red, yellow, black, brown and green), but also of faience and glazed gold. Seen in the strong sunlight – in the variegated pillars of the cloisters – all this colour scintillates with an extraordinary beauty, as it does in the churches themselves, where the play of light catches these little facets of colour in the intricacy of their jewel-like patterns. An example of the perfection of this type of Cosmati work is to be found in the *ambone* and its neighbouring paschal candlestick in S. Lorenzo fuori le Mura. There were usually two *ambones*, for reading the Epistles and the Gospel respectively; but in this unusual single *ambone* the priest recited both, facing in different directions. It is formed by great discs and rectangles

of porphyry, surrounded by exquisitely delicate mouldings and mosaic. In the centre of the projecting pulpit is a finely carved eagle. The adjacent candelabrum has a classically moulded base and a Corinthian capital, the spiralling of the shaft of the column being inset with mosaic. Seen, as it was intended, by candlelight, it flickers into life, the spiral sparkling with its iridescent gems.

The most striking item of furnishing in a Roman church – that feature which first catches and fixes the attention of the visitor as he enters – is undoubtedly the high altar and above it the canopy, or *baldacchino*. The latter may be of the utmost simplicity or of the sumptuous magnificence in bronze and gold of Bernini's colossal *baldacchino* in St Peter's. Many of those in the older churches were both designed and executed by the Cosmati, and the surfaces that lent themselves to decoration – the architraves of the canopies and the altar-frontals – they frequently inlaid with mosaic. In the churches of S. Clemente and S. Cesareo are to be found those earlier and simpler types; in S. Clemente, four slender columns of *pavonazetto* marble support a classical architrave on which rest six small columns, supporting the gable-end of the canopy. As the twelfth century progressed the Roman *baldacchini* became more elaborate, an intermediate stage being reached in that of S. Agata dei Goti, until the three-tiered type evolved, as is seen in S. Giorgio in Velabro and S. Lorenzo fuori le Mura (1149). With the arrival of the Sienese Arnolfo di Cambio there appeared the Gothic influence in the canopies of S. Cecilia in Trastevere (1283) and S. Paolo fuori le Mura (1285). In Rome this early Gothic seems uncomfortably out of place, lacking the simple classicism and serenity of the Cosmatesque *baldacchini* and the aerial lightness of the fully developed Gothic style; it seems over-elaborate, fussy, overdressed. Arnolfo's work, however, was not without imitators: in S. Giovanni in Laterano, Urban v, with a contribution from Charles v of France, ordered Giovanni di Stefano of Siena to raise a great Gothic canopy (1367) over the high altar; even the earlier, more sober, *baldacchino* (1294) in S. Maria in Cosmedin, signed by Deodatus, the third son of Cosmas the Younger, shows this alien Gothic influence.

The earliest church floorings, as seen in the lower churches of S. Clemente or S. Crisogono, were simple affairs; at the

RIGHT Viewed through the pines and shrubs of the Forum, the twelfth-century campanile of S. Francesca Romana rises beside the massive ruins of the Basilica of Maxentius (or of Constantine; fourth century AD). The campanile is unusual in that the top three storeys have double openings, each subdivided by slender colonnettes.

most, birds and animals were depicted on a neutral ground of mosaic, with perhaps a border of geometrical design. The Romans were to rise to better things. In the beautiful little Byzantine Chapel of S. Zeno in S. Prassede, the pattern on the ninth-century pavement (the earliest example in Rome's churches of *opus sectile*) is formed by a disc of red porphyry, set in a mosaic design of porphyry, serpentine and white marble. It was, however, the more elaborate interlacing patterns of *opus alexandrinum* which, in the hands of the Cosmati during the twelfth and thirteenth centuries, became such a magnificent feature of Roman churches. The resuscitation of this style of polychrome marble flooring came about in the eleventh century at Monte Cassino, where Abbot Desiderius had imported mosaicists from Constantinople. The glorious Cosmatesque pavements in coloured marble are thus, once again, Byzantine in inspiration. How much the Byzantine mosaicists in turn owed to Hellenistic paving is another matter. The designs are essentially geometrical: a large round (or square) of red or green porphyry is set in an interlacing framework of white marble, which is filled in by patterns composed of coloured marble *tesserae* of diverse shapes — squares, triangles, circles, polygons, stars, lozenges, ellipses and so on — producing a chromatic richness that has been described as that of an oriental carpet or of a bed of flowers.

The porphyry used so freely by the Cosmati came entirely from classical columns, sawn to provide the circles and squares employed in their pavements and church furniture. Red porphyry — so prized by the ancient Romans that it came to be known as 'imperial purple' (Italians referred to it as *rosso antico*) — was especially sought after from the time of Claudius and came from Egypt, from quarries on the Red Sea. Green porphyry (*verde antico*) was derived, like much of the most precious marble, from the Peloponnese in Greece.

An outstanding example of Cosmatesque *opus alexandrinum* is the beautiful central strip (1128), which continues in the choir, at S. Clemente (p. 92). Other early specimens of this magnificent, very Roman, form of church paving are to be found in S. Maria in Cosmedin (1123), S. Crisogono (1130), S. Croce in Gerusalemme (1144), S. Maria Maggiore (1145) and S. Maria in Trastevere (1148, but reset during the last century). The splendid example in S. Lorenzo fuori le Mura (p. 90), so intricate in its interlacing and in its intervening patterns of mosaic, dates from almost a century later, being laid in the course of Honorius III's reconstruction of the church. And as late as the beginning of the fifteenth century Pope Martin V followed this Roman tradition in his Cosmatesque pavement at S. Giovanni in Laterano (p. 99). Besides their work in the older of these churches, the Cosmati have left for the perpetual delight of posterity the pavements at S. Alessio, S. Benedetto in Piscinula, S. Francesca

PAGE 118 The Savelli tomb (usually known as that of Luca Savelli, d. 1266) in S. Maria d'Aracoeli contains the bodies of members of three generations of the family. Above a richly decorated ancient sarcophagus, the funeral urn, inlaid with mosaic and bearing the Savelli arms, is surmounted by a Gothic *aedicule* enclosing a statue of the *Virgin and Child* (early fourteenth century).

PAGE 120 The nave of the restored church of S. Maria in Cosmedin. The paving, of *opus alexandrinum*, is a beautiful example of Cosmati work.

PAGE 121 In the tribune of S. Maria in Cosmedin rises the *baldacchino* by Deodatus, the third son of Cosmas the Younger (1294), which exhibits the influence of Arnolfo di Cambio's Gothic canopy in S. Paolo fuori le Mura. The episcopal throne (twelfth century) has arms in the shape of the Apulian lions. The paving near the altar is a rare example of eighth-century *opus sectile*.

Romana, SS. Giovanni e Paolo, S. Giovanni a Porta Latina, S. Maria in Domnica, S. Saba, S. Maria d'Aracoeli and SS. Quattro Coronati – to mention only the best known.

It was not only on the greater or more frequented churches that the Cosmati lavished the riches of their exquisite art. In three small churches in the vicinity of the huge ruins of the Baths of Caracalla – S. Balbina, S. Cesareo and SS. Nereo ed Achilleo – there survive works by them that should not be overlooked by admirers of their felicitous conjunction of marble and mosaic.

S. Balbina is a church dating from the Constantinian age, erected above the house of the Consul Lucius Fabius Cilone – further evidence of the early conversion to Christianity of members of the senatorial class. It contains the highly distinctive funeral monument to Stephanus de Surdi (1303), a moving work full of dignity and richly ornamented in mosaic by Giovanni, son of Cosmas. The choir, reconstituted in 1939, contains fragments of first-century mosaic found under the Via Imperiale. Behind the high altar stands the thirteenth-century episcopal throne, its marble rubbed and burnished with age, of the type that the Cosmati appear to have derived from antiquity.

S. Cesareo (p. 93) is simply a rectangular hall, its austerity softened by the splendour of the blue and gold ceiling, emblazoned with the arms of Pope Clement VIII (Aldobrandini). It is remarkable for its sanctuary, pulpit, altar-frontal and episcopal chair, all work of the highest quality by the Cosmati. As an illustration of the deterioration in taste and execution in the art of mosaic that set in after the time of Cavallini and Torriti – the age of the Cosmati – may be cited the mosaics executed during the seventeenth century for the apse and sanctuary arch by the Cavalier d'Arpino.

The beautiful little church of SS. Nereo ed Achilleo was once known as the Titulus Fasciolae. There is a legend that St Peter, fleeing from the Mamertine prison, dropped here a bandage (*fascia*) that had bound his leg (which had been injured by his chains), and that this was picked up and preserved in an oratory built on this spot by a pious Roman matron. This ancient building was thoroughly restored in 1597 by the church's titular, Cardinal Baronius, who left an inscription imploring his successors, 'for the love of God' and 'the merits of these martyrs', not to alter it in any way. The existing work here by the Cosmati is particularly precious. Fragments of the original paving are to be seen in the presbytery. The reconstituted twelfth-century marble choir is surrounded by a screen, and this, the *ambones* and the *confessio* are all richly decorated with a mosaic inlay. The sixteenth-century *baldacchino* is raised on four pillars of beautiful African marble. Behind is an unusual episcopal throne, flanked by two lions, of Romanesque robustness and vitality, which are reputed to be of the school of Vassallettus. On the back is carved an excerpt from a homily of St Gregory the Great, spoken over the graves of the martyred Nereus and Achilleus, soldiers in the Imperial service; the passage was placed there by Cardinal Baronius in the mistaken belief that the reading took place on this spot. If we ignore the crude paintings of the Mannerist Pomarancio and retain in our mind's eye the beauty of the sanctuary, with the early ninth-century mosaics of the *Transfiguration* on the tribune arch, the impression of this little church is one made memorable 'by its simplicity, its elegance, its austere and mystical beauty' – as the Frenchman Battifol described it.

The departure of the Pope and the papal court to Avignon at the beginning of the fourteenth century put an end to this late mediaeval flowering of Roman art. But there remain many churches in which the visitor to Rome will come, often unexpectedly, upon the work of the Cosmati, affording him a glimpse of the artistic perfection achieved in their essentially Roman art.

LEFT The original church of SS. Quattro Coronati was founded in the fourth century but rebuilt and enlarged in the seventh and eighth centuries. After its destruction by the Normans under Robert Guiscard, it was rebuilt, diminished in size, *c.* 1110, the earliest columns (from different classical buildings) and the Byzantine-inspired *matronea* being retained. The paving is Cosmatesque.

ABOVE The resplendence of the glittering mosaics used by the Cosmati can be seen in this reconstituted pulpit in S. Cesareo. The panels of *verde antico* act as a foil to the brilliance of the mosaics (thirteenth century).

RIGHT The ancient church of SS. Nereo ed Achilleo decorated for a Roman wedding. The screen in marble, porphyry and inlaid mosaics has been reassembled from the original by the Cosmati (twelfth century). The high altar is also Cosmati work.

6
The Patronage of the Renaissance Popes

By September 1420 the sojourn of the Papacy in Avignon was over and the Great Schism, during which there were two – and even, at one time, three – popes, had ended. The Colonna Pope Martin V entered Rome, to find what Petrarch had so vividly described seventy years earlier: '... the churches were abandoned by those who received their titles and honours from them, left so desolate as to be without roofs and doors, the walls in ruins, the interiors open to flocks and herds. . . .' With the return of the popes and cardinals a rejuvenated Rome raised itself from apathy and abasement and went to greet the dawning Renaissance with open arms. No sooner had Martin V taken up residence in the Vatican than he gave orders to a commission of cardinals and bishops to begin the rebuilding of Rome's parish churches, and provided funds for this purpose. He himself set about restoring the derelict S. Giovanni in Laterano and the church of SS. Apostoli, building beside the latter the great palace in which his family have lived to this day. He brought to Rome Masaccio, Masolino, Gentile da Fabriano and Vittore Pisano to work in his restored Lateran – but all their frescoes in that church have perished. The only surviving Roman paintings which might possibly have been executed by Masaccio are those in S. Clemente, and these are more generally attributed to Masolino. The memorial to Martin V is the beautiful pavement and tomb (c. 1443) in S. Giovanni in Laterano.

Since the days of Pietro Cavallini and his school Rome had produced few artists of more than mediocre ability, and henceforth popes and cardinals looked elsewhere for architects, sculptors and painters – particularly to Florence, the true cradle of the Early Renaissance. An exception should be made for the Roman sculptor Paolo Romano (d. 1477), whose work may be seen on the tomb of Cardinal Vulcani in S. Francesca Romana, on the Carafa monument in S. Maria del Priorato, on the tomb of the Cardinal of Hertford in S. Cecilia in Trastevere, and on the monument to Cardinal Stefaneschi in S. Maria in Trastevere. One should also mention the native-born painter Antoniazzo Romano, whose work, perhaps unfairly neglected, can be found in many Roman churches. But henceforth it was 'foreigners' who took the lead in every branch of the arts. The sojourn of the two Florentine artists, Brunelleschi and Donatello, in Rome has been regarded as having a crucial impact on the whole development of Italian *quattrocento* art. Both were drawn there by the study of antiquity – in the true awakening spirit of the Renaissance. Donatello left only two works in Roman churches: the much-worn tombstone of Archdeacon Crivelli in S. Maria d'Aracoeli, and the beautiful tabernacle (1432) in the Chapel of the Sagrestia dei Beneficiati in St Peter's.

The architecture of the High Renaissance in Rome, which culminated in the masterpieces of Bramante and Michelangelo, owes an immeasurable debt not only to Brunelleschi but also to two other early fifteenth-century Tuscans, Filarete

RIGHT The pleasant little Renaissance cloister at S. Onofrio (mid-fifteenth century). The upper arcade is supported by octagonal columns of the period, the lower by antique columns. It was in the monastery here that Torquato Tasso died on 25 April 1595, on the eve of being crowned with laurel on the Capitol.

and Leon Battista Alberti, as well as to Leonardo da Vinci. The first three spent long periods in Rome. Brunelleschi's study of classical buildings and his precise measurement of the Pantheon gave him the expertise that allowed him to complete the cupola of Florence's cathedral, the wonder of the age. Filarete made the bronze doors of St Peter's for Eugenius IV, and Alberti put his services as architect and town-planner at the disposal of Nicholas V. Alberti, who had rediscovered Vitruvius, set out his theories, as Vitruvius had done, in ten books: *De re aedificatoria*. For Alberti architecture included philosophy, mathematics and antiquity; everything obeyed the requirements of proportion and harmony. He found that in classical buildings the column, in its various orders, was the controlling modular unit of design. Like Brunelleschi, he had in mind a building whose every part 'conspired to form a beautiful Whole'. The principle he enunciated became the canon of the architects of the High Renaissance in Rome: 'The harmony and concord of all the parts achieved in such a manner that nothing could be added or taken away or altered except for the worse.' An aesthetic whole, that is, consists of the perfect blending of the ideally self-sufficient parts of the building.

When the discerning and cultivated Pope Eugenius IV returned to Rome in 1443 from a nine-year absence in Florence, he continued his predecessor's work in the restoration of the city churches, St Peter's and S. Giovanni in Laterano. He cleared away the booths that cluttered up the entrance to S. Maria ad Martyres (the name by which the Pantheon was known), thus exposing to view the magnificent columns, entablature and pediment of that masterpiece. While the cathedral of Ostia was being repaired, the remains of Monica, the mother of St Augustine, were discovered and by the Pope's orders were brought to Rome and placed in the Augustinians' church of S. Agostino in a tomb executed by Isaia da Pisa (*c.* 1450). It was Eugenius IV who called to Rome the painter-monk from Fiesole, Fra Angelico, who lived in the Dominican monastery attached to S. Maria sopra Minerva and died there in 1455. Fra Angelico's principal work in Rome was done for Nicholas V in the Chapel of St Lawrence (or Cappella di Nicolò V) in the Vatican. These frescoes, glorious in their freshness of colour, depict scenes from the lives of St Lawrence and St Stephen, and are some of the most touchingly beautiful paintings in Rome. It was Eugenius IV who presented to the Order of Hieronymites the newly founded (1419) church and monastery of S. Onofrio on the Janiculum, where the stricken poet Tasso was later given shelter. The Pope summoned from Como the architect and sculptor Andrea Bregno, who, with the school of sculptors that he founded, contributed greatly to the adorn-

---

PAGE 128 Detail of the Renaissance tomb of Nicola da Forca Palena of the Order of Hieronymites, let into the wall by the entrance to the monastery he founded at S. Onofrio in 1419.

PAGE 130 The entrance to the cloister attached to S. Salvatore in Lauro. In the grace and refinement of the architectural forms, the cloister reflects the discriminating taste of the Renaissance.

PAGE 131 Off the cloister, in the former monastery at S. Salvatore in Lauro, is a charming Renaissance courtyard where oleanders and magnolias bloom. Behind the fountain is an arched doorway, flanked by saints in scallop-topped niches, with a bust in an oval setting above.

ment of Rome's churches, particularly with monumental tombs; but the initiation of the great period of Roman sculpture coincided with the arrival of Mino da Fiesole *c.* 1473.

When in 1447 the humanist Pope Nicholas V assumed the triple crown, he surrounded himself with scholars and lovers of the arts; it was he who founded the Vatican Library. He used to say that there were two objects on which it was worth spending money: books and buildings. Nicholas V wished to glorify the Papacy and Rome by the embellishment of the city, the strengthening of its walls and the restoration or the building of its churches. 'It is of vital necessity', he said, 'to confirm the masses in their weak and menaced faith by the visible evidence of greatness.' To aid him in this work he summoned Alberti to Rome, with whose assistance plans were drawn up for the re-establishment of the Leonine City and for the rebuilding of both the Vatican and St Peter's. Advised by Alberti and the Florentine Rossellino, Nicholas V began work on St Peter's. The foundations of the new

Sixtus IV appointing Platina as Papal Librarian; painting by Melozzo da Forlì.

church had only risen a few feet at his death. Of the Vatican, where he visualized a papal palace that would rival in splendour the Imperial buildings on the Palatine, only his chapel was completed; it was decorated by Fra Angelico.

Nevertheless, Nicholas V carried out the restoration or rebuilding of some forty churches for the Jubilee of 1450, among them S. Maria Maggiore, S. Paolo and S. Lorenzo fuori le Mura, S. Stefano Rotondo, S. Teodoro and the Spanish church, S. Giacomo degli Spagnoli, on the Piazza Navona. Cardinal Latino Orsini rebuilt *c.* 1450 the church and monastery of S. Salvatore in Lauro, whose beautiful Renaissance cloister has to this day survived the eighteenth-century alterations to the church. Isaia da Pisa's monument (*c.* 1450) to Eugenius IV was brought to this church from Old St Peter's.

Pope Calixtus III (Borgia) relinquished his predecessor's ambitious plans. Constantinople having fallen to the Turks

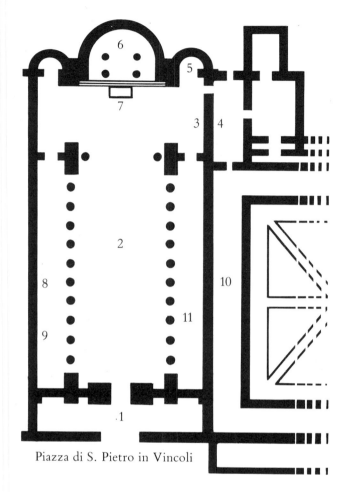

Piazza di S. Pietro in Vincoli

S. Pietro in Vincoli

1 Façade and portico (c. 1475), attributed to Baccio Pontelli or
   Meo del Caprina.
2 Nave with antique columns.
3 Mausoleum of Julius II with *Moses* (c. 1515) by
   Michelangelo.
4 Antesacristy with *Liberation of St Peter* (1604) by
   Domenichino.
5 *St Margaret* (seventeenth century) by Guercino.
6 Tribune with painting (1577) by G. Coppi.
7 *Confessio* containing the chains of St Peter.
8 Byzantine mosaic (c. 680) of St Sebastian.
9 Tomb of Cardinal Nicolò da Cusa (d. 1464) by A. Bregno.
10 Cloister, attributed to G. Sangallo (1489–1503), with well-
   head (c. 1517) attributed to A. Sangallo the Younger
   assisted by Simone Mosca.
11 *St Augustine* by Guercino.

in 1453, the Pope was concerned above all with the Turkish threat and devoted much energy to the aggrandizement of his own family. However, he did restore the venerable S. Prisca on the Aventine. Pius II, too, was more occupied with attempts to restore S. Sofia to Christian hands than with the programme of church restoration launched by Nicholas V, whose works were left unfinished. It was during these years that the pleasure-loving Venetian Cardinal Pietro Barbo, later Pope Paul II, built his great palace (the Palazzo Venezia) and restored and largely rebuilt (1455–71) his titular church of S. Marco, which adjoined it. The Renaissance portico and loggia of travertine collected from the Colosseum are attributed to Giuliano da Maiano or to Alberti.

With the first of the two della Rovere popes – Sixtus IV (1471–84) – Rome began to assume its modern aspect. Of humble origin, this family (said to have descended from fishermen from the Ligurian coast, near Savona) and their relatives, the Riario, raised the Papacy to a degree of magnificence that outshone the courts and capitals of Christendom. Adopting Alberti's plans, Sixtus IV widened and paved the city's streets, opening up new thoroughfares to the Vatican and constructing a new bridge over the Tiber, the Ponte Sisto. Among the many Roman churches rebuilt or embellished by this pope were S. Maria del Popolo and S. Maria della Pace. The cloister of S. Giovanni dei Genovesi in Trastevere, one of the most beautiful of Rome's Renaissance cloisters, was begun under Sixtus IV, and has been attributed to his favourite architect, the Florentine Baccio Pontelli.

Sixtus IV's nepotism was notorious. The description of the magnificence of the reception given in his palace at SS. Apostoli by his nephew Cardinal Pietro Riario for Princess Lucrezia d'Aragona reads like a passage from the *Arabian Nights*. Another nephew, Cardinal Giuliano della Rovere, afterwards Pope Julius II, ordered Baccio Pontelli to erect the portico, with its elegant octagonal columns, to his titular church of S. Pietro in Vincoli, and instructed Giuliano Sangallo to design the adjoining monastic buildings and cloisters. Similarly, the Cardinal of S. Pietro in Vincoli, as Giuliano was usually known, employed Baccio Pontelli in the construction of the impressive portico to SS. Apostoli, of which he was also titular cardinal. This consists of an arcade of nine arches, which are raised, again in the style of the Florentine Renaissance, on octagonal columns, with the della Rovere arms on the capitals, supporting half-columns of the Ionic order against pilasters. The balustrade (1681), with the statues of Christ and the Twelve Apostles, was added by C. Rainaldi.

Sixtus has given his name to one of the most famous

The Temptation of Christ (*c.* 1481) by Botticelli in the Sistine Chapel.

buildings in the world: the great hall which constitutes the Sistine Chapel in the Vatican, begun in 1473. Yet even the name of its architect is uncertain; some have attributed it to the little-known Giovanni de' Dolci, but there is reason to think that the Pope entrusted the plan to his favoured Baccio Pontelli. The chapel is divided by an exquisite marble screen, the joint work of Mino da Fiesole, Andrea Bregno and Giovanni Dalmata, who are also responsible for the beautiful balustrade of the choir. Originally the walls were to be covered with frescoes, the scenes on the left-hand wall, from the Old Testament, to be paralleled on the right by representations from the New Testament, according to a scheme seemingly devised by Sixtus' learned librarian, Platina. The vaulted ceiling represented the azure sky, studded with golden stars. The artists chosen were all Tuscan or Umbrian, and Vasari declares that Botticelli was given supreme charge by the Pope. There are three paintings by him: the second on the left (from the *Last Judgement* end), the *Youth of Moses*; the fifth, the *Punishment of the Rebels*; and the second on the right, the masterly *Temptation of Christ.* Perugino (with the help of his accomplished pupil, Pinturicchio) seems to have played the leading role in the execution, being originally responsible for six paintings, of which three perished to make way for Michelangelo's *Last Judgement.* Of

those that remain, the fifth on the right, *Christ giving the Keys to St Peter*, which must rank among his masterpieces, is highly significant of the stage which Renaissance painting had reached. There is a mastery of the control of space, light and grouping of figures; in the two triumphal arches, Antiquity joins hands with Christianity in the contemporary *tempietto* in the central background. This centralized temple recurs in Pinturicchio's *Death of S. Bernardino* in S. Maria d'Aracoeli. It remained for two later popes, Sixtus' kinsman, Julius II, and Paul III, to commission from Michelangelo the ceiling paintings and *Last Judgement* that are the chief glories of the chapel (see p. 143).

Of the Renaissance painters engaged on the Sistine Chapel it is perhaps Pinturicchio, the fellow-townsman and pupil of Perugino, whose work is best represented in Roman churches. He was constantly employed by the della Rovere family and by the Borgia Pope Alexander VI for whom he painted the splendid Borgia Apartments in the Vatican. In *c.* 1486 he was engaged on the Bufalini Chapel in S. Maria d'Aracoeli, where he depicted scenes from the life and death of S.

Christ giving the Keys to St Peter (*c.* 1481) by Perugino in the Sistine Chapel.

Bernardino, the Sienese saint who had been canonized in 1450. No one catches better than Pinturicchio the quality of Italian Renaissance life – a life lived so much in spacious squares, where beautiful men, women and children, dressed with all the brilliance of this colourful age, are set against the arcades and loggias of the revived classical architecture. Colour, light and space are all conveyed with an elegant ease; he delighted in his world and we share in his delight. Even his *Burial of S. Bernardino* in this church, where the emaciated saint on his bier is attended by members of the Bufalini family (the donors of the picture), is placed in such a square, with life going on in the background: two half-naked cherubs dance in the presence of death, and a swaddled child in a cradle symbolizes the continuity of life, while the soul of the saint is escorted to heaven by angels (p. 142).

Some of Pinturicchio's best work for the della Rovere family was done in Sixtus iv's favourite church of S. Maria del Popolo. According to popular legend this church was built on a spot haunted by the malign spirit of Nero (who was buried nearby at the foot of the Pincian Hill), until Pope Paschal ii exorcized it by building a chapel there. In 1472

Sixtus iv erected the present church and the adjoining monastery – possibly to the designs of Baccio Pontelli and Andrea Bregno – and gave the latter to the Augustinians. Here the German monk Martin Luther stayed in 1511. The Renaissance façade is structurally functional, faithfully reproducing the height and breadth of the nave and aisles. The delicately sculptured central doorway bears the arms of Sixtus iv, and in the tympanum is a *Madonna and Child* in relief of the school of Bregno. In the mid-seventeenth century Bernini, carrying out alterations to the church for Alexander vii, added the broken convex cornices at the angles of the attic, the swag of oak-leaves adjoining the central section and the Chigi heraldic device crowning the pediment. But in the main it is a Renaissance façade.

Within, S. Maria del Popolo is an interesting architectural amalgam: the nave and aisles have retained the Cistercian cross-vaulting, but the whole has undergone a seventeenth-century sea-change (1655) at the hands of Bernini, with a wealth of figures of saints and angels in stucco. At either end of the transept Bernini has also employed his illusionism in the marble frames and stucco figures for the paintings over the altars. The apse, or retrochoir, was lengthened by Bramante on the orders of Julius ii; it contains two monumental tombs (the masterpieces of Andrea Sansovino, both executed for

The Conversion of St Paul (1601), one of the masterpieces by Caravaggio in S. Maria del Popolo.

Julius II), those of Cardinal Girolamo della Rovere and of the Pope's personal enemy, Cardinal Ascanio Sforza, brother of Ludovico il Moro, Duke of Milan. Designed in the form of triumphal arches, the tombs are adorned with figures of the Virtues, reliefs of the Madonna and Child in the lunettes and exquisitely carved decorative motifs. On the vaults of the presbytery are some of the most delightful of Pinturicchio's paintings.

But it would require a volume to do justice to the artistic treasures contained in S. Maria del Popolo: Raphael's beautiful Chigi Chapel; the sculpture of Renaissance masters, such as Bregno, Lorenzetto and Mino da Fiesole, together with those of the High Baroque, such as Algardi and Bernini; paintings by Sebastiano del Piombo and Annibale Carracci. In the Chapel of the della Rovere (the first chapel leading off the right-hand aisle), above the altar, is Pinturicchio's *Adoration of the Child Jesus*. This painting might be seen as the quintessence of the spirit of the Early Renaissance, with its devotion, its reverence for homely, everyday objects and activities, its delight in landscape,

buildings, bridges and distant mountains suffused in a diaphanous blue. No greater contrast can be imagined than the changed temper of a century later, as exemplified in the two masterpieces (1601–2) by Caravaggio in the chapel to the left of the high altar, *The Conversion of St Paul* and *The Crucifixion of St Peter* – almost overpowering in their tenebrous realism. To understand this almost complete reversal of values demands an investigation of the transformation that came over Italian art with the passing of the great trio of the High Renaissance in Rome – Bramante, Raphael and Michelangelo.

Among the few remaining Renaissance church façades in Rome, apart from that of S. Maria del Popolo, are those of S. Agostino and S. Pietro in Montorio. S. Agostino was built at the expense of the opulent French Cardinal d'Estouteville by Giacomo di Pietrasanta in 1479, and is rather a forbidding-looking building. Approached by a high flight of steps, it consists of two orders, the lower storey divided by pilasters into three sections, the central door being surmounted by a pediment, the doors on either side by eye-windows. The upper, with its great central circular window under the pediment, is bound to the lower storey by means of massive ungainly volutes. Very different is the elegant façade of the little church of S. Pietro in Montorio on the Janiculum, built on the site where, during the Middle Ages, St Peter was erroneously believed to have suffered martyrdom. Its design is attributed either to the school of Andrea Bregno or to Meo del Caprina. It, too, is approached by steps, here formed from a double ramp. It consists simply of two storeys, framed by corner pilasters and a pediment, the upper being divided from the lower portion by a shallow cornice. A rectangular doorway with plain mouldings, a rose-window and a shield in the centre of the tympanum are its sole decoration.

It might have been thought that Alexander VI (Borgia, 1492–1503) would have been too preoccupied with his vacillations of policy and with the private and public concerns of his large family to attend to Roman building. During his pontificate, however, besides his fortification of the Castel S. Angelo and his work on the Vatican (the Torre di Borgia, and the Borgia Apartments decorated by Pinturicchio), he both restored and built churches. In 1518 he ordered the Florentine Antonio Sangallo the Younger to erect for the

RIGHT *Jonah and the Whale* (1520), in S. Maria del Popolo, was carved by Lorenzetto from a design by Raphael. As if to heighten the sculpture's affinities with the antique, the face of Jonah bears a strong resemblance to Antinous, the favourite of the Emperor Hadrian; the block of marble from which it was hewn came from the Roman Temple of Castor and Pollux.

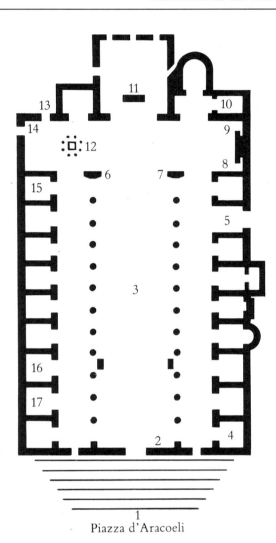

Piazza d'Aracoeli

S. Maria d'Aracoeli

1 One hundred and twenty-two steps leading to the church.
2 Monument to Cardinal Ludovico d'Albret (d. 1465) by A. Bregno and, removed to wall, tombstone of Giovanni Crivelli (d. 1432) by Donatello.
3 Nave divided from aisles by twenty-two columns of mixed origin. Cosmatesque paving (thirteenth century) and ceiling with naval symbols commemorating the battle of Lepanto (1571).
4 Bufalini Chapel or Chapel of S. Bernardino with frescoes (*c.* 1486) by Pinturicchio.
5 Passage leading to the Piazza del Campidoglio; mosaic (eighth century) over the exterior of the door.
6 and 7 Two pulpits (reconstructed) by Lorenzo di Cosma and his son Giacomo (*c.* 1200).
8 Tomb of Pope Honorius IV (d. 1287).
9 Tomb of Luca Savelli (*c.* 1287) in Roman sarcophagus.
10 Santa Rosa Chapel with mosaics (thirteenth century).
11 High altar with *Madonna* (tenth century) and, to the left, monument to Cardinal G. B. Savelli (d. 1498) attributed to the school of A. Bregno.
12 Circular monument to St Helena with porphyry urn, resting on an ancient altar said to have been erected by the Emperor Augustus after a prophesy from a Sybil.
13 Entrance to room containing the *Santo Bambino.*
14 Monument to Cardinal Matteo d'Acquasparta (d. 1302) attributed to Giovanni di Cosma, with fresco by P. Cavallini.
15 Chapel of S. Margherita da Cortona.
16 Chapel of St Anthony of Padua with painting (*c.* 1449) by Benezzo Gozzoli.
17 Chapel of the Crib.

Aragonese and Catalans the church of S. Maria di Monserrato, today known as the Spanish Church. (It is ironical that the two Borgia popes, Calixtus III and Alexander VI, should for centuries have lain forgotten in their wooden coffins and that they should only have been buried here in 1881 on the intervention of the King of Spain.) Also in 1495, King Louis XII of France, to commemorate the successful invasion of Naples, founded Trinità dei Monti on the Pincian Hill. Building only got under way in 1502, and the church was eventually consecrated by Sixtus V in 1585. In 1499 Alexander VI began to build the church of S. Rocco for the guild of Tiber innkeepers and boatmen, and the following year saw the founding of the church of the German

nation, S. Maria dell'Anima, the architect most probably being Andrea Sansovino, who certainly carved the group over the central doorway, *The Madonna between Two Souls in Purgatory.* But, in terms of artistic importance, the two chief events of Alexander VI's pontificate were the arrival in Rome in 1496 of Michelangelo Buonarroti and in 1499 of Donato Bramante. Michelangelo's first Roman commission was the exquisitely beautiful *Pietà*, carved for the French Cardinal Villiers de la Grolaye and now in St Peter's. In 1501 he returned to Florence.

Bramante was born and brought up as a painter in Urbino, whose court, under the great Federigo di Montefeltro, was one of the most enlightened in Italy. He was employed for a period in Milan, where he turned his attention to architecture, influenced in this decision by the work of the advanced Florentine architects and of that supremely talented man, Leonardo da Vinci. In several of the churches which he designed in Milan, Bramante developed an idea which had

LEFT *The Madonna del Parto* (1521) by Jacopo Sansovino in S. Agostino is much venerated by Roman mothers, as is attested by the numerous ex-votos, lighted lamps and votive candles that constantly surround her.

S. Maria del Popolo

1 Façade.
2 Chapel of the della Rovere family, with *The Adoration of the Child Jesus* (c. 1485) by Pinturicchio and tomb of Cardinal Cristoforo and of Domenico della Rovere by A. Bregno and Mino da Fiesole.
3 Tombs of Giovanni della Rovere by follower of A. Bregno (1483) and Bishop G. Foscari (d. 1463) by Vecchietta.
4 Tombs of Giovanni Borgia, son of Alexander VI and brother of Lucrezia and Cesare Borgia, and of their mother Vannozza Cattanei.
5 High altar.
6 Apse by Bramante with *Madonna del Popolo* (thirteenth century?) and murals by Pinturicchio on the vault; stained glass by G. de Marcillat.
7 Tombs of Cardinal Ascanio Sforza (d. 1505), brother of Ludovico il Moro, and of Cardinal G. B. della Rovere by A. Sansovino.
8 Cerasi Chapel with *The Conversion of St Paul* and *The Crucifixion of St Peter* (1601–2) by Caravaggio and *Assumption* by Ann. Carracci.
9 Mellini Chapel with monument to Cardinal G. Mellini (c. 1630) by A. Algardi.
10 Chigi Chapel designed and decorated by Raphael for Agostino Chigi (d. 1512) and his brother Sigismondo (d. 1526), with sculpture by Lorenzetti and Bernini.
11 Baptistery.
12 Tomb of G. B. Gisleni (d. 1672).
13 Passage to sacristy.
14 Sacristy with altar by A. Bregno for Cardinal Rodrigo Borgia, later Alexander VI.

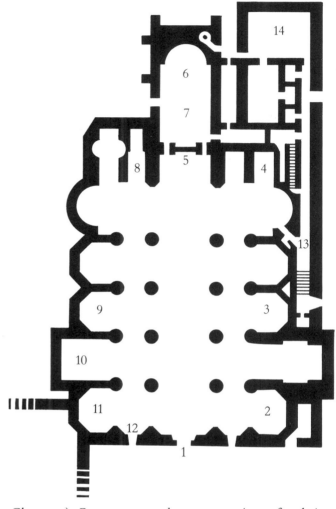

already been put forward: that of the centrally-planned, as opposed to the customary longitudinally-planned, church. After he came to Rome, he may have been employed on the magnificent palace, the Cancelleria, which was being built for Cardinal Raphael Riario and was paid for partly out of the cardinal's gaming wins from Franceschetto Cibo. The vast palace included the church erected in 380 by Pope Damaso in honour of St Lawrence – S. Lorenzo in Damaso. Bramante was to rebuild this church in the Cancelleria, removing the ancient columns for use in the courtyard and altering its original orientation. The Bramantesque form of a nave separated from the aisles by square piers remains, but the richness of the nineteenth-century marbles and gilding (by Valadier and Vespignani) have obscured the harmony of the original design. The portal is by the sixteenth-century architect Vignola.

In addition to his immense works at the Vatican (in the Belvedere and Damasus Courts) and in St Peter's (see Chapter 9), Bramante created two masterpieces of ecclesiastical architecture in Rome: the cloister at S. Maria della Pace (1500–4) and the Tempietto of S. Pietro in Montorio (1502). In Bramante the architectural ideas of the Early Renaissance, of Brunelleschi and Alberti, have reached their fulfilment; with him enters the grandeur of the Roman High Renaissance. In the cloister at S. Maria della Pace (his first Roman work, commissioned by Cardinal Oliviero Carafa) Bramante achieves perfection of harmony and proportion. On the ground floor the arcades are formed by rectangular

RIGHT The Bufalini Chapel in S. Maria d'Aracoeli was decorated by Pinturicchio with *Scenes from the Life of S. Bernardino of Siena* (c. 1486). The saint was a fervent supporter of the Osservanti or reformed Order of Franciscans. In the *Transfiguration* he stands holding a book in which is written, 'Father, I have made manifest Thy name to all men', between a youthful St Louis, Bishop of Toulouse, and St Anthony of Padua.

piers, with attached pilasters of a delicately moulded Ionic order, resting on plinths and passing through the pronounced string course at the springing of the arches. Above the rounded arches is a severely articulated entablature. This supports an open gallery, where slim columns alternate with the continuation of the piers and attached pilasters, both with Composite capitals. Above, a typical Roman architrave replaces the rounded arches of the ground floor. This upper gallery is a pure delight in its dignity and grace, the strong Roman sunshine making an arresting contrast of light and shadow.

Built on the spot on the Janiculum Hill where, as I have mentioned, St Peter was at one time believed to have been crucified, the Tempietto of S. Pietro in Montorio has been said to be sculptural, rather than strictly architectural, in its perfection – a reliquary in stone. At first sight it may seem austere in the absence of decoration, save for the purely classical metopes and triglyphs, the shell-tops of the niches and the coat of arms in stone. Its beauty derives entirely from its harmony and proportion, the ratio of height to width on the ground floor reappearing in the second storey. The colonnade is of the severe Tuscan Doric order, used in the Tempietto for the first time in modern Roman architecture. Here has been realized afresh the classic architectural ideal of contained space, lost since antiquity.

After the intermission of the very brief pontificate (1503) of Pius III, the della Rovere Cardinal of S. Pietro in Vincoli ascended the papal throne as Julius II (1503–13). The impetus given by this remarkable man to the Roman High Renaissance brought it to its full flowering. In 1505 the Pope, on the advice of Giuliano Sangallo, summoned Michelangelo to Rome. The master's first commission was to prepare a design for Julius' own tomb, which was intended to be on a magnificent scale. Forty statues were to adorn it; at the summit the figures of Heaven and Earth were to support the sarcophagus in which the pope was ultimately to be buried. Then Julius commissioned Bramante to draw up plans for the rebuilding of St Peter's in a manner worthy of the Papacy and of his own glory, in the centre of which his own tomb would in due course be placed. The tomb, however, was never completed; other commissions intervened, including the titanic undertaking of the painting of the Sistine ceiling.

Michelangelo Buonarroti shared with his patron that masterfulness of spirit, that imaginative irritability, which the Italians expressively call *terribilità*, yet even he had to bend to Julius' imperious will. When it was first proposed to him that he should decorate the entire vaults and ceiling of the Sistine Chapel with fresco, he protested, declaring that he was a sculptor, with no experience of painting, and suggesting Raphael in his stead. But on 27 July 1508 he mounted the

PAGE 142 *The Burial of S. Bernardino* (c. 1486) by Pinturicchio in the Bufalini Chapel in S. Maria d'Aracoeli. The baby in the cradle, the dancing cherubs and the everyday events depicted in the background symbolize the continuity of life; at the top on the right the saint's soul ascends to heaven.

PAGE 144 The beautiful cloister of S. Maria della Pace (1500–4) was the first major work executed by Bramante (for Cardinal Oliviero Carafa) on his arrival in Rome from Milan and Urbino. It marks the return to the architectural canons of antiquity in Renaissance Rome.

PAGE 145 In his 'reliquary in stone', the Tempietto of S. Pietro in Montorio, a masterpiece of harmonious proportion, Bramante realized the Renaissance ideal. Michelangelo compared him to the artists of antiquity: 'One cannot deny that Bramante was as worthy an architect as any in ancient times.'

ABOVE Michelangelo's *Creation of Man* (1508–12) in the centre of the Sistine Chapel ceiling.

LEFT A Renaissance *ciborio* or tabernacle by an unknown artist, possibly Florentine, in SS. Quattro Coronati (late fifteenth century).

scaffolding (from which, metaphorically, he was not to descend until four years later), and there he worked, lying on his back for days on end, with lime and colour running into his eyes, nose and mouth, nearly choking him (it was said that for some time afterwards he could only read a letter by holding it above his head). What he created, together with the *Last Judgement*, painted over twenty years later, constitutes one of the most stupendous works ever achieved by the imagination and hand of a single genius. He succeeded in presenting nothing less than the story of the Creation, according to Genesis, and the spiritual history of humanity. This immense composition contains no fewer than three-hundred figures. Symbolic of Michelangelo's thinking is his magnificent *Creation of Man*, in the centre of the ceiling. In this, the Omnipotent, Omniscient and All-Compassionate, in a cloud of angels, stretches out his hand towards the beautiful recumbent figure of the newly created Adam, who also reaches out to touch the fingers of his Creator. But their fingers do not touch; for Michelangelo the gap was only closed in the mysteries of the

Incarnation and Redemption. That Christ's coming was foretold is represented in the majestic figures of twelve prophets and sibyls.

When the painting of the Sistine Chapel ceiling was completed, work was to be resumed on Julius' tomb. But this was never done, for at this juncture Julius II died. It is ironical that almost all that remains in Rome of this Pope's megalomaniacal monument is the single, but awe-inspiring, figure of Moses (p. 152) in the della Rovere church of S. Pietro in Vincoli.

It was Pope Paul III (1534–49) who called on the aging Michelangelo to paint the *Last Judgement*. Much had happened in the interval, including the beginnings of the Northern Reformation and the cataclysmic Sack of Rome by the mercenary army of the Emperor Charles V in 1527, and it seems that something of the changed temper of the times is revealed in Michelangelo's great apocalyptic vision of the final scene. It took five years of unremitting labour before, on All Saints' Day, 1541, exactly twenty-nine years after the unveiling of the ceiling, this mighty work was revealed. Pope Paul fell on his knees in admiration; but the critics were not long in voicing their disapproval, the hypocritical Aretino adding his voice to their censure of this display of nudity. In 1564, after Michelangelo's death, the Council of Trent was to condemn such works as unsuitable for the adornment of places of worship. A hack painter was appointed to clothe some of the nudes, thereby earning for himself the derisive sobriquet of 'Breeches'.

In the summer of 1508, at the invitation of his countryman Bramante, Raphael, then aged twenty-five, arrived in Rome. The son of a painter and something of a poet, Raphael had been brought up in close contact with the court of the cultivated Duke Guidobaldo di Montefeltro and the Duchess Elisabetta Gonzaga of Urbino. Later he had studied in Perugia under Perugino and in Florence, where his good looks, charm and outstanding ability were quickly noticed. After Bramante introduced him to Pope Julius II and to the Sienese banker Agostino Chigi, Raphael immediately acquired commissions. In 1509 Julius, recognizing his extraordinary talents, set Raphael to repaint the Stanza della Segnatura in the Vatican, destroying frescoes by such earlier masters as Bonfigli, Piero della Francesca, Andrea del Castagno, Sodoma and Signorelli in order to make way for Raphael's work.

If Michelangelo has been seen to have possessed characteristics both Olympian and Titanic – a Zeus and a Prometheus – Raphael seems to have attributes more usually associated with Apollo. Not only was he endowed with a magnificent gift of design, consummate draughtsmanship and a refined colour sense; he was also able to imbue his work with a lyrical quality. Far removed from the Promethean struggles in which Michelangelo engaged, Raphael appears to have been blessed with a harmony, both within himself and with the world, that produces in his work an impression of balance, graceful fluency and ease. Besides his masterpieces in the Vatican Stanze and his numerous portraits, his continuation after Bramante's death in 1514 of his building in the Belvedere Court and on the Cortile di S. Damaso, the beautiful 'grotesque' decorations in the Vatican Palace, and his architectural work in the Palazzo Vidoni Caffarelli and the Villa Madama – besides all this activity, Raphael created the Chigi Chapel in S. Maria del Popolo and paintings in two Roman churches: the *Prophet Isaiah* (1512) in S. Agostino and the *Sibyls* (1514) in S. Maria della Pace.

With the exception of St Peter's (see Chapter 9), the only ecclesiastical work which can be attributed to him with certainty is the little church of S. Eligio degli Orefici, near the spot where he planned to build himself a palace, before death overtook him in 1520 at the early age of thirty-seven. At S. Eligio, the church of the College of Goldsmiths, Raphael was influenced by Bramante's interest in centrally-planned churches, this example being designed as a Greek cross, with a drum and hemispherical dome at the crossing; the harmonious effect is heightened by the interplay between the

Detail of *The School of Athens* by Raphael in the Vatican Stanze showing a self-portrait by the artist (in the black cap). Standing beside him is the painter G. A. Bazzi (1477–1549) who was known as Il Sodoma.

white and greys of the walls and architectural members.

During the pontificate of Leo X (1513–21) the Renaissance in Rome reached its zenith, and this was reflected in the magnificence and luxury of the papal court. Although the Pope preferred literature to the visual arts, Raphael was kept employed on the Stanze. His best-known pupil, Giulio Romano, painted the beautiful *Holy Family and Saints* (1522), now over the high altar in S. Maria dell'Anima. Giulio was then a young man of twenty-three; his early promise had not yet succumbed to the pornography of Aretino, nor to the Mannerist excesses which characterize his later work. Church-building was of little interest to the worldly Pope Leo, though, while a cardinal, he had restored his titular church of S. Maria in Domnica. The Renaissance portico (1513), Bramantesque in style, which he erected here, has been attributed wrongly to Raphael; it is in fact the work of Andrea Sansovino. Leo X commissioned, as the national church of Florence (the city where he was born and brought up), the church of S. Giovanni dei Fiorentini – a work, it must be confessed, unworthy of the aesthetic Florentines. Michelangelo, Raphael and Peruzzi are all said to have had a hand in proposing its design, but the one which found favour with Leo (for whom the decisive factor may have been expense) was by Jacopo Sansovino. Subsequently many architects were employed in its building, the façade by Alessandro Galilei only being completed in 1734. However, the high altar, some monuments and the Falconieri Chapel in the crypt are by Borromini, who is buried there. The sybaritic Leo x's principal interests did not lie in church construction.

Like S. Maria del Popolo, the Dominican church of S. Maria sopra Minerva (p. 25) is a repository of art treasures, so that the visitor is confronted with an embarrassment of riches, many of them dating from the Renaissance. It might have been thought that this, rather than S. Giovanni dei Fiorentini, was the national church of the Florentines, with its tombs of the Medici Leo x and Clement vii and of Diotisalvi Nerone (who was exiled for conspiring against the Medici in 1466), and the beautiful late sixteenth-century monument by an unknown, possibly Tuscan, artist to Virginia Pucci Ridolfi, the niece of the celebrated Florentine historian Guicciardini. It also contains the statue of the *Redeemer with his Cross* (c. 1520), by one of Florence's greatest sons, Michelangelo, in whose eyes the human form was one of the most perfect of God's creations.

Among the treasures in S. Maria sopra Minerva are two of special interest: the tomb of Fra Angelico and the preserved body of St Catherine of Siena. The painter-monk is represented on his tombstone in his Dominican garb, the face mummy-like in death, the hands that created so much beauty reverently crossed; they are remarkable for their attenuated fingers. The great St Catherine, the patron saint of Italy, was in her lifetime looked on as an honorary Roman. She lies beneath the Gothicized high altar (1855), in a sepulchre (1430) by Isaia da Pisa. In 1637 Cardinal Antonio Barberini removed to this church the walls of the room in which the saint died. Now covered with frescoes by the native-born Antoniazzo Romano and his school, they can be seen in a chapel behind the sacristy. A beautiful *Annunciation* by Antoniazzo in the Chapel of the Annunciation in the middle of the right-hand aisle shows him to have been under-rated as a painter. A quite magnificent angel makes the momentous announcement to Mary as she is in the act of presenting marriage dowries to poor girls, who are shown against a background of gold – small figures, dressed in white, beside the founder of a confraternity established for this purpose: the Dominican Cardinal Torquemada (d. 1468),

uncle of the infamous inquisitor. Antoniazzo was associated with the much greater painter Melozzo da Forlì, who is represented here in the St Raymond Chapel, also in the right-hand aisle, where there stands the splendid tomb of Bishop Giovanni de Coca, by Andrea Bregno, set in a Renaissance frame. Above this Melozzo has depicted Christ, clothed in white within a pink-gold mandorla, between two angels who sound their brazen trumpets, the billowing folds of their garments revealing their sturdy young limbs. In the Capranica Chapel to the right of the high altar is the sole example in the church of the work of Fra Angelico – his *Madonna and Child* (c. 1449), thought to have been painted for a standard.

Three other tombs are too precious to be passed by. At the end of the right-hand aisle is that of Bishop William Durand (d. 1296), set within a Gothic frame, on which angels draw back curtains to reveal his recumbent figure, covered by material whose delicately carved folds flow over on to the front of his tomb. Above, in mosaic, are the Madonna and Child, shown with St Dominic, St Privato and the kneeling bishop. This thirteenth-century work is by Giovanni di Cosma. To the left of the entrance is a masterpiece by Mino da Fiesole: the monumental tomb to Francesco Tornabuoni (d. 1480), who is shown lying on his side on an exquisitely sculpted urn whose legs are formed by sphinxes. Above, between two heraldic shields, is a powerfully moulded medallion (from whose centre radiate tongues of fire), completing this admirable composition. Mino created one other tomb in this church: that of Giovanni Alberini (d. 1473) in the Frangipane Chapel. Here Mino made use of a splendid antique Greek sarcophagus (possibly of the fourth century BC), showing Hercules struggling with the Nemean Lion; the tranquil rigidity of the figure of the deceased is in complete contrast with the ferocious struggle taking place below.

Despite the high quality of all these works, the chief glory of S. Maria sopra Minerva is in the Carafa Chapel (or Chapel of St Thomas Aquinas), which is entirely decorated with the magnificent murals and vault paintings (1488–92) of another Florentine, Filippino Lippi. In this chapel lay the body of St Thomas Aquinas until his relics were removed to Naples in 1511, and Filippino's paintings (the only examples of his marvellous work in Rome) are a fitting tribute to the theological labours of the saintly doctor. In *The Annunciation* over the altar, in a beautiful Renaissance frame, Mary's attention to the great news is seen to be somewhat distracted by St Thomas's presentation of Cardinal Oliviero Carafa, whom she receives with all the graciousness of a great lady. Above, to the jubilation of a band of angels, the majestic figure of the Virgin is borne aloft on her triumphant way to heaven. To the right of the chapel are two scenes, both equally

S. Maria sopra Minerva

1 Façade (seventeenth century) with Renaissance central doorway (1453).

2 Gothic nave (c. 1280).

3 Tomb of Diotisalvi Neroni (1482), a Florentine exiled by Piero de'Medici.

4 Monument to Virginia Pucci Ridolfi (d. 1568).

5 Chapel of the Annunciation by Carlo Maderno, with *Annunciation* (c. 1460) by Antoniazzo Romano.

6 Aldobrandini Chapel by G. Della Porta and C. Maderno, with *The Last Supper* by Federico Barocci and monument to Salvestro Aldobrandini and Luisa Dati, parents of Clement VIII, by Della Porta.

7 Chapel of St Raymond of Penafort with monument of Cardinal Giovanni Diego de Coca (d. 1477) by Andrea Bregno and murals by Melozzo da Forlì.

8 Carafa Chapel with paintings by Filippino Lippi, *The Annunciation* and *St Thomas Aquinas confuting Heretics* (1488–92) (the two young men in the latter picture are thought to be Leo X and his cousin Clement VII), and monument to the Carafa Pope Paul IV (d. 1559), designed by Pirro Ligorio.

9 Tomb of William Durand, Bishop of Mende (d. 1296), by Giovanni di Cosma.

10 Rosary or Capranica Chapel with stucco ceiling by Marcello Venusti (1573) and tomb of Cardinal D. Capranica (d. 1458) by follower of A. Bregno.

11 High altar with sarcophagus containing the body of St Catherine of Siena (d. 1380) and statue of the saint by Isaia da Pisa; behind the altar the tombs of two Medici popes, Leo X and Clement VII, both designed by Antonio Sangallo the Younger (1536); on the floor a memorial stone to the humanist Pietro Bembo (d. 1547).

12 Statue of the *Redeemer with his Cross* (1519–21) by Michelangelo.

13 Tomb of Fra Angelico, who died (1455) in the adjoining monastery.

14 Sacristy and the remains of the room where St Catherine of Siena died, with painting (1482) by Antoniazzo Romano.

15 Chapel of St Dominic (1725) by Fil. Raguzzini.

16 Tomb of Andrea Bregno (1506) attributed to L. Capponi.

17 Tomb of Maria Raggi (1643) by Bernini.

18 Chapel with monuments to Maria Colonna-Lante, Giulio Lante della Rovere and their daughter Carlotta.

19 Grazioli Chapel with painting, *The Redeemer*, attributed to Perugino and statues, *St Sebastian* (fifteenth century) attributed to M. Marini and *St John the Baptist* by A. Bonvicino (1603); also tombs of B. and A. Maffei (early sixteenth century) attributed to L. Capponi.

20 Tomb of Francesco Tornabuoni (d. 1480) by Mino da Fiesole.

21 Passage leading to the cloister and the Dominican monastery.

22 Cloister.

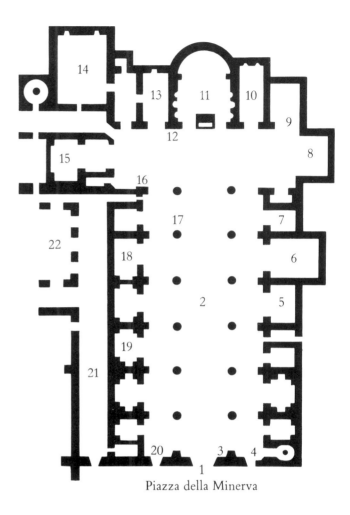

Piazza della Minerva

admirable in their composition. Above, St Thomas kneels before the Crucifix, with, beside him, the volumes of his works, which Christ acknowledges with the words, 'Well hast thou written of me, Thomas'. Below, the *Triumph of St Thomas Aquinas*, one of the greatest works of the Florentine master, shows his skill in the composition of his groups of figures in the foreground and in his handling of the recession in space to the intricate architectural setting in which the Saint, between the female personifications of Grammar, Dialectics, Rhetoric and Philosophy, confounds his adversaries. In all this wealth of form and magnificent colour Filippino Lippi achieves the allegorical glorification of St Thomas and the Roman Church.

The brief pontificate of the Emperor Charles V's tutor, the Dutchman who took the name of Adrian VI (1522–3), could not have been in greater contrast, in its austerity, with

An early drawing of the Late Renaissance façade, attributed to Giacomo Della Porta, of S. Luigi dei Francesi.

the golden age of Leo X, but his piety left no mark on the churches of Rome. Even his great monumental tomb in S. Maria dell'Anima (p. 155), designed by Baldassare Peruzzi, is diminished by the beauty of Giulio Romano's *Holy Family*, which adjoins it. Nor was his luckless successor to add to the city's churches. As a cardinal in 1518, Giulio de' Medici had begun the national church of the French, S. Luigi dei Francesi, whose Late Renaissance façade (with the salamander of François I in relief) was perhaps by Giacomo Della Porta (p. 157). But when Giulio de' Medici became Pope

Clement VII (1523–34) he was caught in the toils of his own devious policy towards the northern powers of France and Germany and by the zeal of the Reformation. When the early fog lifted on the morning of 6 May 1527, the *landsknechts* of the Emperor Charles V under the Constable of Bourbon poured through a breach in the walls of the Leonine City. The Pope narrowly escaped, to take refuge in the Castel S. Angelo, and the Eternal City suffered all the horrors and devastation of a sack. From the battlements Clement could witness the destruction of S. Spirito and burning palaces and churches. When, after seven months' captivity, the Pope escaped, Rome was a scene of desolation; little remained of all the accumulated artistic treasures of the Roman Renaissance.

7
The Stylization of Style: Mannerism

With the Sack of Rome in 1527 the optimistic, balanced world of Renaissance humanism was rudely shattered. In Rome the plague of 1522 and the artistically sterile pontificate of that good but philistine man, Pope Adrian VI, followed by the Sack, brought about an exodus of artists from the Eternal City. Adrian VI himself had wished to destroy Michelangelo's masterpieces in the Sistine Chapel, referring to them as nothing but 'una stufa d'ignudi' (literally, but euphemistically, 'a hot-house of nudes'). Saving what they could – often only their lives – the artists fled; but, wherever they settled, they disseminated the Roman style. Of the painters, Pierino del Vaga introduced this *maniera* to Florence in 1522, Giulio Romano to Mantua two years later. Parmigianino returned to his native Emilia in 1527. The Florentine Rosso successfully carried the style to Fontainebleau in 1530, where he was soon joined by Primaticcio. Thus this Italian – and, in particular, Roman – attitude to innovation in art became widely diffused.

The recently revived term 'Mannerist' is used to describe an artistic style which, originating in Rome *c.* 1520, continued beyond 1580 (a year described as a 'watershed'), until it came in contact with the Counter-Reformation. The Italian word *maniera* is equivalent to 'style', or 'stylish'; Mannerism is the stylish style. From the outset the term

'Mannerist' was one of praise. Vasari thought his own century, the sixteenth, superior to the preceding because it had style. Raphael and Castiglione, writing to Leo X, castigated Gothic as 'devoid of all grace, entirely without style [*maniera*]'. Shearman has said that 'self-conscious stylization is the common denominator to all Mannerist works of art'. Grace, difficulties effortlessly overcome, complexity, variety, richness were all ingredients in this consciously sought-after style. Patrons looked to the greatest artists for something (anything, the choice was theirs alone) stupendous. This 'mannered' style was expressed primarily in painting and sculpture, and was already evident in works by artists of the High Renaissance, such as Michelangelo and Raphael. It can be seen in the former's *Ignudi* in the Sistine Chapel or in his *Christ* in S. Maria sopra Minerva. But the term also applied to architecture. Raphael found Bramante to 'fall short of the best antique style in decorative richness of materials'. Serlio, writing in 1540, remarked that 'it is a splendid thing if an architect is abundant in inventions, because of the consequent diversity of things that happen in the structure . . . a source of great pleasure to the eye and satisfaction to the mind'. The decorum, proportion and harmony of the art and architecture of the High Renaissance were to be dissolved during this intervening period, until, a century later, a new synthesis was to be found in works of the High Baroque.

Michelangelo's last undertaking in Rome, designed and begun the year before his death at the age of eighty-nine in 1564, was the conversion of the huge ruins of the Baths of Diocletian (built in 305) into the Carthusian church of S.

LEFT The great figure of *Moses* (*c.* 1515) in S. Pietro in Vincoli was but one of the statues ordered by Julius II from Michelangelo for the Pope's mausoleum projected for the New St Peter's. Although the statue retains the serenity of the Renaissance ideal, its force presages the shift towards Mannerism.

Maria degli Angeli. Alterations were carried out in the eighteenth century by Vanvitelli, but the whole titanic conception is essentially Michelangelo's. As you enter from the vestibule, you pass Jean-Antoine Houdon's statue of the founder of the Order, St Bruno, of which Pope Clement XIV once remarked that so lifelike was it that the Saint would speak, had not the rules of his Order forbidden him. The church is in the shape of a Greek cross, and the impression given, when one stands at the crossing, in what was the *tepidarium* of Diocletian's great Baths, with its monolithic Corinthian columns of antique red granite, is one of sheer immensity. Not since antiquity, it seems, had human genius been equal to such a structural task until a Michelangelo undertook it. But in S. Maria degli Angeli man is dwarfed; confronted with the colossal, one feels that one's humanity is diminished, rather than augmented and exalted. It is too stupendous.

If in S. Maria degli Angeli the Antique fails to join hands with Christianity, it is quite the opposite in a little church on the ancient Via Flaminia, a short way beyond Bernini's Porta del Popolo: the Tempietto di S. Andrea. This is by the Modenese architect Vignola, and was erected for Pope Julius III in 1554. As a prelate at the Vatican, Julius was imprisoned with Clement VII in the Castel S. Angelo during the Sack of Rome; after escaping on 30 November, St Andrew's Day, he built this church in fulfilment of a vow made to the saint on that day. Vignola, a disciple of Michelangelo, here breaks new ground by crowning his small oblong building with an elliptical cupola. Renaissance

architects had seen perfection of form in centrally-planned churches, covered by a hemispherical dome. S. Andrea is pleasing in its simple austerity: its façade of *peperino* is divided into three bays by pilasters, doubled at the extremities; its central doorway is surmounted by a pediment and flanked by window niches. Above, the flat wall surface is broken by an angular pediment and is crowned by a pronounced cornice from which rise the drum and cupola. The harmony and proportion without are also found within – the interior has all the charm of an architectural decorum which is still that of the Renaissance. The façade and interior are here in equilibrium; later, as Mannerist tendencies gained strength, the façade came to bear little or no relation to the inside of the church.

The church of S. Spirito in Sassia was severely damaged, in fact, almost destroyed, during the Sack and was rebuilt by Antonio Sangallo the Younger *c.* 1540 – less the façade, which was built by Ottaviano Mascherino, to designs left by Sangallo, some half-century later. The façade maintains much of the spirit of the architecture of the Renaissance, in that parts, while contributing to the satisfying composition of the whole, retain their independence and individuality, quite in the sense demanded by Alberti. The front of S. Spirito is of two storeys, joined by plain concave volutes. The lower storey is articulated by Corinthian pilasters into five bays; the central bay, which contains a portal of simple moulding and pediment, is slightly wider than the outer ones, these being of equal width and decorated similarly, with a niche and two square tablets. The higher storey of three bays repeats the lower, with the exception that the central section contains a large eye-window, with, above, the coat-of-arms of Sixtus V. It is surmounted by a triangular pediment. Again, the interior is distinguished by the elegance of its harmonious proportions. S. Spirito has been called by Wölfflin 'the *schema* for all later façades'. The façades of Roman churches are a fascinating study, reflecting as they do not only architectural changes, but what lie behind these: historical and artistic movements and altered liturgical needs.

In S. Caterina dei Funari (rebuilt 1560) the façade (attributed by some to Giacomo Della Porta, though it is more likely to be by Guidetto Guidetti) still follows the style of S.

LEFT Medallion portrait of Michelangelo Buonarroti from *Die Blauen Bücher*, 1929.

RIGHT Honoured in death as he seldom was in life, the Flemish Pope Adrian VI, formerly tutor to the Emperor Charles V, is buried in S. Maria dell'Anima in a majestic tomb designed by Baldassarre Peruzzi (after 1523). The allegorical figures are by Michelangelo Senese; the bas-relief showing *Adrian VI's Entry into Rome* is attributed to N. P. Tribolo.

PROH DOLOR

QVANTVM REFERT IN QVAE TEMPORA VEL OPTIMI CVIVSQ

VIRTVS INCIDAT

HADRIANO VI PONT MAX EX TRAIECTO INSIGNI INFER GERMANIAE VRBE
QVI DVM . . RVM HVMANAR MAXIME AVERSATVR SPLENDOREM
VLTRO A P . . CERIB OB INCOMPARABILEM SACRAR DISCIPLINAR SCIENTIAM
. . . CASTISSIMI ANIMI MODERATIONEM

Spirito, but a greater richness is apparent in the decoration, particularly in the opulent swags of fruit in the area of the capitals and in the free-standing columns that support the pediment of the doorway. S. Caterina has been said to exhibit a 'timid elegance'.

There is nothing timid about the façade of Giacomo Della Porta's Madonna dei Monti (1580), which is considered that architect's masterpiece. Here we can see a distinct Mannerist break with the earlier ideals. The church's strength and elegance are strangely at odds with the poor quarter known as the Suburra in which it stands. In Roman times this district had an unsavoury reputation as the haunt of pimps and prostitutes. In the church of the Madonna tendencies which were tentatively appearing in S. Caterina have been carried further. This is a beautifully compact façade, the two orders powerfully wedded by the scroll-like volutes. But Della Porta has concentrated all the force of his composition in the central sections, which are marked by superimposed pilasters, leaving the outer bays on the lower storey bare of all ornament, apart from a string course. The strong moulding of the tablets above the niches is repeated in the moulding over the portal, which penetrates into the area of the capitals. Above, a well-proportioned window corresponds to the portal, its segmental pediment, as opposed to the triangular one of the latter, adding to the 'richness'. Inside the church, over the high altar,

is a popularly venerated *Madonna with the Child and Saints*, a work dating from the end of the fourteenth century. Here is the resting-place of St Joseph Labre, a Frenchman who, out of humility, led the life of a beggar and was found dying in the neighbourhood by a butcher, who cared for him until his death, shortly afterwards, on Ash Wednesday, 1783.

In his design for S. Luigi dei Francesi, which was begun by Clement VII while he was still Cardinal de' Medici but was not consecrated as the French national church until 1589, Della Porta (if the façade is in fact by him) has strengthened the central section in accordance with the Mannerist tendency, but he has maintained the Renaissance tradition in giving each of the bays its independence, while subordinating them to the whole design. The salamanders in spheres, the emblem of François I, were said to have been carved by 'a certain Master Gian, a Frenchman'.

But the finest example of this continued development of the church façade is undoubtedly that of S. Susanna (1603, the national church of American Catholics), designed by the architect of the façade of St Peter's, Carlo Maderno. It has a fastidious richness, since both members and decoration were handled with masterly control. The design progresses from the central section outwards, from columns to half-columns and from half-columns to the angular pilasters. The outer bays have their decorative tablets, but the strongest effect

PAGE 156 The scholarly Vignola's *Rule of the Five Orders in Architecture* (1562) was widely accepted and studied. Some years earlier Vignola had shown his technical mastery in the Tempietto di S. Andrea (1554) on the Via Flaminia, a masterpiece of the sober elegance that was one aspect of Roman Mannerism.

PAGE 157 The façade of S. Luigi dei Francesi, the national church of the French, is impressive in its porous Roman travertine. Beneath the statue in a niche by the French sculptor P. Lestache (1758), a circular medallion contains a salamander in high relief, the device of François I.

PAGE 159 Carlo Maderno's beautiful façade to S. Susanna (1603), showing his sure sense of architectural design and decorative detail, marks an important step in the evolution of Mannerism to Baroque. The statues in the niches are by his namesake and contemporary Stefano Maderno.

·D· RVSTICVCIVS ·A·

comes from the magnificent doorway and window (loggia) above and from the elaborately moulded niches, with their statues – those in the upper storey being by the architect's namesake, the talented Stefano Maderno. The severity which was seen earlier, even in Della Porta, gives way here to a rich plasticity which heralds the High Baroque.

For centuries religious-minded men had called for the reform of the Church 'in head and members'. If the Sack of 1527 had a traumatic effect on those living in Rome and on Catholics everywhere, the Protestant revolt in Northern Europe was far more profoundly felt, in that it broke the unity of Christendom and posed a religious and intellectual threat to the Roman Church in its organization and in its most cherished dogmas. The work of reform, inaugurated by Julius II at the Lateran Council in 1512, received a fresh impetus after the Sack. This rejuvenation, the Counter-Reformation, was stimulated by a series of energetic popes, like the ascetic Paul IV (1555–9), and by the crucial Council of Trent, which concluded twenty years of thoroughgoing discussion at its last session in December 1563. For two generations 'the climate of Rome was austere, anti-humanist, anti-worldly, and even anti-artistic' (Wittkower).

Reform of the Church from within resulted not only in the far-reaching decrees of the Council of Trent, but in the emergence of two religious movements whose influence was to prove dynamic: the Society of Jesus, founded by St Ignatius of Loyola, and the Oratory of St Philip Neri. St Ignatius' *Spiritual Exercises* had been approved by Paul III as early as 1548, eight years after the Society had been confirmed in its constitution by the same pope. The Oratory, founded by St Philip Neri, had grown out of informal meetings of priests and laymen; it was formally recognized by Gregory XIII in 1575 and its practical base was established at the church of S. Maria in Vallicella. These two movements, so different in their outlooks but united in their desire for the spiritual welfare of the Church, were to exercise a profound influence on Roman artists and architects, who had received new directives from the decrees of Trent. Henceforth, all artistic endeavour was to be subservient to the aims of the Church. It was also to be clear, simple and intelligible to all; it was to be

Elevation of Il Gesù, showing the façade designed by G. Della Porta, and the interior by Vignola.

realistic; and it was to provide an emotional stimulus to piety. It was clear that much Mannerist art contravened the Council's canons.

In designing the great church of Il Gesù for the newly founded Society of Jesus, begun in 1568 at the expense of Cardinal Alessandro Farnese, Vignola created a new type of church to meet changed needs, a type that was to become established throughout the entire Catholic world. It is confusing, however, to speak of a 'Jesuit style'. Of the Council of Trent's three *desiderata*, the creators of Il Gesù seem chiefly to have sought to fulfil the third: the emotional stimulus to pious devotion. On Vignola's death in 1573 the work was continued by Giacomo Della Porta, who designed the façade, the cupola and the circular chapel to the right of the tribune. A comparison of Vignola's design for the façade with the one which was built will illustrate how ideals still influenced by the Renaissance had given way to Mannerism, and, on entering the church, one will see how Mannerism has in turn been superseded by the lavish magnificence of the Baroque. Della Porta has retained the articulation in both storeys by the coupled pilasters of Vignola's original design, but, whereas Vignola distributed the architectural elements of niches containing statues so that they possessed a Renaissance independence within the whole design, Della Porta has concentrated everything on the massiveness of his central section. This is accentuated by the double pediment which forms the triumphal arch of the main doorway, the *aedicule* of the window above and the scrolls of the extremely powerful volutes. The effect is to produce that peculiarly Roman form of *gravitas* – gone is all the lightness of the Renaissance, to be replaced by a solemn, majestic grandeur.

In the interior the basilican aisles have been done away with, the space being occupied by three dark lateral chapels with low rounded arches, separated by huge coupled fluted pilasters. The eye is irresistibly drawn forwards past the crossing, lit by light pouring in from the drum and cupola above, to the high altar. The original altar was replaced in 1834 by the present one, designed in a style of restrained Neoclassicism. But from all sides one is greeted with a profusion of polychrome marble, sculpture in bronze and stucco, and gilding – and no paintable surface is left unpainted. Above the rich entablature of the nave and the gilded cornice, statues of saints in immaculate white stucco (by E. A. Raggi) point towards the gorgeousness of the ceiling painting, the seventeenth-century Genovese Baciccia's *Triumph of the Name of Jesus* (p. 230). Here, from the initial letters of the Holy Name – barely visible, on account of the encompassing incandescent light – rays pour forth to illuminate, among the brilliance of the angelic host, the aerial figures of the adoring faithful, crowds unrestrained by the bounds of the framework – an extraordinary *tour de force* of chromatic illusionism.

The restraint of the high altar is only a foil to the altars in the transepts. The rich High Baroque altar (1674) in the right-hand transept, that of St Francis Xavier, designed by Pietro da Cortona, has above it a powerfully realistic painting of the death of the saint by the seventeenth-century Carlo Maratta. On the left is the Chapel of the Sacred Heart, by Giacomo Della Porta, filled with colour from the frescoes (1599) by Baldassare Croce and from the well-known painting above the altar, the *Sacred Heart of Jesus*, by the eighteenth-century Pompeo Batoni. All this richness, however, is but a foretaste of that of the Chapel of St Ignatius of Loyola (1696) in the left-hand transept; here, under the altar, in a tomb of gilded bronze, lies the body of the saint (p. 222).

The chapel was designed by the Jesuit Andrea Pozzo, who employed the foremost artists of his time to create a sepulchre worthy of the founder of his Society. The result is an exuberant abundance of precious marbles, porphyry, agate, lapis lazuli, gilt, silver-work and paintings. The statue of the saint is partly of silver. The original by P. Legros was entirely in that metal, but had to be melted down by Pius VI, in order to meet the voracious demands of Napoleon after the

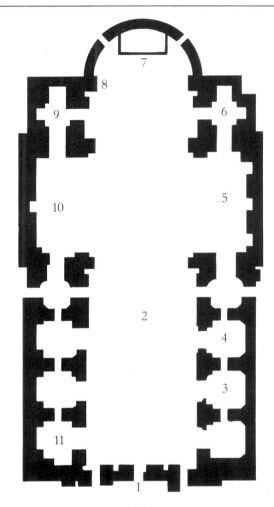

Piazza del Gesù

Il Gesù

1 Façade (1575) by G. Della Porta.
2 Nave by Vignola with painting on the ceiling, *Triumph of the Name of Jesus* (1672–85), by Baciccia and stucco figures by E. A. Raggi.
3 Chapel of the Passion.
4 Chapel of the Angels.
5 Altar of St Francis Xavier (1674–8) by Pietro da Cortona.
6 Chapel of the Sacred Heart, attributed to G. Della Porta, with frescoes (1599) of B. Croce.
7 High altar (1834–43) by A. Sarti.
8 Altar in memory of S. Roberto Bellarmine with bust (1622) by Bernini.
9 Chapel of S. Maria degli Astalli containing the *Madonna of the Street* (early fifteenth century).
10 Chapel of St Ignatius of Loyola (1696–1700) by A. Pozzo with statues by P. Legros, B. Ludovisi, L. Ottoni and G. Théodon.
11 Chapel of S. Francesco Borgia with altar by A. Pozzo and paintings (*c.* 1660) by P. F. Mola.

The decoration in a window alcove of the Theodoli Chapel in S. Maria del Popolo is an example of the continuation of the Mannerist style in the seventeenth century. Two *gesso* angels support a painting of St John in an oval frame.

Treaty of Tolentino (1797). The sphere (the world) which is raised by the cherub is of lapis lazuli. For decorative luxuriance this chapel is among the richest in Rome. But piety is not always the handmaiden to the highest art and this chapel is not to everyone's taste.

Next door to the chapel (to the left, that is, of the tribune) is the little Chapel of S. Maria degli Astalli, which contains a much venerated *Madonna of the Street* dating from the early fifteenth century, a treasure from the church that had to be demolished to make way for Il Gesù. It is said to have been originally situated on the wall of a house in a street leading to the Capitol – hence this chapel is popularly known as St Mary of the Street.

It is natural to couple with Il Gesù the other great Jesuit church, S. Ignazio, built in 1626 to the design of a member of the Society, the learned mathematician Orazio Grassi, at the expense of Cardinal Ludovico Ludovisi, nephew of Pope Gregory XV. The approach to S. Ignazio by the piazza is made delightful by an incongruity. Nothing could be more dissimilar from the Roman gravity of the church front, which owes much to Il Gesù, than the charming little square designed by Filippo Raguzzini (1727). This could be the setting for a Venetian comedy by Goldoni – scenographically a most decorative Rococo *jeu d'ésprit.* Unlike its exemplar, S. Ignazio lacks a cupola, although one was designed for it by Father Andrea Pozzo. However, in compensation, there is close by an observatory belonging to the Collegio Romano, from which the time-ball gives warning for the old cannon to be trundled out every day from its shelter on the Janiculum to fire the signal of noon, to the delight of schoolchildren.

Another of Rome's curiosities is the ceiling in *trompe l'oeil* (c. 1685) in S. Ignazio painted by this same Father Pozzo

LEFT The richly gilded ceiling in S. Maria d'Aracoeli was erected in commemoration of the celebrated Christian naval victory at the battle of Lepanto (1571) against the Turkish fleet.

ABOVE The decorative elegance of the early seventeenth century is shown in the ceiling of S. Giovanni in Laterano, where in a formal pattern picked out in gold against a blue ground Clement VIII (1592–1605) has placed the arms of his family – Aldobrandini.

(pp. 220–1). From a spot marked in the nave the visitor looks up – apparently through the columns and arches of a magnificent classical building, crowded with figures – to behold what seems to be the pure empyrean, where he sees the triumphal *Entrance of St Ignatius into Paradise*. It is an astonishing feat of perspectival architectural illusionism. Also by this extra-ordinarily talented Jesuit are the figures around the non-existent cupola (he has simulated one on canvas) and, in the transept, the rich altar, beneath which, in an urn of lapis lazuli, are the remains of S. Luigi Gonzaga. The sculpture in high relief, the *Glory of S. Luigi Gonzaga* (1698), is by P. Legros (p. 235). The church also contains works by one of the finest of the High Baroque sculptors, Alessandro Al-gardi: the statues *Magnificence* and *Religion* (1650) on the wall of the entrance, and the frieze of *putti* around the interior.

The church of St Philip Neri's Oratorians, S. Maria in Vallicella (or the Chiesa Nuova), was begun in 1575 to designs by Martino Longhi the Elder. The impressive façade (1605) by Fausto Rughesi is of two orders divided by pilasters, its central doorway being prominently set within twin columns, with a segmental pediment containing the figures of the Madonna between two angels. Above, it is distinguished by a finely proportioned window and statues in their niches. The interior is of an extraordinary richness – this in a church that St Philip Neri wanted simply whitewashed. In the nave, angels of white stucco support oval frames, containing scenes from the Old and New Testaments by various artists of differing quality. But S. Maria in Vallicella is remarkable for the series of paintings by the High Baroque painter and architect Pietro da Cortona. In the nave vault is his *Vision of St Philip Neri during the Building of the Church* (1664). The pendentives to the cupola (there is no drum) contain the figures of his *Isaiah*, *Jeremiah*, *Ezekiel* and *Daniel*. The cupola itself is filled by Pietro's majestic *Glory of the Trinity*, where his power of composition is magnificently demonstrated. Particularly arresting are his foreshortened figures of God the Father and God the Son: among all these figures nothing is cluttered, all is composed. In the apse is his glorious *Assumption of the Virgin*, where the same qualities are displayed. Furthermore, in the sacristy is an earlier example of his work on the ceiling, *Angels with the Instruments of the Passion* (1634). This sacristy (1629), which is considered one of the most beautiful in Rome, is by P. Marucelli. It also contains, on the altar, a fine group in marble, *St Philip Neri and an Angel* (1640), by Algardi. And this is not all: S. Maria in Vallicella glories in the only works remaining in a Roman church by Peter Paul Rubens: the *Virgin in a Glory of Angels* and two groups of saints in the tribune by the high altar (1606–8). These are among the earliest of Rubens' major

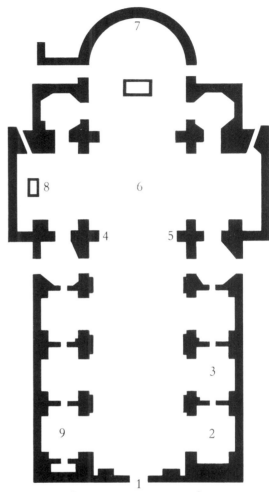

Corso Vittorio Emanuele

S. Andrea della Valle

1 Façade (1655–63) by C. Rainaldi.
2 Lancelotti Chapel (1675) with sculpture by E. A. Raggi.
3 Strozzi Chapel (c. 1616) attributed to G. Della Porta with copies of the *Pietà* between the figures of *Leah* and *Rachel* by Michelangelo.
4 Tomb of Pius II (d. 1464) attributed to Paolo Taccone and an unknown follower of A. Bregno (c. 1470).
5 Tomb of Pius III (d. 1503) by the Ferrucci.
6 Cupola with the *Glory of Paradise* (c. 1621) by G. Lanfranco and the *Four Evangelists* (1621–8) on pendentives by Domenichino.
7 Apse with frescoes by Domenichino (1624–8) and Mattia Preti (1650–1), stucco-work by A. Algardi.
8 Altar of S. Cajetan of Thiene (1912) by C. Bazzani.
9 Barberini Chapel with *St Martha* (seventeenth century) by F. Mochi and *St John the Baptist* (early seventeenth century) by Pietro Bernini.

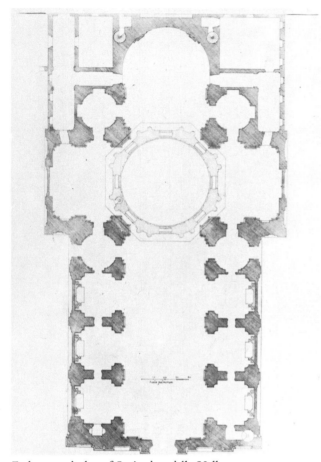

Early ground-plan of S. Andrea della Valle.

works. Admirers of the Flemish painter regard the few years which he spent in Rome as decisive for his development. It was said of him while he was there, 'He learned good taste and painted in a good Italian style [*maniera*].'

Not far from Il Gesù, in the Corso Vittorio Emanuele, stands the great church of S. Andrea della Valle, begun in 1591 to the designs of G. F. Grimaldi and Giacomo Della Porta. But other prominent architects had a hand in its construction: in 1622 Carlo Maderno raised the elegant drum and cupola, inferior only to St Peter's in size; and in 1655 the Baroque architect C. Rainaldi built the imposing travertine façade (p. 177). In this building the richness that we have seen evolving in Roman churches is conspicuously marked by the almost entire replacement of the earlier pilasters (here used only at the angles of the lower storey) in favour of half-columns. The plasticity of the surface is vitally enhanced by the breaking of the horizontal line with recessions and projections. This broken line is most clearly seen in the pediment. The volutes that formerly served to link the lower

storey to the attic have given way to statues – or would have given way to them, since only one was made, the winged angel, on the left, by Ercole Ferrata. The niches (which take the form of *aedicules*, each with its agitated statue), the medallions above them, supported by cherubs, and the figures which flank the Chigi arms on the segmental pediment of the ornate central doorway, all contribute to make the façade of S. Andrea della Valle one of the most outstanding among those of Rome's churches.

Within, the wide nave, with its single order of giant pilasters reaching to the springing of the barrel vault, and the visual pull forwards, from the light coming from the drum and cupola at the crossing of the transept – these effects give a feeling of spaciousness and grave dignity. By the last piers before the crossing are the monumental tombs of the two Piccolomini popes. On the left is that of the Renaissance humanist Aeneas Sylvius Piccolomini (Pius II), whose lively memoirs, which he continued to write after becoming pope, give a fascinating picture of his times. The sculptor is unknown, but was possibly of the school of Andrea Bregno (*c.* 1470). On the sarcophagus are represented Pius II's celebrated reception in Rome of the head of the Apostle St Andrew; above are the Madonna and Child to whom Pius is presented as cardinal by St Paul and as pope by St Peter. Opposite is the tomb of Francesco Todeschini Piccolomini (Pius III), an early sixteenth-century work, modelled on the tomb of Pius II, by the Florentine sculptors F. and S. Ferrucci.

The frescoes of the cupola (*c.* 1621) are by Lanfranco, who worked in competition with Domenichino, whose *Evangelists* are on the pendentives. Lanfranco's figures in this, his presentation of the *Virgin in Glory*, form a strange, swirling vortex of movement, a chromatic merry-go-round; it is difficult to see precisely what is taking place, but it is clearly something highly momentous, as befits its subject. In the triumphal arch and apse, above the gilding and the stucco figures (youthful work of Algardi), are Domenichino's *Scenes from the Life and Death of St Andrew*. Below are further *Scenes* by the Calabrese painter Mattia Preti. These three painters were influenced by the Bolognese tradition, which was in opposition to Mannerism which was still lingering on.

The variety of Roman church-building during this period between the High Renaissance and the High Baroque is exemplified by the churches of SS. Domenico e Sisto, S. Giacomo degli Incurabili and S. Gregorio Magno.

The Dominican church of SS. Domenico e Sisto is admirably placed, approached as it is by beautiful high double-ramped steps (1654), the work of Orazio Torriani (p. 206). This upward thrust is continued by the church

The apse, presbytery and cupola of S. Andrea della Valle are of a lavish richness of colour and gold. Lanfranco painted the *Virgin in Glory* (*c.* 1621) in the cupola in competition with Domenichino who was engaged on the *Four Evangelists* on the pendentives. The *Scenes from the Life and Death of St Andrew* (1624–8) in the presbytery and apse by Domenichino are framed by gilding and stucco figures, the youthful work of A. Algardi.

façade of two storeys, articulated by coupled pilasters, with a rich doorway and statues in niches, and crowned by a pediment, from which rise up eight flaming candelabra. More than one architect had a hand in it, working between 1575 and 1655, though the original plans were possibly by Giacomo Della Porta. The lower storey is thought to be by Nicola Torriani; the upper, perhaps also by him or by another seventeenth-century architect, Vincenzo Della Greca. The decoration of the interior is rich in polychrome marble, the first chapel on the right, designed by Bernini, possessing a fine group, *Noli me tangere* (*c.* 1649), by E. A. Raggi. Although this sculpture is in marble, Raggi worked much in stucco, in the use of which he was one of the finest exponents of his age. Particularly arresting is the fresco on the ceiling of the nave, the *Apotheosis of St Dominic* (1674), the work of the Bolognese Domenico Maria Canuti, in which the effect of ethereal space has been most successfully conveyed and the whole scene, one of lightness and grace, has been set in the rich *trompe l'œil* framework of Enrico Haffner (p. 219).

In the fourteenth century two Colonna cardinals set up a hospital, on the Via del Corso, for sick pilgrims who entered the city by what was then the Porta Flaminia, attaching to it a chapel, or oratory. By the generosity of Cardinal Salviati this church of S. Giacomo degli Incurabili was rebuilt at the end of the sixteenth century by Francesco da Volterra, who used an elliptical plan, the first of its kind in Roman churches. It was he who raised the lower storey of the façade, employing columns of the Doric order, the upper storey, with Corinthian pilasters, being completed in 1600 by Carlo Maderno, who built the central balcony, with its shell-like niche. In the hands of architects of the High Baroque this elliptical plan, with radial chapels, adopted by Francesco da Volterra, was to undergo spectacular developments.

On the Coelian Hill, and overlooking the Palatine Hill, stood the family palace of Pope Gregory the Great, which he converted into a monastery, with its oratory (575) dedicated to St Andrew. Gregory's church and monastery were reconstructed in the Middle Ages, possibly after damage or destruction by Robert Guiscard's Normans. After these, too, had suffered through the lapse of time, in 1629 Cardinal Scipio Borghese commissioned G. B. Soria to rebuild the church of S. Gregorio Magno — or, rather, the courtyard, or *atrium*, to the church. Soria's façade — the 'palace' type of church front — resembles in its architectural elements that of S. Sebastiano on the Appian Way, built by Flaminio Ponzio and Giovanni Vasanzio some twenty years earlier. The lower storey of S. Sebastiano is formed of an arcade of three bays, separated by double Ionic columns; in the upper storey, three windows of a simple moulding, with segmented pediments, correspond to the lower bays; the whole is surmounted by a

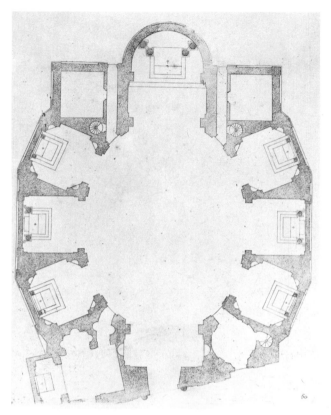

Early ground-plan of S. Giacomo degli Incurabili.

triangular pediment. Soria has made use of the raised position of his site by approaching the building with a broad flight of steps of extremely low tread, flanked by simple walls, thus anticipating the horizontal effect which he required for his façade. This is divided into three compartments, the central section, which is flanked by coupled pilasters, projecting slightly forwards. In each bay is a round-headed doorway, above which is the Borghese eagle. The three corresponding windows of the upper storey rise above a balustrade and are capped — those to the sides by triangular pediments, the central (and slightly wider) window by a segmental pediment. Only this central section is crowned by a high-angled gable. The horizontality is accentuated by deep architraves and projecting cornices. S. Gregorio Magno, which is looked on as Soria's masterpiece, has all the Roman massiveness and produces a sense of solemn decorum, even majesty.

The interior of the church was rebuilt by the eighteenth-century Roman architect Francesco Ferrari, who preserved at the end of the right-hand aisle the little chapel and the room in which St Gregory lived and slept (his episcopal chair still remains). To the left of the church, in what was once a Benedictine cemetery, with its somewhat forlorn cypresses, stand three chapels — today, alas, in a sorry state of disrepair.

ABOVE In the basilica of Constantinian foundation, S. Agnese
fuori le Mura, the coffered and richly decorated ceiling is of
1606, but it has been many times restored, the last being by Pius
IX in 1855 – 'PIUS IX P[ontifex] M[aximus] REST [auravit]
ORN [avit].'

RIGHT S. Giovanni Decollato is a repository of
paintings of the mid-sixteenth-century school of Roman
Mannerism. The *Baptism of Jesus* is by the Florentine Jacopino
del Conte (1541).

The central chapel (1607), designed by Flaminio Ponzio, may have been built over Gregory's original oratory, which was possibly destroyed, as mentioned above, by Robert Guiscard. That to the right is reputed to be on the site of a chapel of the Pope's mother, St Sylvia; that on the left, the Chapel of St Barbara, contains the table from which, each day, St Gregory personally served twelve poor people. One day, it is said, the number was increased by the presence of an angel. The chapels were decorated by frescoes of Domenichino and Guido Reni (p. 13).

Soria executed further commissions for the connoisseur-cardinal Scipio Borghese, notably the façade (p. 205, 1626) of S. Maria della Vittoria (in which he seems to have been influenced by Maderno's S. Susanna), and in the same year he began a thorough restoration of the church of S. Crisogono in Trastevere. In both he maintained the high standard of Roman church-building, but in neither does he give a hint of those reinvigorating innovations that were so soon to culminate in the splendours of the Roman High Baroque.

8
Baroque and Beyond

It has already been said that the 1580s marked a watershed for art and architecture in Rome. The accession in 1585 to the papal throne of the energetic Sixtus V may be seen as inaugurating a new era: the Rome that we see today now began to take shape. The anxieties and hesitations that were symptomatic of the crisis – the Counter-Reformation – through which the Church had passed gave way to a new feeling that the Church had saved itself from within, that the tide of the Northern Reformers had been halted and turned back. During the transitional period from Sixtus V – that great builder of straight streets, wide squares, churches and palaces, that irrepressible raiser of obelisks – to the death of Paul V in 1621, it was increasingly felt by those concerned with these matters that Mannerism was unable to fulfil the counter-reformatory requirements. It was too esoteric, too academic, too backward-looking or, rather, too inward-looking. What was wanted was something at once more popular and dynamic, something that responded to the more hopeful, even euphoric, mood of the Catholic Restoration. The exuberant new style of Baroque – which met these needs – came into its own in the 1620s and held the Roman stage for some fifty years. This period corresponded roughly with the pontificates of Urban VIII, Innocent X and Alexander VII, which spanned the years 1623–67. From the last decade of the sixteenth century Rome resumed its earlier rôle as the European capital of much that was most progressive in the visual arts. But before we discuss the Baroque phase, we must notice the work of two groups of artists, working slightly earlier, whose impact on the art of the Roman churches was hardly less dramatic, though very different, both from the art of the Baroque period and from each other.

Just before the turn of the century there arrived in Rome from Northern Italy two painters entirely dissimilar in their styles but both remarkable for their talents, who, both in themselves and through their followers, were to make a major contribution to the decoration of Roman churches: Michelangelo Merisi (called Caravaggio, from the name of his birthplace, near Bergamo) and Annibale Carracci, from Bologna. It seems curious today that Caravaggio, this man of the people, this bohemian who was in constant trouble with the police, who painted pictures that one would have thought appealed directly to the popular taste, should have been rejected by the people and first accepted and appreciated by connoisseurs among the higher ranks of the Church hierarchy. It was possibly through the agency of Cardinal Francesco del Monte that in 1597 Caravaggio received his first commission for a monumental religious work, the paintings for the Contarelli Chapel in S. Luigi dei Francesi. Over the altar is *St Matthew and the Angel*, on the left wall the pensive, deeply moving *Christ calling St Matthew* and, opposite this, one of the most arresting of his works, the *Martyrdom of the Saint*. All three of these oils were painted between 1597 and 1602. The dramatic intensity of Caravaggio's vision is such that it tends to draw the spectator

RIGHT S. Maria in Campitelli (1663–7) by Carlo Rainaldi. The grandeur of the deeply fluted columns and pilasters of the Corinthian order is enhanced by the suggestiveness of the perspectives as one passes from the spaciousness of the Greek cross to the area beneath the splendid cupola.

LEFT The Contarelli Chapel in S. Luigi dei Francesi contains three masterpieces by Caravaggio, painted between 1597 and 1602, relating to the life of St Matthew. One of these, the violent *Martyrdom of the Saint*, can be seen here through an arch of the nave.

ABOVE Another of the series by Caravaggio, *Christ calling St Matthew*, in the Contarelli Chapel of S. Luigi dei Francesi.

into the region, the orbit, of the picture plane; he participates in the representation rather than acting (as he would if he were looking at a picture painted in the classical Renaissance tradition) as a disinterested, appreciative observer. So close becomes this involvement that at times, as in *The Conversion of St Paul* (p. 136) in S. Maria del Popolo, the events portrayed seem to break out of the picture's frame into the space occupied by the beholder. The composition is regulated, held together, and the accents are placed on the planes that the artist wishes to stress, by the play of light out of the densest obscurity – this *tenebroso* being the quality most associated with Caravaggio. His darkness has a real opacity – an absence, or denial, of light; it is light alone that brings volume

to his forms and highlights the transitory moment, the emotional (and spiritual) *raison d'être* of the action – its immediacy, its presence here and now. The spectator becomes an active sharer in the emotional experience.

Caravaggio's realism, which may have been overstressed by his critics, is nevertheless based on traditional elements; but it appeared to his contemporaries, as it may still appear to us, as revolutionary. His *Madonna with the Serpent* (now in the Borghese Gallery) was rejected by the clergy for this very reason. Apart from his work in S. Maria del Popolo, there is his fine *Madonna of the Pilgrims* (1605) in the church of S. Agostino. Despite his stormy life – and he fled Rome after killing a man in a gambling quarrel – Caravaggio's work is deeply religious in feeling and impact.

In S. Luigi dei Francesi there is also, however, a work of a quite different kind: Domenichino's *St Cecilia before the Judges*. In this picture St Cecilia, refusing to sacrifice to the pagan gods, expresses her will with a graceful turning of her head and body, and by a raising of her hands, that appear highly sophisticated and Mannerist. Domenichino was a follower of the school represented by the brothers Annibale and Agos-

tino Carracci, and their cousin Lodovico Carracci: they stood in opposition to the Caravaggisti, being (especially Annibale) strongly classical in bent.

Annibale Carracci arrived in Rome from Bologna, his reputation already established, in 1595, and for the next nine years he was engaged on works in the Farnese Palace. His magnificent ceiling in the gallery, with its centre-piece, the *Triumph of Bacchus and Ariadne*, placed him in the great tradition of mural painters, from Giotto and Masaccio to Raphael and Michelangelo, so that for three centuries the Farnese ceiling was spoken of in the same breath as Raphael's Stanze and Michelangelo's Sistine ceiling. Annibale's religious work is to be seen in only two Roman churches: in S. Maria del Popolo (where his *Assumption* in the Cerasi Chapel has to bear comparison with Caravaggio's two masterpieces there) and in S. Maria di Monserrato, the Renaissance church begun in 1518 by Antonio Sangallo the Younger, and now the national church of the Spaniards, which contains his highly competent *S. Diego*. His brother Agostino, who assisted him in his great mythological works,

ABOVE LEFT The *Assumption* by the Bolognese painter Annibale Carracci (1560–1609) in S. Maria del Popolo.

ABOVE The *Holy Trinity*, one of the finest paintings by Guercino (1591–1666) from Ferrara, in S. Maria della Vittoria.

RIGHT S. Andrea della Valle was begun in 1591 to the design of G. F. Grimaldi and Giacomo Della Porta. In 1608 Carlo Maderno took over the building, and it was he who raised the cupola (1622). In 1655 Carlo Rainaldi began the magnificent façade in travertine. The single angel is by his contemporary Ercole Ferrata.

has left one painting in a Roman church: a characteristic *Madonna di Loreto* in S. Onofrio. Members of the school established by the Carracci, however, have contributed much to the pictorial embellishment of Roman churches.

Guido Reni and Francesco Albani appeared in Rome *c.* 1600, to be followed shortly by Giovanni Lanfranco and Domenichino, and, somewhat later, *c.* 1621, by Guercino. Works by both Reni and Domenichino can (or could) be

seen in the Oratory of St Andrew at S. Gregorio Magno, and the apse of the adjoining Chapel of St Sylvia contains frescoes (1608) by the former. Reni also painted the once much-admired *Crucifix* in S. Lorenzo in Lucina and the figures of saints in the sumptuous Palatine Chapel at S. Maria Maggiore. His best-known work, however, is the glowing, aerial *Aurora* ceiling in the casino of the Palace Rospigliosi on the Quirinal. Albani is responsible for the choir in S. Maria della Pace (1612–14). Besides his cupola in S. Andrea della Valle and other works, Lanfranco decorated the Chapel of St Augustine in S. Agostino. Guercino was much sought after by private connoisseurs, but also executed many paintings in Roman churches: the large *St Augustine and St John the Evangelist* over the right-hand transept in S. Agostino; the *St Philip Neri in Adoration* in an inner chapel of S. Maria in Vallicella; the *Holy Trinity* over the altar in a chapel in S. Maria della Vittoria; and works in S. Pietro in Vincoli and S. Nicola in Carceri.

Unlike the paintings of Annibale Carracci, or such a work of Reni as his spirited *Aurora* – which suggest a certain hedonistic relaxing among the higher clergy from the dogmatic didacticism of the edicts of the Council of Trent – much of the church painting of this period, with its highly charged emotion, had a wide popular appeal. The connoisseurs appreciated it for its painterly qualities; the mass of the people for its emotive religiosity or its only too apparent devotional sensibility. The painters, therefore, had the best of both worlds.

Already at the turn of the century Carlo Maderno's S. Susanna heralded the advent of the High Baroque. His work on the interiors of S. Maria della Vittoria and S. Andrea della Valle allowed him little scope, although his dome for the latter, based clearly on Michelangelo's St Peter's, has a massive grandeur. Henceforth he was engaged on the completion of St Peter's (see Chapter 9). Changed conditions, however, required new churches. St Charles Borromeo was canonized in 1610, and within a short period three churches were begun in his honour: S. Carlo al Corso, S. Carlo ai Catinari and S. Carlo alle Quattro Fontane. From the accession of Urban VIII in 1623 Rome, with its palaces and churches, took on a new look, with an exuberance of outward forms that would have shocked the austerity of the counter-reformatory popes and the founders of the reforming

LEFT In 1624 Bernini, at the age of twenty-six, was commissioned to rebuild the ancient church of S. Bibiana, his first architectural work. In the niche behind the high altar, also designed by him, he placed his statue of the saint holding her martyr's palm (1626).

religious Orders. The new movement, that seemed to sum up and express all the vitality and the latent sensuousness of the age, was inspired by three men of genius: Gian Lorenzo Bernini, Francesco Borromini and Pietro da Cortona, whose births occurred within three years of each other at the close of the sixteenth century.

Bernini was born in Naples in 1598, the son of a Neapolitan mother and a Florentine father. The latter, Pietro Bernini, was an indifferent Mannerist sculptor, with a flabby sense of form which was in the strongest contrast with that of his famous son. Gian Lorenzo worked with his father in the family studio which still stands in the Piazza dell'Esquilino. It was while he was working with him on the Pauline Chapel at S. Maria Maggiore that the young prodigy came to the notice of Cardinal Scipio Borghese, for whom he carved those youthful works that are now in the Borghese Gallery. As early as 1624 he was commissioned to execute the great *baldacchino* in St Peter's, and on Carlo Maderno's death in 1629 he was appointed 'Architect to St Peter's'. His powers of concentration and of physical labour (even when we take his band of collaborators into account) were immense – churches, chapels, funeral monuments, statues, fountains and the colonnade in front of St Peter's were all crowded into the pontificates of the Barberini, Pamphilj and Chigi popes. Apart from these achievements, he was painter and poet, a man of courtly manners, a good husband and father – and a devout Catholic, whose bedside reading was St Ignatius' *Spiritual Exercises*. Bernini was the personification of the Catholic Restoration.

In 1624 he was commissioned to design the façade of the little church of S. Bibiana, which today is perilously close to the railway lines that lead into the Stazione Termini. The façade of S. Bibiana is hardly revolutionary; instead of developing Maderno's type at S. Susanna, Bernini went back to the 'palace' type of church front embodied in Ponzio's S. Sebastiano or Soria's S. Gregorio Magno. Over an open arcade of three bays, of which the central projects slightly, he placed a bold *aedicule* (forming a loggia), whose deeply indented pediment breaks the sky-line above the balustrade of the two adjoining bays. The interior of the church is interesting for two essays in the developing Baroque: Bernini's first commissioned religious statue (of S. Bibiana) and Pietro da Cortona's first important cycle of frescoes (of incidents from the life of the saint). In his statue Bernini expressed that type of seventeenth-century devotional sensibility that was to become familiar through the paintings of Guido Reni.

In 1658, almost simultaneously with building churches at Castelgandolfo and Ariccia, Bernini started on what was to be his most important contribution to ecclesiastical architec-

S. Andrea al Quirinale

1 Portal.
2 Chapel of St Francis Xavier, with painting (1706) by Baciccia.
3 Chapel of the Flagellation, with painting (1682) by Giacinto Brandi.
4 Entrance to the monastery containing the room where King Carlo Emanuele IV of Savoy, who abdicated his throne, died in 1819, and the Chapel of St Stanislaus Kostka with a monument (c. 1690) by P. Legros.
5 High altar with *Crucifixion of St Andrew* by Borgognone (1698); above, an aureole with cherubs and angels (c. 1670) by E. A. Raggi.
6 Altar of St Stanislaus Kostka, with painting (c. 1687) by C. Maratta.

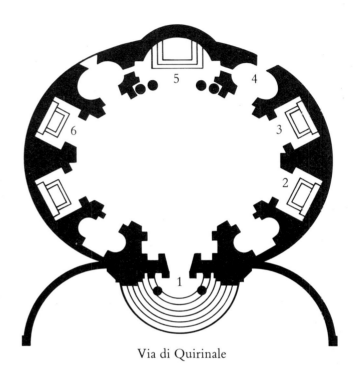

Via di Quirinale

ture: S. Andrea al Quirinale, which was commissioned by Cardinal Camillo Pamphilj for novices of the Jesuit Order. To appreciate Bernini's art one has to remember that he makes no distinction between the material means of realizing his idea, which was often literary – the *concetto*, as the Italians called it. This is particularly evident in his sculpture: he chooses to represent one particular crucial moment, the climax of dramatic action. But it is also evident in the architecture of S. Andrea. The plan is oval, the longer transverse axis being parallel with the street. The façade is striking, the quadrant walls leading the eye to the *aedicule* formed by two Corinthian pilasters, supporting a strongly accented triangular pediment, which constitutes the door-way; this in turn is preceded by a protruding semicircular portico, raised on two Ionic columns and surmounted by the Pamphilj coat-of-arms. Inside the church the high altar is likewise placed in an *aedicule*, but concave this time and with a segmental pediment, broken in the centre to form a deeper concave space, in which the figure of St Andrew appears at the moment when he is about to ascend to heaven. The

LEFT Bernini considered his church of S. Andrea al Quirinale, erected between 1658 and 1671 for Cardinal Camillo Pamphilj, as his only completely satisfying work. From the elliptical cupola cherubs in stucco descend in joyful animated movement and grace.

distribution of light reinforces the *concetto*, as do the stucco *putti* above the windows, who carry garlands and martyrs' palms, the naked fishermen with their nets and oars, and the sea-shells, all of which symbolize St Andrew's trade. The architecture, the multicoloured dark marbles, the white and gold of the dome, the sculpture, the light – everything subserves Bernini's aim of achieving an essentially theatrical (but at the same time devotional) effect.

This desire of Bernini to unify all the visual arts in the service of one overwhelming impression is no better exem-plified than in his celebrated *Ecstasy of St Teresa* (1645) in the Cornaro Chapel in S. Maria della Vittoria. He had already experimented with the potentialities of concealed and directed light in the Raimondi Chapel in S. Pietro in Montorio (c. 1642). He was to repeat the experiment as late as 1674 in the Altieri Chapel in S. Francesco a Ripa, with his monu-ment to the Blessed Ludovica Albertoni (p. 199). It has been said that Bernini conceived the Cornaro Chapel as one huge painting. In fact, the vaulting is frescoed, with angels rolling back the clouds to reveal the azure empyrean, from which they descend on to the wall, in one place breaking the window-line with flowing robe and foot. The light of the upper regions, even on the ornate pediment of the *aedicule* above the altar, is in strong contrast with the dark marble columns which support the latter and form a frame within which St Teresa lies in a swoon, transfixed by the power of

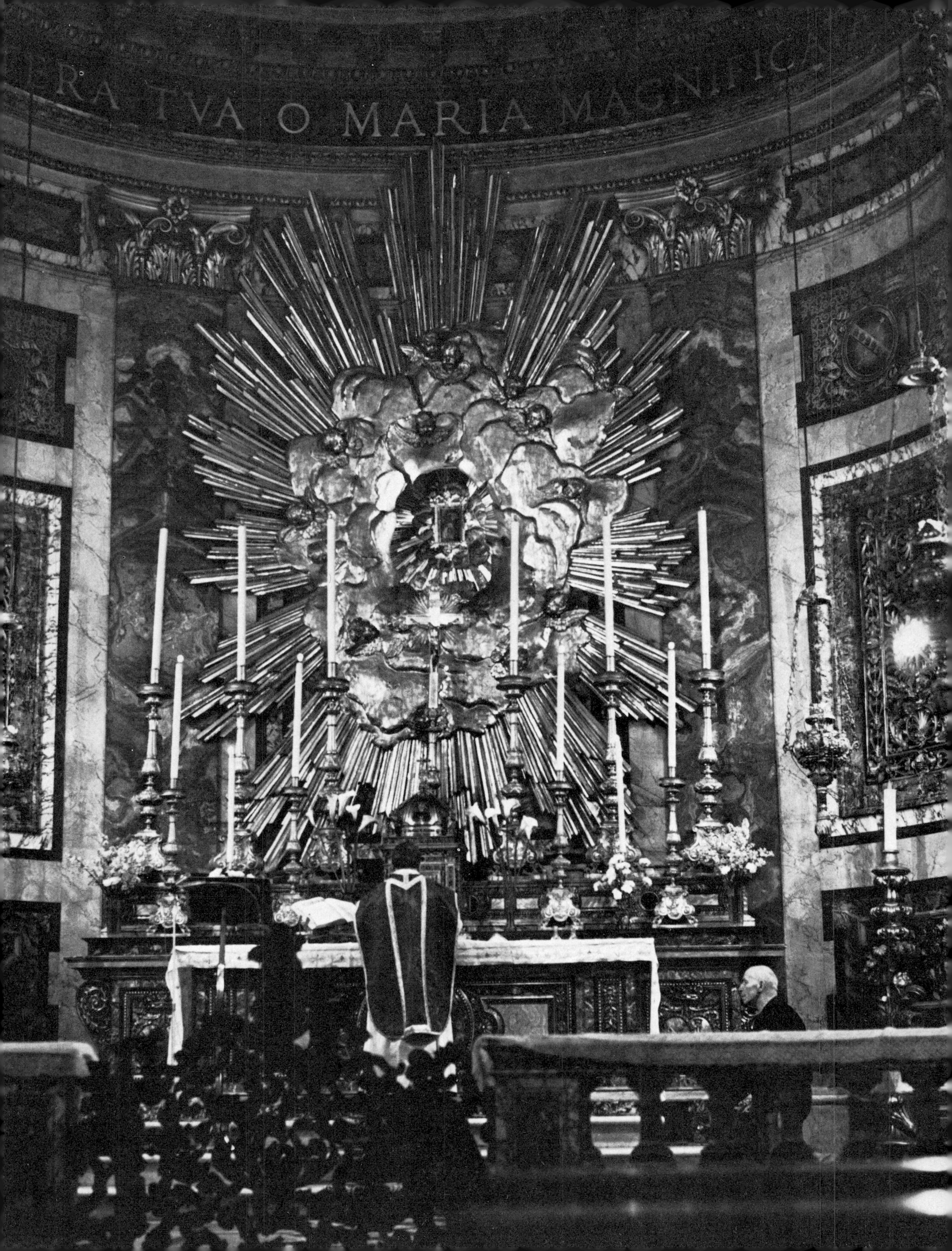
RA TVA O MARIA MAGNIFICA

divine love. The harbinger of this overwhelming, trans-forming love is represented by a beautiful smiling angel, who poises the arrow that has already penetrated the very depths of her being. The celestial light that encompasses the two figures comes not only from a concealed overhead source, but is reinforced by actual shafts of metal. This dramatic scene is witnessed as if from theatre boxes by figures of the Venetian Cornaro family, carved by Bernini and his assistants. It is perhaps not surprising that the sophisticated eighteenth-century Président de Brosses should have made a remark to the effect that if this was divine love he could well understand what was meant.

To appreciate the extraordinary versatility of Bernini's genius one should not fail to see his *Habakkuk* (1655) in S. Maria del Popolo (p. 198), the angels (1668) that were once on the Ponte S. Angelo and are now in S. Andrea delle Fratte, the remarkable portrait bust (1668) of Gabriele Fonseca in S. Lorenzo in Lucina and his stupendous works at St Peter's.

The ripples from the giant waves of approval and disapproval that greeted the ecclesiastical architecture of Francesco Borromini in his own day have reached our own era. A relative of Carlo Maderno, he, too, was born near the Lake of Lugano. After arriving in Rome *c.* 1620, he was first

Self-portrait by Gian Lorenzo Bernini (1598–1680)

PAGE 182 Bernini has been described as the last universal genius of the Italian Renaissance. In the Cornaro Chapel in S. Maria della Vittoria his *Ecstasy of St Teresa* and its setting (1645) seem to combine the arts of architecture, sculpture, painting – even literature.

PAGE 183 In 1833 fire destroyed the miraculous picture of the *Madonna of Prague*, 'Our Lady of the Victory', with its setting among clouds and gilded rays designed by Bernini, above the high altar in S. Maria della Vittoria. A copy of the painting has been placed in a restored setting by Prince Alessandro Torlonia.

PAGE 185 A finial – with its exquisitely crisp cutting of the stone – designed by Borromini (*c.* 1658) for the Tempietto di S. Giovanni in Oleo, now in S. Giovanni a Porta Latina.

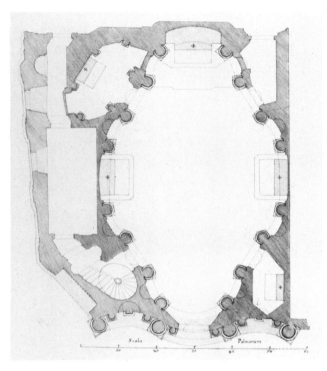

ABOVE LEFT Early engraving of the ground-plan of S. Carlo alle Quattro Fontane begun by Borromini in 1638.

ABOVE Francesco Borromini (1599–1667) by an unknown artist.

RIGHT Bernini's Fountain of the Rivers (1651) in the Piazza Navona, with the façade (1653–5) of S. Agnese in Agone by Borromini behind. Although these two architects worked together at one time, Borromini, with his melancholic temperament, must have suffered from the overwhelming success of his supremely talented rival.

employed as stone-carver and architectural draughtsman under Maderno at St Peter's and elsewhere; then, after the latter's death in 1629, he worked for Bernini on his great *baldacchino* in St Peter's and on the Palazzo Barberini. In his personality he was quite different from Bernini, being a brooding, melancholic man. It may be that his difficult temperament stood in the way of his swift advancement. Certainly, his chance to display his own highly personal architectural talents did not come until 1634, when he was commissioned to build for the Spanish Discalced Trinitarians the monastery of S. Carlo alle Quattro Fontane. Four years later he was entrusted with the design of the little church which adjoins the monastery, and worked on this at the same time as Pietro da Cortona was building SS. Luca e Martina. Rudolf Wittkower regarded these two churches as among the 'incunabula' of the Roman High Baroque.

Borromini's art was revolutionary in that he discarded the Renaissance principle of humanistically motivated architectural planning that had existed for Brunelleschi, Alberti, Bramante and even Bernini – the basic principle that a unit or module (usually the diameter of a column) should be multiplied in order to form proportions which were felt to be commensurate with the human scale. Borromini did not think in humanistic terms, but geometrically and plastically: he would plan an overall geometric configuration which could, in turn, be divided geometrically. Not for him was the Berninian *concetto* – in its place were mass and, above all,

structure. If there was a Borrominian *concetto*, it was architectural and sculptural. The apparently wilful and aimless undulations or meanderings that have disturbed so many people who have seen Borromini's buildings are in fact coherent and logical elements in the architect's highly original and brilliantly executed inventions, and there are reputable precedents for all of them. An account of S. Carlo will give an idea of the essential geometry on which all Borromini's designs, however bold, are firmly based.

The charming little cloister at S. Carlo consists of an elongated octagon, the columns being bound by a continuous cornice, and the breaks at the corners avoided by convex curvatures or quadrants. The plan of the interior of the church is based on two equilateral triangles, with a common base on the transverse axis of the building. The lofty,

prominent columns are grouped in fours, constituting triads
of undulating bays, with larger recesses at the high altar and at
the opposite ends of the transverse axis. A powerful
entablature allows the eye to follow with ease the sinuous line
of the perimeter. The use of pendentives, enclosing circular
medallions between the rounded arches, made possible the
construction of an oval dome, its deep coffering of octagons,
hexagons and crosses brilliantly lit from the lantern and from
the windows concealed by the stylized leaves above the
cornice. Far from being rebuffed by the complexity, the eye is
entranced and stimulated to wander at will as it comprehends
this little Baroque masterpiece (p. 197).

The façade was not finished for over thirty years – in fact, it
was Borromini's last work, completed in 1667. It is of the
'palace' type, formed by two storeys of equal value, each
consisting of three bays, the lower with a convex central
section, flanked by two concave bays, while all three divisions
of the upper storey are concave. A strong undulating
entablature joins the two tiers, but above there is an upper
entablature and balustrade broken by a larger oval medallion,
supported by angels and crowned by a typical Borromini
segmental-pointed pediment. Below this is a pagoda-like
aedicule, whose pronounced convexity parallels the central

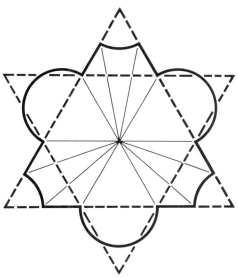

TOP Early engraving of the ground-plan of S. Ivo alla
Sapienza.

ABOVE Plan of S. Ivo alla Sapienza (1642–50) by Borromini
illustrating its geometrical structure based on a regular star-
hexagon.

section beneath. Above the entrance is a niche formed by two angel-faced hermes, whose wings create an arch above the statue of St Charles Borromeo by E. A. Raggi. This absence of intervening wall and the close conjunction of structural and sculptural elements are in keeping with much Roman High Baroque architecture, and contribute here to Borromini's brilliant solution of the problem presented by a restricted space. The whole church would fit into one of the piers that support the dome of St Peter's.

In 1642 Borromini began the church of S. Ivo alla Sapienza. This stands at the end of the courtyard, designed by Giacomo Della Porta, of the Palazzo della Sapienza (which houses the National Archives) in the Corso del Rinascimento. On entering S. Ivo one may well gasp with surprise at the architect's daring – all these concavities, convexities and slanting walls seem so complex. One is at first bewildered; then the eye, following the giant pilasters upwards beyond the pronounced entablature and cornice, is drawn into the white and gold dome, and finally to the point where all these contrasting planes find their perfect solution in the simple circle of the lantern (p. 228). Again Boromini has based his plan on the equilateral triangle – here, in fact, on two triangles, which so interpenetrate that they form a star-hexagon, their points of interpenetration being on the circumference of a circle. Lines drawn from the points of the star form a perfect hexagon. The concave recesses are determined by circles with a radius of half the side of the hexagon; the convex endings of the opposite recesses are formed by circles of the same radius, with their centres at the other three apices. In this way one is presented with concave recesses and recesses with slanting walls and convex ends, facing each other across the church. The effect is marvellously stimulating, both intellectually and aesthetically.

Despite the strong entablature the star shape is carried on into the dome, the gilding following the line of the pilasters, and each of the segmental bays is pierced by a window. The vertical thrust is of tremendous force. An architectural symphony in white and gold – the latter in the Chigi stars, the papal armorial bearings and the angels' heads under the lantern: such is the interior of Borromini's spectacularly original church of S. Ivo.

Nor is the exterior less remarkable (p. 208). Borromini carries on in the church façade the arcade motif of Della Porta's courtyard, placing the Chigi emblem at either end. A huge hexagonal drum repeats in its convex faces the triads within, superimposed pilasters strengthening the meeting-points of the convex sectors. Above is a stepped pyramid, with curious buttresses carrying on the line of the lower pilasters; this in turn is crowned by a lantern formed of double columns separating concave recesses. This powerful upward movement is continued by an extraordinary, ornate spiral of stone, capped by an iron 'onion' and a ball. Rome had seen nothing that could rival this architectural strangeness, this fantasy in stone – or rather, this fantastic display of structural inventiveness.

While pursuing the construction of S. Ivo, Borromini was simultaneously rebuilding S. Giovanni in Laterano (see p. 97), continuing with the Rainaldis' (father's and son's) S. Agnese in Agone in the Piazza Navona, and building the apsidal exterior of S. Andrea delle Fratte. The commission for the continuation of S. Agnese (built over the spot where, traditionally, the youthful saint was exposed naked to the public gaze) was given to Borromini by the Pamphilj Pope Innocent X, who wished to make the piazza on which the family palace stood (and still stands) the finest in Rome. It was he who allowed Bernini to display the extraordinary imaginativeness of his *concetti* in the colossal Fountain of the Rivers (1651), which occupies the centre of the piazza.

The Rainaldis' original design for S. Agnese was for a centrally planned building in the shape of a Greek cross. This was virtually retained by Borromini, but he strengthened the architectural element of the magnificent red Corinthian columns, so that they underline the octagonal form of the crossing. The interior of S. Agnese presents an appearance of sumptuous richness in marble and gold; it is a veritable repository of High Baroque sculpture and painting – sculptural works by Ercole Ferrata, Alessandro Algardi and E. A. Raggi, and paintings mainly by Cirro Ferri (in the cupola) and Baciccia.

With the exterior, Borromini had a freer hand at first (later he was superseded), and the result is one of Rome's most satisfying Baroque façades. The concave central section, with its attic, is flanked by two beautifully designed towers. The twin columns of the triumphal-arch doorway are continued in the coupled pilasters of the lofty drum, which in turn are repeated in the ribs of the cupola and lead the eye up to the single columns of the lantern. This derivation from Michelangelo's St Peter's is one of the most elegant domes of all Rome's churches; it completes a façade that delights by the harmony of its proportions and by its perfect symmetry.

The extraordinary dome and tower that Borromini added to the unfinished S. Andrea delle Fratte at about this time (1653) are best seen from the Via Capo le Case. The dome (which is also unfinished and is in rough brickwork) bears little relation, like that at S. Ivo, to the interior which it encases. By means of four projecting buttresses Borromini creates four faces that correspond in their rhythm to the lower storey of S. Carlo alle Quattro Fontane, the convex bay of the 'drum' being flanked by the two concave bays of the buttresses. This strange structure was to be crowned by a

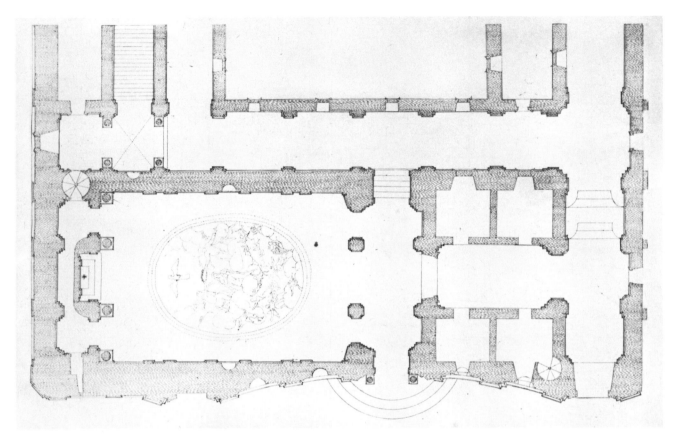

Early engraving of the ground-plan of the Oratory of St Philip Neri by Borromini.

lantern with concave recesses above the convex 'drum' below. Even stranger is the adjoining tower, where each of the five storeys differs radically from the others, though it retains a bizarre homogeneity, even to the topmost inverted scrolls, surmounted by their spiky crown.

Borromini's use of brickwork, which he moulded with a wonderful sense of plasticity, is also exemplified in the little-known church of S. Maria dei Sette Dolori (1662), in the Via Garibaldi in Trastevere, under the Janiculum – just opposite the Bosco Parrasio, where, during the seventeenth century, the famous Academy of the Arcadians met. Here, too, the façade is unfinished. The interior is of an extreme elegance, with lofty Corinthian columns articulating the walls and supporting an entablature and cornice which encompass the changing line of the perimeter and surmount, without a break, the semicircular arches. Light comes pouring in from the clerestory, to illuminate a building of an extraordinary grace and charm. More sombre is Borromini's church of the Collegio di Propaganda Fide (1662), but here the interest lies in the use he makes of cross-ribs in his ceiling – a Gothic reminiscence of a kind which is never far away in his architecture.

Also of brick, but of a very fine finish, is the façade of the

Oratory of St Philip Neri, which Borromini began as early as 1637. This most engaging building is next door to S. Maria in Vallicella. Here, too, Borromini shows his preference for the curvilinear, even to the characteristic segmental-pointed pediment. The secular style of the windows belies the fact that behind part of the façade is a small oratory. Its somewhat austere interior is constructed with a single order of half-columns on the altar wall, and, on the sides, a rhythmic sequence of pilasters. It is pleasant to know that, in keeping with the origins of the Oratorians, concerts are held in this church in the winter, as in several other Roman churches, notably in S. Marcello al Corso, and S. Maria d'Aracoeli.

Borromini's difficult nature seems eventually to have caused his death: he took his own life in 1667, at the age of sixty-eight.

The third member of this great trio of artists of the Roman High Baroque, Pietro da Cortona, has only recently begun to receive his due. Like Bernini, but unlike Borromini, he was extremely versatile, being esteemed as painter, architect and

The Arch of Septimius Severus in the unexcavated Forum; on the right is the church of SS. Luca e Martina. Eighteenth-century engraving by G. B. Piranesi.

designer of sculpture, though he did not himself sculpt. Coming to Rome in 1612 or 1613, he seems quickly to have obtained employment, and, recognizing his talents, Cardinal Francesco Barberini, nephew of Urban VIII, obtained for him in 1624 the commission to paint the fresco cycle in S. Bibiana. He was then twenty-eight. In 1633 he began work on one of the most exciting examples of illusionist painting in Rome: the ceiling fresco of the Gran Salone in the Barberini Palace, *The Glorification of Urban VIII's Reign* – a magnificent feat of sheer painterly bravura. The Barberini bees alone would evoke an apiculturist's admiration. In the following year his colleagues elected him president of their confraternity, the Academy of St Luke, and he received his first big architectural commission: the rebuilding of the church of the Academy. While work was in progress on his own tomb in the crypt (made at Pietro's own expense), the body of S. Martina had come to light, and her name, with that of the Evangelist Luke, was adopted for the new church. Pietro da Cortona has the distinction of having created, in SS. Luca e

Martina, the first of the completely homogeneous great churches of the Roman High Baroque, antedating the masterpieces of Bernini and Borromini.

The façade is in two storeys, between markedly projecting piers, faced by twin pilasters, the main body of the building swelling gently in a convex curve. The four Ionic half-columns of the lower storey are continued by Composite pilasters in the upper; but whereas, over the entrance doorway, there are two plain uncapped pilasters, above it there are two Composite half-columns, framing an elegant window. There is a sharp contrast between clearly defined and seemingly malleable, almost modelled, elements, the carefully framed panels of flowers and palms contrasting with the decorative motifs that surmount the building, especially the large central armorial shield supported by reclining figures. This contrast is paralleled in the dome, the austere angularity of the pediments of the windows of the drum giving way to the soft curves of the decorative features which mask the beginning of the curvature of the cupola and are repeated in the lantern. It seems that some of the characteristics of the painter of the Barberini Palace ceiling reappear in the architect of the exterior of SS. Luca e Martina.

The originality of the façade prepares one for the interior.

Here the impression is of brilliant light and dignified grandeur, the latter emanating from the perfect articulation of the wall-space by the homogeneity of the Ionic columns and pilasters. The plan is of a Greek cross with apses. In contrast to the lush colour and crowded incident of the Barberini Palace ceiling, here all is white and restrained in movement; yet there is a sense of richness, which derives partly from the vistas provided by receding columns and pilasters, and by the screening columns of the apsidal ends, and partly from the stucco-work and the elaborate coffering and ribs of the vaulting. The effect is that of complete architectural control, of harmonious serenity. Below, in the lower church of S. Martina, Pietro designed an altar of gilded bronze. Besides a memorial to the architect himself (who left his large fortune to the Academy of St Luke), there are a monument to the architect Soria and a *Pietà* in terracotta by Algardi.

In 1656 Pietro built the magnificently spectacular façade and portico to the *quattrocento* church of S. Maria della Pace, in the Via della Pace. To come on it unexpectedly, shut in as it is in a maze of narrow streets, is a pleasant surprise; yet what a pity that Alexander VII did not complete the scenographic square which he had planned in front of it! The façade may be looked on as being composed in three zones, or fields, in relation to the spectator. The middle zone, that of the upper storey, its convex centre held in by projecting piers, resembles

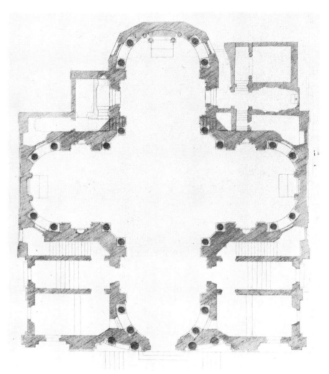

Early engraving of the ground-plan of the upper church of SS. Luca e Martina.

PAGE 193 Seen between the pine-trees in the region of the Forum is the sixteenth-century church of S. Maria di Loreto. The original plans have been attributed both to Bramante and A. Sangallo the Younger, but the windows and niches of the drum, the cupola and the elaborate lantern are by Jacopo Del Duca, who worked on them between 1577 and 1585.

PAGE 194 The lavishly decorated Sistine Chapel in S. Maria Maggiore was designed in 1585 by Domenico Fontana for that assiduous builder Sixtus V (Peretti). The paintings in the cupola and pendentives are by *cinquecento* Mannerists.

PAGE 195 The cupola of S. Carlo ai Catinari, erected (1612–20) for the Barnabites by Rosato Rosati, is considered one of the most elegant in Rome. In the pendentives Domenichino has represented the *Cardinal Virtues* (1630).

G.B. GAULLI - (BACICCIA)
S. ANNA - 1675

PEREGIT TANDEM EXTREMVM ANN MDCLXXI
A E NEC PLAVSVS EXACTVRVS NEC PLANCTVS SED
IN ADITV   IN EXITV
AVE   SALVE

IN NIDVLO MEO MORIAR

the façade of SS. Luca e Martina. Before it is a semicircular portico (the front zone), supported on four pairs of Doric columns and having all the appearance of a little Greek temple. In the third, rear, zone the large concave wings enclose all within their enfolding arms. This interplay of concave and convex was also preoccupying Bernini and Borromini at this period. Another High Baroque feature of S. Maria della Pace is the encased pediment, where a triangle encloses a segment. Below this the entablature is broken to make way for the armorial bearing of Alexander VII. The boldness of Pietro's design is as arresting as it is satisfying – this, in a church where Bramante and perhaps Baccio Pontelli had had a hand.

Another striking example of High Baroque boldness is the façade of S. Maria in Via Lata, which Pietro began in 1658. The alignment of the Corso, on which it stands, may have ruled out the possibility of a curved façade. Here Pietro reversed the process which he had adopted at SS. Luca e Martina: the central section of an open arcade, topped by an even more prominent loggia, is flanked by recessed bays. A firmly moulded triangular pediment caps the central section; as at S. Maria della Pace, it encloses another, segmental, pediment, but here the segment is formed by a rounded arch which joins the two broken halves of the straight entablature above the columns, with their highly decorative capitals.

There are few decorative features, the whole bold effect being achieved by the strong contrasts of light on the surface planes and by the deep shadow in the recesses of the entrance portico and of the first-storey loggia. The portico, too, is of great interest. A coffered barrel vault is borne on two lines of columns, one row of which screens the wall of the church, which seems to run on, as does the vault, not stopping at the apsidal end. Pietro thus gives the illusion that the apses are in a larger area, shut out from the eyes of the beholder.

Pietro da Cortona's great dome for the church of S. Carlo al Corso (in the street of that name), built in 1668, is without doubt one of the most beautiful of all examples of this characteristic feature of Rome's Baroque churches. It illustrates the path which the architect had followed and the advances which he had made during the years since he had created the dome of SS. Luca e Martina, which betrays a certain affinity with Mannerism. The dome of S. Carlo, by contrast, is a serene, essentially classical, masterpiece. Piers of superimposed pilasters divide the drum into bays, where high rectangular windows, with severely moulded frames, are flanked by screening columns. Above is an entablature, with a pronounced cornice from which the line of pilasters is continued in curved brackets topped by shells. Between the brackets are oval windows with softly moulded frames; in the centre of each frame is a cherub's head and above it a

---

PAGE 196   Soaring above the gilt and bronze of Bernini's majestic *baldacchino* in St Peter's, the cupola seems to float on air and light. This, Michelangelo's masterpiece and the most perfect of all cupolas, was completed by Giacomo Della Porta (1590). The perfection of the architecture and the brilliance of light mitigate the indifference of the mosaics, based on the cartoons (1605) the Cavalier d'Arpino designed for Clement VIII.

PAGE 197   S. Carlo alle Quattro Fontane (S. Carlino) occupied Borromini for all his working architectural life. The cloister, which he began in 1634, was his first independent ecclesiastical work. In 1638 he began the church, the façade of which was uncompleted at his death in 1667. Inside,

the rhythmic movement of the undulating walls is firmly bound by the pronounced architrave. Light from concealed windows floods the elliptical cupola, with its geometrical coffering.

PAGE 198   Bernini's *Habakkuk* (1655) in the Chigi Chapel in S. Maria del Popolo. Bernini has depicted the angel plucking at Habakkuk's hair to arouse him into setting off for Babylon, to take his dinner to Daniel in the lion's den.

PAGE 199   Monument to the Blessed Ludovica Albertoni (1674) by Bernini in S. Francesco a Ripa. Bernini has brought off one of his celebrated 'conceits' in having apparently disembodied angels' heads gaze on the recumbent figure. Above is a painting by Baciccia (G. B. Gaulli) of the *Madonna and Child with St Anne* (c. 1675).

PAGE 200   The macabre monument in S. Maria del Popolo erected by the Polish architect G. B. Gisleni to himself in 1670. He died two years later in 1672. An inscription on the side can be translated 'Neither living here nor dead there'. The medallions contain the symbolic metamorphosis of a caterpillar into a butterfly.

An eighteenth-century engraving of the façade of S. Maria in Via Lata which Pietro da Cortona began in 1658.

triangular cornice. The line of the cornice – triangular over the windows, flat over the brackets and broken by the shells – acts as a modulation between the entablature of the drum and the ribbed cupola. A beautiful lantern, formed by shallow scrolled volutes and arched recesses and surmounted by a ball and cross, completes this dome which, after that of St Peter's, must be accounted the finest of any Roman church.

Where the three great masters of the Roman High Baroque led the way, others were to follow, but not in a spirit of slavish imitation: some were highly individualistic architects in their own right. Carlo Rainaldi began the construction of the great church of S. Maria in Campitelli, in the Piazza Campitelli, in 1663 for Alexander VII. In its impressive grandeur Rainaldi's church-front (p. 212), which Wittkower has conveniently termed the 'aedicule façade', is typical of Roman ecclesiastical architecture of the period. It is characterized by two great central aedicules (each enclosing another), the lower breaking into the ground of the aedicule occupying the upper storey, and this in turn breaking into the area of the pediment. Particularly notable are the columns (both outer and recessed) and the use of triangular and segmental pediments, those covering the central section being deeply indented and broken. The columns and windows of the flanking bays are reminiscent of those of the Capitoline palaces.

The interior is no less imposing. The eye moves from one majestic free-standing column to another, to the pilasters in the nave, to its chapels, to where the light streams into the circular area beneath the dome, and eventually comes to rest in the twilight of the tribune and the high altar. The whiteness is only broken, and most effectively, by the gilding. The sense of space and size of which one is conscious on entering the church comes largely from the transverse axis,

and the width of the chapels, but, even more, from the length of the main axis. In every way the grandeur of the exterior is matched by the impressiveness of the interior (p. 173).

Simultaneously with his work on S. Maria in Campitelli (and on the great façade of S. Andrea della Valle, in the Corso Vittorio Emanuele), Rainaldi was engaged on those twin churches that make so effective an introduction to Rome for the visitor entering from the Porta del Popolo (or Porta Flaminia): S. Maria di Montesanto and S. Maria dei Miracoli (p. 210). The site of the former was narrower than that of the latter; Rainaldi solved the problem of how to make the churches present to the Piazza del Popolo, where they stand, an impression of identical size and shape by designing an oval dome over an elliptical plan for S. Maria di Montesanto (on the left) and a round dome for S. Maria dei Miracoli (on the right). The resemblance of the former church to a Greek temple is due to the intervention of Bernini, who in 1673 continued the work on the building, using columns taken from his demolished campanile at St Peter's. Two years later, the church was completed by Carlo Fontana. To Rainaldi also fell the task of integrating the apsidal end of S. Maria Maggiore, which he achieved with outstanding effect.

Another remarkable church of the Roman High Baroque is SS. Vincenzo ed Anastasio, built between 1646 and 1650 for Cardinal Mazarin by Martino Longhi the Younger in the vicinity of the spectacular Fountain of Trevi. The façade of this little church is highly original, and appears to owe little to other contemporary architecture, apart from its assurance and brio. Its most distinguishing feature is Longhi's bold use of triads of free-standing columns on both storeys to form the central bay. Above the central doorway the inner and outer columns of each triad are held together by segmental pediments, the upper one broken, to be joined to the central female bust by ornamental swags. It is this decorative richness that gives SS. Vincenzo ed Anastasio its gay exuberance. Reclining on the pediment of the elegant rectangular window two angels support the blazon, and above, besides Mazarin's cardinal's hat, there are two cherubs, sounding a fanfare of praise.

Carlo Fontana had served Bernini, Pietro da Cortona and Rainaldi as architectural draughtsman. Perhaps his own most successful Roman work was S. Marcello al Corso (1682), but here there is a falling away from the invigorating sureness of High Baroque into something more academic: a

RIGHT The expressive statue of S. Carlo Borromeo by Attilio Selva from Trieste (d. 1970), seen against the apsidal end of S. Carlo al Corso. The dome, with its beautifully articulated drum, cupola and lantern – perhaps the finest in Rome after St Peter's – is by Pietro da Cortona (1668).

CONCORDIAE INTER GENTES ADSERTOR
AVSPICE CHARITATE
DVCTV IVSTITIAE ET PACIS SVASV
LATERANENSIBVS PACTIONIBVS
ITALIAE DEVM RESTITVIT
DEOQVE ITALIAM

PIVS XI PONT MAX

QVI FIDE PIETATE SAPIENTIA
REBVS GESTIS

Late Baroque classicism, which seems to herald the *Settecento*. Fontana's façade (p. 209) has movement and is formally 'correct' and pleasing, but it seems to lack the full-blooded robustness which we associate with the generation of architects who had just passed away.

At the dawning of the eighteenth century the face of Rome – with its churches, palaces, monuments, fountains and obelisks – was, by and large, very similar to what the visitor sees today. Competent architects existed, and important churches like S. Giovanni in Laterano (Galilei), S. Maria Maggiore (Fuga) and S. Croce in Gerusalemme (Passalacqua) (pp. 236–7) received their present façades, while other churches were built, rebuilt or restored. But the chief change came with the creation of those scenographic features which give us so much pleasure today: in 1723 Francesco De Sanctis constructed in travertine his magnificent Spanish Steps, leading from Pietro Bernini's beautifully maritime Fountain of the Barcaccia (1627) to Trinità dei Monti; in 1727 Filippo Raguzzini designed his delightful ochre-stuccoed Piazza S. Ignazio; during the years 1732–62 Nicola Salvi created that monumental masterpiece, combining architecture, statuary and water, that has drawn so many thousands of admirers – his celebrated Fountain of Trevi. In the 1790s Giuseppe Valadier (who was a Roman, despite his surname) began the designs which gave to the Piazza del Popolo its present form.

If the centre of the most progressive movements in art and architecture passed elsewhere during the eighteenth century, Rome became the goal of the grand tourist, the delight of the connoisseur and the haven of the academic. The century, so slow-moving and sedate in Italy, ended in the cataclysm of the Napoleonic Wars. The nineteenth century, with all the turmoil and upheaval that accompanied the reunification of Italy, was hardly propitious to church-building, although Pio Nono was assiduous in the work of repair and restoration, using the architects Vespignani, father and son, for this purpose. During the present century restoration has owed much to the knowledge and taste of A. Muñoz. With Rome once more the national capital, its churches and their priceless contents were declared a national heritage and passed under the supervision of the Ministry of Fine Arts: the four basilicas of St Peter's, S. Giovanni in Laterano, S. Paolo fuori le Mura and S. Maria Maggiore alone remained directly under papal control.

We may fittingly end this chapter by discussing what is, perhaps, the last church built in Rome during the eighteenth century to be typical of the period: S. Maria del Priorato, the little church of the Sovereign Order of the Knights of Malta on the Aventine. This was rebuilt and decorated in 1765 by an architect more celebrated for his engravings, the Venetian Giovanni Battista Piranesi. Beyond the lovely church of S. Sabina and that of SS. Bonifacio ed Alessio, the Via di S. Sabina debouches into the Piazza dei Cavalieri di Malta – a characteristic Piranesi *capriccio*, walled in and decorated with obelisks, steles and monsters. At the end on the right a drive leads to the church. A far cry from the suggestive plasticity of the High Baroque is the austere Neoclassical style of Piranesi's façade (p. 238), with its single order of fluted pilasters, its doorway surmounted by a simple eye-window, the whole being crowned with a triangular pediment. The interior is of a dazzling whiteness, which is taken up in the stucco of the medallions and Maltese crosses. The high altar is also of stucco; it has a large globe, surrounded by *putti*, and a sculptured group, *St Basil in Glory*, showing the saint supported by angels, all to Piranesi's designs. The church contains some interesting tombs, two formed from Roman sarcophagi, and a third, that of Monsignor Bartolomeo Carafa (d. 1405), which is among the few surviving works of the Roman sculptor Paolo Romano.

From a charming garden nearby (beside the church of S. Sabina) there is a magnificent view over the intervening cupolas and towers of Rome to where, against the blue sky, there rises Michelangelo's crowning masterpiece, the ethereal dome of St Peter's.

RIGHT S. Maria della Vittoria was begun for Cardinal Scipio Borghese by Carlo Maderno in 1603. The façade was designed in 1626 by G. B. Soria, who was clearly greatly influenced by the neighbouring church of S. Susanna, also by Maderno. The lion at the foot of Domenico Fontana's Fountain of Moses (1587) is a copy of an ancient Egyptian original in the Vatican.

ABOVE The double flight of steps (1654), attributed to Orazio Torriani, leading up to SS. Domenico e Sisto, is a forerunner to the celebrated Spanish Steps (De Sanctis, 1723). They contribute to the pronounced upward thrust of the seventeenth-century façade, the lower storey of which is thought to be the work of Nicola Torriani, the upper of Vincenzo Della Greca.

RIGHT Bramante may have designed the hexagonal addition, with its cupola and lantern, to the *quattrocento* S. Maria della Pace, erected for Sixtus IV by Baccio Pontelli. The campanile (1502) behind, of S. Maria dell'Anima, is by an unknown architect: above gothicized pediments and pinnacles, a conical spire rises, covered with majolica tiles of white, green, blue and yellow.

PAGE 208 S. Ivo alla Sapienza (1642–60) by Borromini. A stepped, pyramidal dome supports a hexagonal lantern, inspired perhaps by the recently-discovered Temple of Venus at Baalbek. This is surmounted by a curious corkscrew spire, said to resemble 'the horn of a Sicilian goat'.

PAGE 209 The Baroque façade (1682) of S. Marcello on the Corso by Carlo Fontana is of two storeys which are linked by palm fronds in place of volutes.

PAGE 210 The lion by G. Valadier at the foot of the ancient Egyptian Flaminian Obelisk (c. 1200 BC) in the Piazza del Popolo. Behind are the twin churches begun by Carlo Rainaldi and completed by Bernini and Carlo

Fontana: on the left S. Maria di Montesanto (1662–75), on the right S. Maria dei Miracoli (1675–9).

ABOVE In S. Maria della Scala the *baldacchino* by Carlo Rainaldi (*c.* 1650) is in the form of an elegant *tempietto*, with attic, cupola and lantern raised on sixteen slender fluted Corinthian-capped columns of oriental jasper.

LEFT In Carlo Rainaldi's masterly design for the façade of S. Maria in Campitelli (1663–7) he dispensed with niches and figurative sculpture. Instead, by means of free-standing columns, projecting members, broken cornices and flat-faced recessions, he sought the rich plasticity, the play of light and shade, that make this one of the most outstanding of Rome's Baroque church-fronts.

ABOVE An early engraving of the elevation of the façade of S. Maria in Campitelli.

ABOVE Beside the main doorway to the church of Gesù e Maria the two funeral monuments to members of the Corno family by Ercole Ferrata and Domenico Guidi illustrate Baroque taste in the second half of the seventeenth century. This monument is to Giulio del Corno who died in 1662.

RIGHT Monument to the Bolognetti family (c. 1675) in the church of Gesù e Maria. Baroque fantasy has represented members of the family as if they were seated in their box at the opera-house or theatre, watching with animated interest the proceedings on the stage. The figures are the work of F. Aprile, F. Cavallini and M. Maglia.

ABOVE Above the high altar of S. Rocco, with its columns of rare breccia from a classical building, is the painting of *St Rocco in Glory* by the Roman Baroque artist Giacinto Brandi (1623–91).

PAGE 217 The sumptuous *baldacchino*, its four columns of rare porphyry bound by fronds of gilded bronze, by the *settecento* architect Ferdinand Fuga in S. Maria Maggiore.

PAGE 218 The interior of S. Maria in Vallicella (the Chiesa Nuova) is remarkable for its chromatic richness. The paintings of the four prophets in the pendentives, the *Glory of the Trinity* in the drumless cupola and the *Assumption of the* *Virgin* in the apse are by Pietro da Cortona (1647–56).

PAGE 219 The spirited ceiling (1674) of SS. Domenico e Sisto is the joint work of the Bolognese painters D. M. Canuti, who painted the centrepiece of the *Apotheosis of St Dominic*, and Enrico Haffner, who executed the *quadratura*.

ABOVE Portrait of Alexander VII
(Chigi, 1655–67) for whom Pietro da
Cortona designed the beautiful façade
and portico of S. Maria della Pace
(1656) and Bernini the incomparable
Piazza of St Peter's (1656–67).

PAGES 220–1 The great fresco (c. 1685)
in the nave vault of S. Ignazio by Father
Andrea Pozzo, where the *Entrance of St
Ignatius into Paradise* is seen between
allegorical representations of the *Four
Corners of the Earth*, constitutes an
astonishing feat of *quadratura* painting.

PAGE 222 The Chapel of St Ignatius of
Loyola in Il Gesù, designed by the Jesuit
Father A. Pozzo (1696), is decorated
with an unsurpassed richness. The statue

of the saint above his altar-tomb is in part
silver, the original by P. Legros having
been melted down by Pius VI to meet the
demands of Napoleon I in the Treaty of
Tolentino. On the pediment, below the
group of the *Trinity*, an angel raises a
lapis lazuli sphere representing the world.

PAGE 223 In the portico of SS.
Bonifacio e Alessio stands the statue in
plaster of Pope Benedict XIII (1724–30),
erected by Cardinal Quirini.

PAGE 224 The dome of St Peter's –
designed by Michelangelo and completed
by Giacomo Della Porta in 1590 – seen
from the Vatican gardens. The beauty of
the proportions of Michelangelo's drum,
soaring cupola and lantern more than

compensates for the not altogether
satisfactory body of the church, where the
windows seem to be squeezed between
the huge pilasters.

PAGE 226 The ornate ceiling of S.
Maria in Trastevere, rich in gilding and
colour, was designed by Domenichino
(1617), who painted the oval centre-
piece, the *Assumption of the Virgin Mary*.

PAGE 227 The magnificent nave ceiling
in S. Giovanni in Laterano was begun
in 1562 (possibly to the design of Pirro
Ligorio) by the Medici Pope Pius IV,
whose arms appear in the centrepiece.
The angels' heads and decorative swags
in the side chapels are part of Borromini's
seventeenth-century restoration.

ABOVE Borromini's interior of S. Ivo alla Sapienza (1642–50), an 'engineering and geometrical masterpiece'.

PAGE 229 In the elliptical Chapel of S. Cecilia in S. Carlo ai Catinari, executed by Antonio Gherardi between 1692 and 1700, the brilliance, movement and gaiety of the stucco-work seems to herald *settecento* Rococo.

PAGE 230 The paintings of the nave vault, cupola and tribune of Il Gesù are all by the Genovese artist G. B. Gaulli (known as Baciccia), executed between 1672 and 1685. The angels in white stucco supporting the nave painting, the *Triumph of the Name of Jesus*, as well as those in the window enclosures, are by E. A. Raggi.

PAGE 231 The nave of S. Luigi dei Francesi is richly decorated in stucco by the French artist Antoine Dérizet (1756); in the vault is the *Death and Glory of St Louis* by his contemporary and compatriot, Charles-Joseph Natoire.

PAGE 232 The *memento mori* motif strikes a macabre note behind the tomb in polychrome marble of Cardinal Cinzio Aldobrandini (1707) in S. Pietro in Vincoli.

PAGE 233 Father Grassi's monument to Gregory XV (Ludovisi) in S. Ignazio. It was during this Pope's pontificate that the Blessed Ignatius was sanctified. The figures of Gregory XV, Faith and Abundance are by P. Legros (1698), the angels by his contemporary, S. Monnot, both French sculptors.

PAGE 234 The tomb of Eleanor Boncompagni in SS. Bonifacio e Alessio. She was a member of the family of Pope Gregory XIII (1572–85).

PAGE 235 One of the two eighteenth-century angels by Bernardino Ludovisi beside the altar of S. Luigi Gonzaga by Andrea Pozzo in S. Ignazio. A high-relief in white marble by P. Legros represents the glory of the saint (1698).

LEFT The interplay of light and shadow on the *settecento* façade of S. Maria Maggiore by the Florentine Ferdinando Fuga (1743).

ABOVE The *settecento* façade of S. Croce in Gerusalemme by Domenico Gregorini and Pietro Passalacqua (1743) presents a play of light on the surface planes offset by the deeply shadowed recesses. Behind rises the rugged Romanesque campanile of 1144.

ABOVE The Neoclassical façade (1765) of S. Maria del
Priorato, the church of the Sovereign Order of the Knights of
Malta, by an architect better known for his engravings, G. B.
Piranesi.

RIGHT The high altar at S. Maria del Priorato with *St Basil in
Glory*, designed by G. B. Piranesi, and stucco-work by T. Righi
(*c.* 1765). In the nave hang the banners of the Knights of Malta:
on the left (from the top down), France, Provence; on the right,
Castile, England and Italy.

CINERIBVS ET MEMORIAE
IOAN BAPTISTAE PIRANESI
DOMO VENETIIS

LEFT Statue of G. B. Piranesi (d. 1798) by Giuseppe Angelini (1735–1811) in S. Maria del Priorato.

ABOVE One of two figures representing *Mildness* and *Modesty* at the foot of the monument to Clement XIV (Ganganelli) in SS. Apostoli, the first Roman work of Antonio Canova (1789).

241

LEFT The extraordinary *settecento* monument in S. Maria del Popolo to Princess Maria Flaminia Odescalchi-Chigi, who died in childbirth aged twenty in 1771. The eagle and the lion, heraldic beasts of the Odescalchi family, express their grief, while cherubs hang the Princess's portrait in an oval medallion studded with Chigi stars.

ABOVE An unusual example of perspective illusionism on the tomb of Cardinal M. Rampolla del Tindaro by E. Quattrini (1929) in S. Cecilia in Trastevere. The Cardinal was Secretary of State to Leo XII (1823–9).

9
The Forum of the World: St Peter's

A book on Rome's churches which excluded its greatest and grandest, St Peter's, would seem as deficient as a study of *Hamlet* in which no reference is made to the Prince of Denmark. Though it might be said that St Peter's cannot be described, but can only be visited, some attempt must nevertheless be made to achieve the impossible. In its vastness and splendour St Peter's symbolizes the grandeur, universality and catholicity of the Church. But to individual men and women, Catholic and non-Catholic alike, its appeal will be something less general – more human and direct. And it is consistent with this essentially human approach when we reflect that, in its architecture and decoration this huge building, on which thousands of men worked and millions were spent, was chiefly conceived and executed by three men: Michelangelo Buonarroti, Gian Lorenzo Bernini and Carlo Maderno. And it arose through the wills of a line of munificent and imperious popes and through the offerings of countless of the nameless faithful. In its inception the New St Peter's was Renaissance; in its completion, Baroque. Yet, in its crypts or grottoes, situated at the level of and around the tomb of the Prince of the Apostles, have been collected monuments, statues and precious objects, often mutilated by the reckless vandalism of the rebuilders, so that the basilica contains art treasures which have accumulated during some 1,900 years of Roman Christianity.

The initiative to rebuild Old St Peter's, which had stood for over 1,000 years and was showing signs of decay, was undertaken in 1450 by the first of the great Renaissance popes, Nicholas V, on the advice of L.B. Alberti and B. Rossellino. Little happened over the next half-century, until the ponti-

ficate of Julius II, the della Rovere pope of irrepressible energy and indomitable will who was determined to erect a building expressive of the power and splendour of the Roman Church. His intention also had a personal aspect, since the new building was to contain the massive monument to himself which he had commissioned from Michelangelo. The architect chosen was Bramante, then at the height of his powers, and on 18 April 1506 Julius II laid the foundation stone of the new church on the present Veronica pier at the crossing.

In accordance with Renaissance architectural ideals, Bramante designed a centrally planned building in the shape of a Greek cross, with each of its four arms constituting a smaller Greek cross. Imbued with the spirit of Antiquity, and spurred on by the magnitude of the Pope's aims, Bramante determined to rival and surpass the grandeur of Imperial Rome – to do no less than raise the dome of the Pantheon on the vaults of the Basilica of Maxentius, whose colossal ruins he had studied in the Forum. But, again in conformity with Renaissance canons, columns of classical proportions would serve as intermediaries to the great piers and arches which would be necessary to sustain the weight of the huge semicircular cupola – so that man would not be dwarfed into insignificance. On the death of Julius II in 1513, and of

RIGHT St Peter's. The much venerated statue of St Peter, whose right foot has been worn away by the kisses of the faithful, is thought to be the work of Arnolfo di Cambio (*c.* 1290?). Behind Bernini's great *baldacchino* (1624–33) the apse contains his setting, in gilded bronze, of the Chair of St Peter (1656–65).

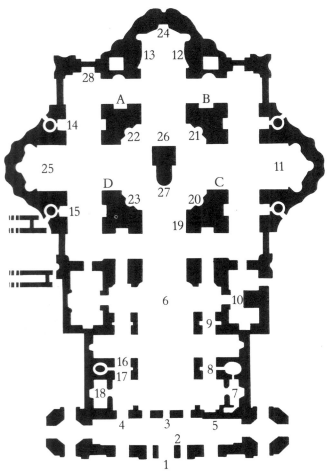

Piazza di S. Pietro

High-relief, *St Leo I meets Attila the Hun* (1650) by Alessandro Algardi in the Colonna Chapel in St Peter's.

St Peter's

1 Façade (1607–14) by Carlo Maderno.
2 Narthex; above the central entrance mosaic of the *Navicella* (1298) by Giotto from Old St Peter's and, on far right, equestrian statue of Constantine (1670) by Bernini.
3 Bronze doors (1433–45) by Antonio Filarete from Old St Peter's.
4 Bronze doors (1964) by Giacomo Manzù.
5 *Holy Door* or *Porta Santa* by Vico Consorti (b. 1902).
6 Nave.
7 Chapel containing Michelangelo's *Pietà* (1497).
8 Monument to Queen Christina of Sweden (*c.* 1702) by C. Fontana and G. B. Théodon.
9 Monument to Countess Matilda of Canossa (*c.* 1630) designed by Bernini.
10 Chapel of the Holy Sacrament with wrought iron by Borromini and *ciborio* (1674) of gilded bronze by Bernini.
11 Right transept.
12 Tomb of Urban VIII (1642–7) by Bernini.
13 Tomb of Paul III (1551–75) by G. Della Porta.
14 Tomb of Alexander VII (1672–8) by Bernini.

15 Entrance to sacristy.
16 Stuart monument (1817–19) by A. Canova.
17 Entrance to the dome.
18 Baptistery.
19 Statue of St Peter (*c.* 1290?) attributed to Arnolfo di Cambio.
20 Statue of St Longinus (1639) by Bernini.
21 Statue of St Helena (1639) by Andrea Bolgi.
22 Statue of St Veronica (1646) by Francesco Mochi.
23 Statue of St Andrew (1640) by Francesco Duquesnoy.
24 Chair of St Peter and window with Bernini's *Gloria* (1656–65).
25 Left transept.
26 *Baldacchino* (1624–33) by Bernini.
27 *Confessio* of the tomb of St Peter by C. Maderno with statue of Pius VI (*c.* 1822) by Canova.
28 Colonna Chapel with high-relief, *St Leo meets Attila the Hun* (1650) by A. Algardi.

A B C and D Giant piers supporting the drum of the dome.

Bramante in the following year, the construction had reached the piers and the arches of the crossing. Raphael, whom Bramante had designated as his successor, wished to lengthen the east arm, so as to form a Latin cross, but his own early death in 1520, followed by delays and disagreements, frustrated his plans. Leo X spent a fortune in merely strengthening the building already achieved: there had been signs of over-hasty workmanship. Then work was further interrupted by the Sack of Rome in 1527.

On 1 January 1547 the Farnese Pope Paul III called in Michelangelo, who was then seventy-two, to take charge – which he consented to do, without payment, 'for the love of God and devotion to the Prince of the Apostles'. He worked on St Peter's for seventeen years, until his death. As with everything else he undertook, Michelangelo has left the indelible imprint of his genius on St Peter's. He reverted to Bramante's Greek cross plan, but stripped it of its humanistic qualities by cutting off the smaller Greek crosses, leaving a square ambulatory and creating gigantic piers to support his dome. All intermediary columns were replaced by a huge order of Corinthian pilasters. Externally, at the rear, Michelangelo's structure impresses chiefly by the immensity of its pilasters, which sustain the heavy attic – in fact, the niches and windows squeezed between the pilasters create a discordant effect. The style is not of the Renaissance (as Bramante's would have been), nor should it be termed Mannerist; it can only be called Michelangelesque. But any defects are forgotten when the eye rises to the graceful coupled columns and perfectly proportioned windows of the drum, and follows up beyond the ornamental swags and the pronounced ribs of the curvature of the soaring cupola to the twin columns of the exquisite lantern, with its crowning orb – a miracle of aerial proportion, one of the most beautiful architectural structures ever conceived and executed by the genius of man. The dome had been completed to the height of the drum at Michelangelo's death in 1564, but he had left a model for his successors, and it was Giacomo Della Porta who, in 1590, under Sixtus V, brought to a conclusion this, the greatest architectural undertaking of the Italian Renaissance. Michelangelo's plan for an entrance portico in the style of that of a Greek temple was never carried out.

The ancient nave and double aisles of the Constantinian basilica were still standing. It was the Borghese Pope Paul V who, despite the opposition of powerful voices such as that of Cardinal Baronius, decided on the destruction of this venerable building, with its *atrium* (containing the famous *cantharus* and pine-cone), its loggia of benediction and campanile. In the course of this wholesale demolition the pickaxe put paid to priceless works of art. Raphael's conception of an elongated eastern arm, forming a Latin cross, was revived, aesthetic or architectural considerations being subordinated to liturgical demands. This project, which destroyed for ever the harmony and proportions of Michelangelo's design, was executed by Carlo Maderno, who extended by 200 feet the nave and aisles, in three bays, but felicitously lessened the dimensions of his piers, so as not to diminish the monumentality of Michelangelo's building. Maderno's palace-type façade has been rightly criticized, chiefly because it blots out much of the drum of the dome from view, when seen from the piazza, and on account of its excessive breadth. But his orders, brute facts and even fortune were all against him. On the death of Paul V in 1621 the new structure, in its grey travertine bareness, was virtually complete.

After his election in 1623 Pope Urban VIII, giving an audience to Gian Lorenzo Bernini, is reported to have remarked, 'It is your great fortune, Cavaliere, to see as Pope Cardinal Maffeo Barberini. But much more is it ours that the Cavalier Bernini lives in our pontificate.' They were men after each other's hearts. What Julius II obtained from Michelangelo in the construction of St Peter's, Urban VIII in the twenty-one years of his pontificate achieved from Bernini in its decoration. But first the new basilica was to be consecrated; this solemn event took place on 18 November 1626, the anniversary of the dedication of Constantine's church by St Silvester 1,300 years earlier.

In 1624 Urban VIII commissioned Bernini, then twenty-five, to construct the huge *baldacchino* over the high altar and the tomb of the Prince of the Apostles, behind the horse-shoe *confessio* of Carlo Maderno. Bernini leapt at the opportunity to achieve that fusion of the arts – in this case, the merging of architecture with monumental sculpture – which was so dear to his aesthetic conceptions. The great height of the *baldacchino* (equalling that of the Farnese Palace) is proportionate to its position directly beneath Michelangelo's huge cupola. The corkscrew pillars have been thought to epitomize the exuberance of Baroque, but in reality they are modelled on the late antique twisted columns which came from Old St Peter's and were now to be used by Bernini in the loggias which he proposed to construct in the great piers, in order to exhibit the Holy Relics. It is in the decoration, where he had the assistance of Borromini, that contemporary Baroque taste is displayed – in the Barberini arms (with their curiously contrasting heads) on the plinths, in the laurel branches, in the vine tendrils (with their *putti* that grow up the columns), in the beautiful gilt angels at the top corners, whose festoons seem to hold in place the scrolls that support the orb and Cross. In the highest portions sculpture comes into its own. Besides the angels and the *putti* holding the symbols of papal

ABOVE The great nave of St Peter's, with Carlo Maderno's addition (1614), seen from the gallery inside the dome.

RIGHT The mosaics in the cupola of St Peter's were based on cartoons by the Cavalier d'Arpino and were executed (c. 1605) during the pontificate of Clement VIII.

ABOVE St Peter's. Detail of the central doors (1433–45) made
by the Florentine Antonio Averulino, known as Filarete, for
Old St Peter's on the orders of Eugenius IV.

RIGHT St Peter's. Detail of the *Holy Door* or *Porta Santa*,
which is opened only every quarter of a century for Holy Year by
the Pope in person, with *Scenes from the Old and New Testaments*
by Vico Consorti (b. 1902).

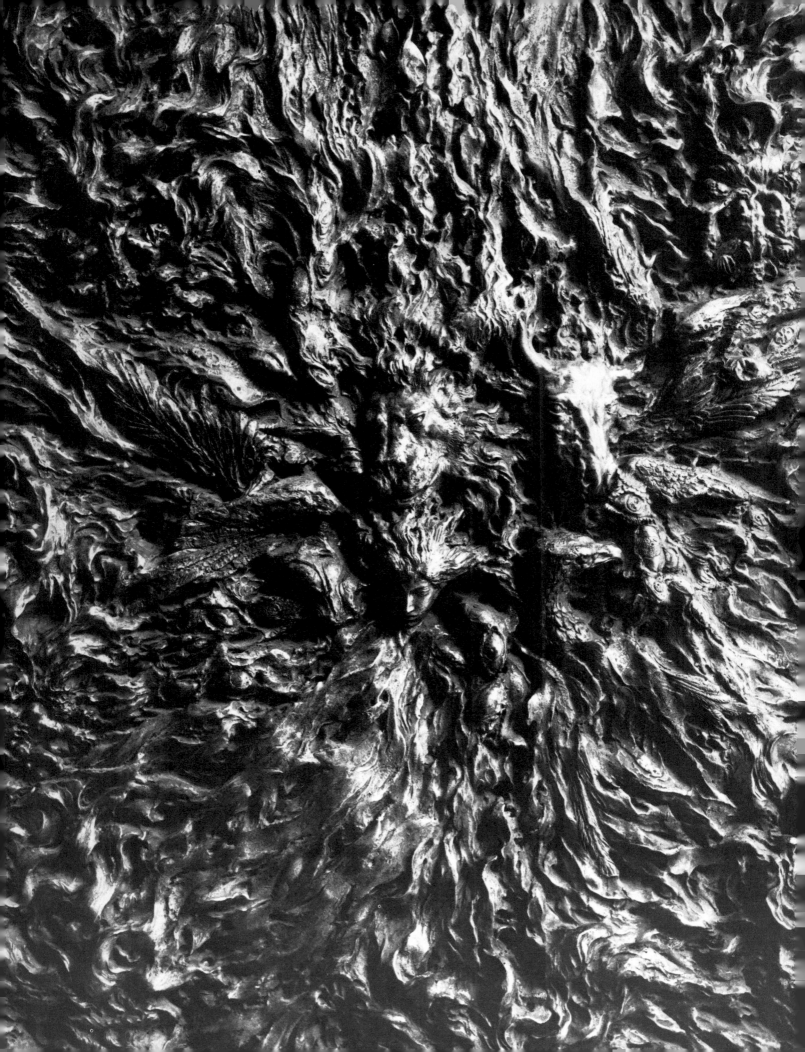

power, are the most realistic Barberini bees. Instead of an entablature there is a kind of canopy-hanging, which also displays the family bees. Tradition has it that, in order to acquire the great quantity of bronze which he needed for the *baldacchino*, Urban VIII stripped the portico of the Pantheon of its gilded bronze tiles and removed others from the roof of St Peter's itself, this act of vandalism giving rise to Pasquino's famous comment: 'Quod non fecerunt barbari, fecerunt Barberini' ('What the barbarians did not do, the Barberini did').

In the piers surrounding the *baldacchino* and beneath his loggias Bernini created great niches to contain four colossal statues, that of St Longinus, with the lance that pierced Christ's side, being carved by Bernini himself. To complete the scenographic effect of this hallowed spot, so revered by Christians, Bernini, using the high altar, with its candles, and the columns and canopy of the *baldacchino* as a frame, devised an extraordinary setting for the reputed Chair of St Peter. Here he pulled out all his stops: multicoloured marbles, bronze, gilt, stucco, metal, glass, light – all was at his disposal, so that he could achieve this, perhaps his greatest, *concetto*. From the agitated, earthly movements of the four Doctors of the Eastern and Western Churches below, to the serenity of the central *cathedra*, and upwards to the heavenly scene, from which descends the Holy Ghost in the shape of a dove,

bathed in yellow light – all this constitutes a theatrical *tableau vivant* before which the devout spectator surrenders, while the agnostic connoisseur turns silently away.

On the death of Carlo Maderno in 1629 Bernini was appointed architect of St Peter's, and, by the work which he carried out there from that time until his own death in 1680, he left the imprint of his hand and taste (as well as that of his followers) on the whole building. One likes to think that the worse than mediocre mosaics were not of his choosing; the blame for those in the cupola (from 1605) can safely be laid at the door of the overrated Cavalier d'Arpino. But the polychrome marbling of the nave piers, the allegorical figures and the medallions in stucco, the triumphal arches of the aisles (with their stucco figures), the marble paving – these were only the background to Bernini's monumental works: the design for the monument to the Countess Matilda di Canossa (1635), the magnificent tomb to his patron Urban VIII (1642–7), the splendid equestrian statue of Constantine the Great (finished in 1670) at the Scala Regia end of Maderno's portico, the tomb of Alexander VII (1672–8; the figures of *Charity* and *Truth*, originally naked, are now decently covered out of respect for the susceptibilities of a more circumspect age) and the decoration of the resplendent Chapel of the Holy Sacrament. In this last Bernini turned goldsmith and designed the beautiful tabernacle of gilded

PAGE 252 St Peter's. Detail of the bronze *Door of Death* by Giacomo Manzù (b. 1908).

PAGE 253 St Peter's. Detail of the bronze *Door of the Sacraments* by Venanzio Crocetti (b. 1913).

PAGE 254 St Peter's. Detail of the bronze *Door of Prayer* by Lello Scorzelli (1972).

bronze and lapis lazuli, modelled on Bramante's Tempietto di S. Pietro in Montorio (p. 145) – the exquisite ironwork of the grille here being by Borromini. But Bernini's masterpiece, one of the grandest examples of civic planning ever carried out, is his flawlessly proportioned colonnade in the piazza of St Peter's.

When, in 1657, Alexander VII set him the task of clearing away the heterogeneous collection of buildings that were grouped round the irregular piazza, to make way for an approach worthy of the grandeur of the basilica, Bernini discarded several alternatives before deciding on the solution that overcame the many problems involved. What he achieved is universally considered a work of genius. From Maderno's façade he threw out two arms, forming a trapezoid which opened into a vast semicircle, which was intended to be completed by a separate section, where the Piazza Pio XII now stands. The colonnade that he constructed consists of four files of free-standing Doric columns, with a simple Ionic entablature, surmounted by a balustrade, on which rise statues, 140 of them, of saints of the Church. The piazza, so majestic in its dignity, so perfect in its harmonious proportions, thus forms an *atrium*, a vast ante-chapel, as it were, in which the pilgrim who enters it feels that he is already within the sacred precincts of the basilica. This, indeed, is 'the forum of the world'. Church and piazza are indissoluble. Again Bernini has accomplished his *concetto* in these colonnades, whose motherly arms, like those of the Church itself, as he himself put it, 'embrace Catholics to confirm their belief, heretics to reunite them to the Church and agnostics to enlighten them with the true faith'.

It is in this huge forum that the Roman crowds gather to watch for the white smoke to issue from the chimney of the Sistine Chapel, and to await, first, the appearance of the senior Cardinal Deacon – who addresses them, the citizens of the Eternal City, with the words, 'I pronounce to you a great joy: we have a pope' – to be followed shortly after by the newly elected pontiff himself. And, on the most solemn feast-days of the Church, as at Easter, this immense forum is a sea of black, packed with pilgrims from every corner of the earth, and in the reverent silence a white figure in the *loggia delle benedizioni*, at the centre of Maderno's façade, the figure of the Bishop of Rome and supreme Head of the Catholic Church, lifts up his hands to pronounce his paternal blessing, 'Urbi et Orbi' – on the City and on the World.

PAGE 256 In the narthex of St Peter's, on the right, stands the spirited equestrian statue of the *Emperor Constantine* (1670) by Bernini.

PAGE 258 The majestic dome of St Peter's seen through the Doric columns of Bernini's colonnade in St Peter's Square.

PAGE 259 St. Peter's. The nineteenth-century statue of *St Peter* by Giuseppe De Fabris (1790–1860) seen under snow against Carlo Maderno's façade (1614) of St Peter's.

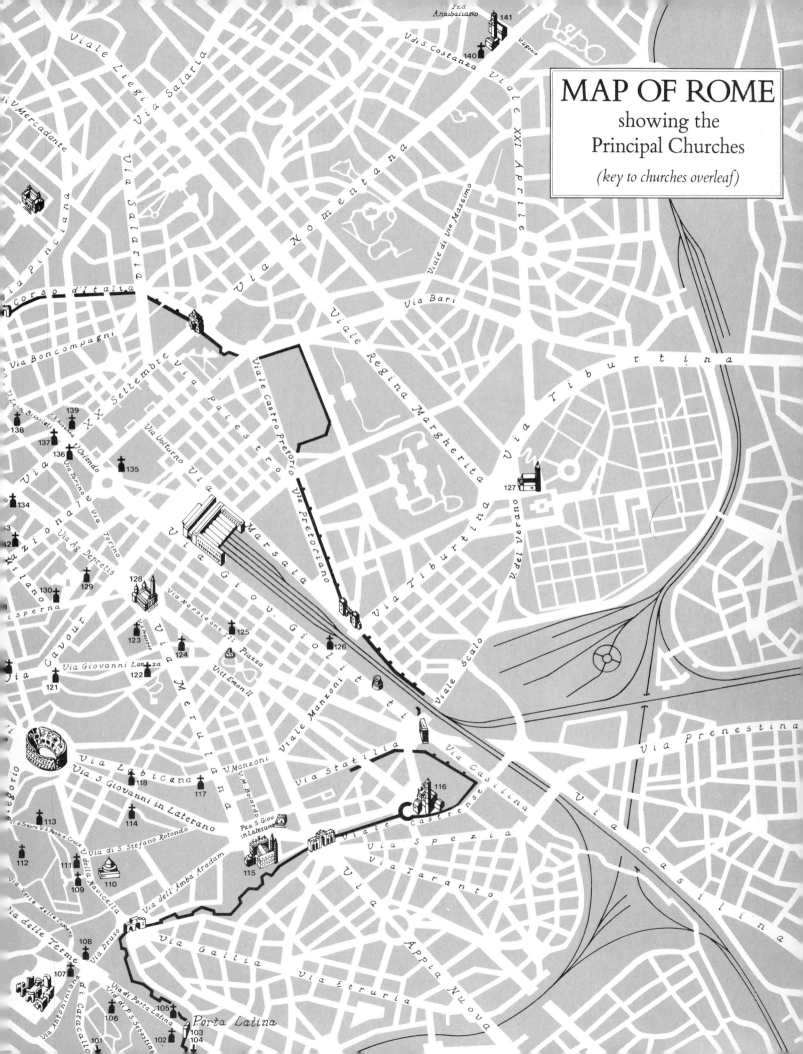

MAP OF ROME
showing the
Principal Churches
(key to churches overleaf)

Key to Churches shown on the Map of Rome

Gazetteer of the Principal Churches in Rome

The asterisks serve as a rough indication of a church's artistic or historical interest. The photographs in this section, showing churches in Rome in the early twentieth century, come from Fratelli Alinari in Rome.

S. AGATA DEI GOTI* Of ancient origin; Arian church during Gothic occupation (6th cent.); reconsecrated by Gregory the Great (593). Cosmati *baldacchino* (12th–13th cents). Externally, remains of ancient buildings.

S. AGNESE IN AGONE or S. AGNESE IN PIAZZA NAVONA** Trad. site of brothel in which St Agatha was exposed. Begun by G. and C. Rainaldi (1652); completed by F. Borromini (1657). Rich Baroque interior; paintings by C. Ferri, S. Corbellini, Baciccia; bas-reliefs and statuary by G. F. Rossi, E. Ferrata, D. Guidi, E. A. Raggi, P. P. Campi; monument to Innocent X (G. B. Maini, 1730); in crypt, Roman remains of Circus of Domitian, mediaeval frescoes, relief by A. Algardi (*c.* 1653).

S. AGNESE FUORI LE MURA** Founded in 324 by Constantia (Costanza, daughter or niece of Constantine) above tomb of the saint; rebuilt by Honorius I (*c.* 625); restored by Adrian I (772), lastly by Pius IX (1855). Apse mosaics (7th cent.); statue of St Agnes (antique torso, additions in gilded bronze by N. Cordier, 1610); Roman candelabrum; altar diptych attrib. to A. Bregno; bust of Christ attrib. to N. Cordier.

S. AGOSTINO*** Built by G. di Pietrasanta (1479). Paintings by Raphael, Caravaggio, Guercino, G. Lanfranco etc.; Byzant. Madonna; high altar by G. L. Bernini; sculpture by A. and J. Sansovino, Isaia da Pisa, L. Capponi etc.

S. ALESSIO: see SS. BONIFACIO E ALESSIO.

SS. AMBROGIO E CARLO AL CORSO: see S. CARLO AL CORSO.

S. ANASTASIA Fourth-cent. *titulus*, built over ruins of 1st cent. AD (can be visited); church mainly 18th cent.; façade by L. Arrigucci; interior by C. Gimacchi, 1722.

S. ANDREA DELLE FRATTE** Existing 12th cent.; in 15th cent. national church of Scots; rebuilt 1612 by G. Guerra, continued by F. Borromini (exterior, drum and campanile). Angels by G. L. Bernini.

S. ANDREA AL QUIRINALE*** By G. L. Bernini (1658). Sculpture by E. A. Raggi; in adjoining monastery sculpture by P. Legros.

S. ANDREA, TEMPIETTO DI* By Vignola (1554).

S. ANDREA DELLA VALLE** Designed by G. F. Grimaldi and G. Della Porta (1591); resumed by C. Maderno (1608); cupola (Maderno, 1622); façade (C. Rainaldi, 1655). Angel on façade (E. Ferrata, 17th cent.); Piccolomini tombs (of Pius II, by school of A. Bregno, *c.* 1470; of Pius III by F. and S. Ferrucci, early 16th cent.); paintings by Domenichino, G. Lanfranco, M. Preti etc.; sculpture by E. A. Raggi, D. Guidi, F. Mochi, P. Bernini; stucco-work by A. Algardi.

S. ANGELO IN PESCHERIA* Founded (770) inside remains of Portico of Octavia (146 BC) and of an ancient fishmarket. *Madonna* (B. Gozzoli or school of). From here in 1347 Cola di Rienzo occupied the Capitol to restore Roman Republic.

S. ANSELMO Church of International Benedictine Seminary; built (1893–1900) by Abate I. de Hemptime.

S. ANTONIO DEI PORTOGHESI National church of the Portuguese. Founded 17th cent.; by M. Longhi the Younger, C. Rainaldi and others. *Madonna with Child* by Antoniazzo Romano; monument by A. Canova (1806).

SS. APOSTOLI** Founded 6th cent.; many times restored, almost rebuilt by F. and C. Fontana (1702–14); portico by B. Pontelli (end. 15th cent.) and C. Rainaldi, who added balustrade and figures of Christ and Apostles (1681). Imperial eagle (2nd cent.) with lion (P. Vassallettus, 13th cent.); sculpture by A. Bregno, L. Capponi, Mino da Fiesole, A. Canova etc.; paintings by Baciccia, S. Ricci, D. Muratori.

S. ATANASIO Greek-Catholic church. By G. Della Porta (1580).

S. BALBINA** Built (4th cent.) on house of consul

L. Fabius Cilone, mentioned 595, restored 1929. Roman paving; tomb of Card. S. Surdi (Giov. di Cosma, 1303); Cosmati episcopal throne, choir, candelabra; 13th-cent. frescoes; 14th-cent. altar; bas-relief by Mino del Reame.

S. BARTOLOMEO DE INSULA* Built on an island in the Tiber at the end 10th cent. for Emp. Otto on ruins of Temple of Aesculapius; many times restored, chiefly 1624 by O. Torriani after a serious flood and again 1852. Marble well (Nicola d'Angelo or P. Vassallettus?); porphyry urn; sculpture from earlier churches; paintings by Ant. Carracci.

S. BENEDETTO IN PISCINULA** Memories of St Benedict; sanctuary of St Benedict; Cosmatesque paving; paintings of 14th, 15th, 16th cents; Romanesque campanile.

S. BERNARDO ALLE TERME Rotunda of Baths of Diocletian converted end 16th cent. for Contessa Caterina Sforza. Stuccos (Cam. Mariani, c. 1600); sculpture by R. Rinaldi.

S. BIBIANA** Founded 5th cent., restored 1220, rebuilt by G. L. Bernini (1624). Frescoes by Pietro da Cortona and A. Ciampelli; high altar, with statue of S. Bibiana by Bernini (1626).

SS. BONIFACIO E ALESSIO* Dedicated first (before 10th cent.) to S. Bonifacio, then (1217) to S. Alessio; rebuilt (1750) by T. De Marchis. Romanesque campanile; Byzant. *Madonna*; Cosmati work; Romanesque crypt; frescoes (12th or 13th cent.); relics of S. Alessio; 15th-cent. cloister.

S. CARLO AI CATINARI** Interior and cupola (1612–20) by R. Rosati; façade (1635) by G. B. Soria; Chapel of S. Cecilia by A. Gherardi (1692). Paintings by M. Preti, Pietro da Cortona, G. Lanfranco, G. Reni, A. Sacchi, Domenichino; crucifix by A. Algardi.

S. CARLO AL CORSO or SS. AMBROGIO E CARLO AL CORSO** Begun 1612 by O. Longhi and M. Longhi the Younger; façade by G. B. Menicucci and Fra M. da Canepina; dome by Pietro da Cortona (1668). Rich decoration; relics of S. Carlo Borromeo; paintings by C. Maratta, G. Brandi and A. Borgognone; Chapel of S. Ambrogio (1513).

S. CARLO ALLE QUATTRO FONTANE or S. CARLINO*** Begun by F. Borromini 1638; cloister also by Borromini (1634). On façade statue, *St Charles praying*, by E. A. Raggi; painting by P. Mignard.

S. CATERINA DEI FUNARI* Erected 12th cent.; rebuilt 1560; façade by G. Guidetti (1564); campanile. Paintings by Ann. Carracci (?), G. Muziano, F. Zuccari.

S. CECILIA IN TRASTEVERE*** Founded before 5th cent. above Roman house; rebuilt for Paschal I (c. 820); added to in 12th cent.; many times restored, especially in the 18th cent. by F. Fuga. Monumental entrance by Fuga (1725). Roman *cantharus* in forecourt; campanile (1113). *Baldacchino* (1283) by Arnolfo di Cambio; sculpture by Mino da Fiesole, Paolo Romano, L. Lotti, C. Aureli, E. Quattrini, S. Maderno etc.; paintings by Antonio da Viterbo (?), school of B. Pinturicchio, S. Conca, G. Reni etc.; Roman *calidarium*; crypt with Roman remains; in adjoining convent (visits Tues. and Thurs. 10 am, Sun. 11 am) *Universal Judgement* by P. Cavallini (1293).

S. CESAREO* Erected on 2nd-cent. Roman site; rebuilt end 16th cent. (by G. Della Porta?). Ceiling (Clement VIII, c. 1600); Cosmatesque pulpit, episcopal throne, frontal; mosaic and frescoes by Cav. d'Arpino (17th cent.); *Madonna and Child* (15th cent.).

S. CHIARA Built for S. Carlo Borromeo (1565) by Francesco da Volterra; façade by C. Maderno.

CHIESA NUOVA: see S. MARIA IN VALLICELLA.

S. CLEMENTE*** Lower church founded before 385 on Roman buildings, destroyed by Robert Guiscard (1084); upper church built for Paschal II (1108), restored by C. S. Fontana (1715). Upper church: 18th-cent. ceiling with fresco by G. Chiari; Cosmati pavement, choir, *baldacchino*, *ambones*, candelabrum; choir screen, with monogram 'Johannes' (Pope John II, 532–5), parts from lower church; 12th-cent. apse mosaic, *Triumph of the Cross*; 14th-cent. fresco, *Jesus, Mary and Twelve Apostles*; Gothic tabernacle (1299); Chapel of St Catherine, with frescoes by Masolino (c. 1431); paintings by S. Conca etc.; sculpture by L. Capponi, G. Dalmata, S. Ghini, school of Isaia da Pisa etc. Lower church: in vestibule frescoes relating to life of St Clement (11th–12th cents); in nave frescoes (9th–12th cents); in r. aisle Roman sarcophagus (1st cent.); frescoes (8th–10th cents). Crypt: Roman buildings; *Mithraeum* (2nd cent.).

S. COSIMATO IN TRASTEVERE* Ancient portal; Romanesque (11th–12th cents) and Renaissance (15th cent.) cloisters; 10th-cent. church, rebuilt 1475. *Madonna and Saints* by Antonio da Viterbo (15th cent.).

SS. COSMA E DAMIANO*** Founded by Felix
IV (527) in Roman buildings; altered by L. Arrigucci
(1632). Sixth-cent. apse mosaics; 13th-cent. *Madonna of
St Gregory* and *Christ on the Cross*; Neapolitan crib
(18th cent.); crypt.

S. COSTANZA*** Mausoleum of Constantine's
daughters and nieces; later baptistery; lastly (1254)
church. Fourth-cent. mosaics.

Eighteenth-century engraving of S. Crisogono.

S. CRISOGONO* Titulus Chrysogoni (crypt on
Roman buildings); church earlier than 499; rebuilt
by G. B. Soria (1626). Eleventh-cent. frescoes;
Romanesque campanile (1124); mosaic *Madonna
with Child* (school of P. Cavallini?).

Eighteenth-century engraving of S. Croce in Gerusalemme.

S. CROCE IN GERUSALEMME (BASILICA
SESSORIANA)*** Attrib. to Constantine
(*c.* 320); built in Sessorian Palace; restored by Lucius II
(for whom campanile was built, 1144); rebuilt for
Benedict XIV by Dom. Gregorini and P. Passalacqua
(1743). Renaissance holy water stoups (late 15th cent.);
Cosmatesque pavement; ceiling fresco, *St Helena ascends
into Heaven* (C. Giaquinto, 1744); tomb of Card. Fr.
Quiñones by J. Sansovino (1536); frescoes attrib. to
Antoniazzo Romano (*c.* 1492); paintings by
C. Maratta, Giaquinto etc.; in Chapel of St Helena
mosaic probably designed by Melozzo da Forlì (before
1484) and Roman statue transformed into likeness of St
Helena; in Gregorian Chapel (1523) *Pietà* by unknown
artist (beginning 17th cent.) and statuettes of St Peter
and St Paul (French, 14th cent.); Chapel of the Relics,

with pieces of the True Cross and thorns from Christ's
Crown; sacristy; library.

SS. DOMENICO E SISTO** Built on site of earlier
church by G. Della Porta, N. and O. Torriani and
V. Della Greca (1575–1655); steps attrib. to
O. Torriani. Rich interior; ceiling by D. M. Canuti and
E. Haffner (1674); in Alaleona Chapel (G. L. Bernini)
statuary by E. A. Raggi (*c.* 1649); polychrome terracotta
Madonna and Child (Florentine, 15th cent.); paintings
by B. Gozzoli (attrib.), F. Mola, F. Allegrini,
G. F. Romanelli etc.

DOMINE QUO VADIS ? Before 9th cent.; rebuilt
17th cent.; façade 1637.

S. ELIGIO DEGLI OREFICI* Built 1516 to design
by Raphael, restored 1962; façade by F. Ponzio (1602).
Paintings by Matteo da Lecce, G. F. Romanelli,
T. Zuccari, G. De Vecchi.

S. EUSEBIO One of oldest *tituli* (4th cent.?); rebuilt
1230 and 1711 (C. S. Fontana); Romanesque
campanile. Altar by M. Longhi; painting by R. Mengs;
16th-cent. choir stalls.

Eighteenth-century engraving of S. Eustachio.

S. EUSTACHIO Trad. Constantinian foundation;
rebuilt 12th cent. and by A. Canevari (1724);
campanile (1196). High altar (N. Salvi, 1739);
baldacchino (F. Fuga, 1746).

FILIPPINI, ORATORIO DEI Begun 1640 by
F. Borromini.

S. FRANCESCA ROMANA or S. MARIA
NOVA* Origin 10th-cent.; many times rebuilt;
façade by C. Lambardi (1615); 12th-cent. campanile.
Cosmatesque paving; sculpture by Mino del Reame,
Paolo Romano, P. P. Olivieri, G. L. Bernini etc.;
mosaics (12th cent.); paintings include *Madonna del
Conforto* (5th cent.), *Madonna and Child* (12th cent.);
memorial (1952) on tomb of Gentile da Fabriano
(d. 1428); crypt (relics of saint).

S. FRANCESCO A RIPA* Built (1231) over chapel
of hospice where St Francis of Assisi stayed (1210);
rebuilt by M. De Rossi (1682). *B. Ludovica Albertoni* by
G. L. Bernini (1674); sculpture by E. Ferrata, D. Guidi,
C. Rusconi, G. Mazzuoli; paintings by S. Vouet,
Baciccia, F. Salviati, D. M. Muratori.

The façade of Il Gesù in the early twentieth century.

GESÙ, IL*** Designed by Vignola (1568); façade
(1575) and cupola by G. Della Porta. Paintings on
nave ceiling – *Triumph of the Name of Jesus* (stucco
angels by E. A. Raggi), as well as the cupola and
tribune by Baciccia (1672–85); Chapel of St Ignatius
of Loyola (A. Pozzo, 1696); altar of St Francis
Xavier (Pietro da Cortona, 1674); Chapel of S. Maria
degli Astalli, with venerated *Madonna of the Street*
(*c.* 1400); sculpture by G. L. Bernini, P. Legros,
B. Ludovisi, L. Ottoni, G. Théodon, C. Rusconi etc.;
paintings by C. Maratta, G. A. Carlone, B. Croce,
P. Batoni, G. B. Pozzi, P. F. Mola, G. Valeriani,
F. Bassano, Pomerancio etc.

GESÙ E MARIA or GESÙ E MARIA AL
CORSO* By C. Rainaldi (1670). Theatrical Baroque
monument to Bolognetti family (*c.* 1675); sculpture by
E. Ferrata, D. Guidi, G. Mazzuoli etc.; rich decoration;
paintings by G. Brandi.

S. GIACOMO IN AUGUSTA or DEGLI
INCURABILI Rebuilt end 16th cent. by Francesco
da Volterra and completed by C. Maderno (1600).
High relief by P. Legros the Younger (*c.* 1700);
Madonna dei Miracoli (15th cent.).

S. GIACOMO DEGLI SPAGNUOLI or
NOSTRA SIGNORA DEL SACRO
CUORE Rebuilt for Jubilee of 1450; restored in 16th
cent. by A. Sangallo the Younger; abandoned early
19th cent.; restored by L. Carimini and reopened 1879.
Angels on façade by Mino del Reame (r.) and
P. Taccone (l.); Renaissance *cantoria* by P. Torrignani;
sculpture by C. Rosselli; frescoes by B. Croce.

S. Giorgio in Velabro and the Arch of Janus Quadrifrons.

S. GIORGIO IN VELABRO** Earlier (6th cent.?)
church rebuilt for Leo II (682–3); many times restored,
lastly in 1926; 12th-cent. campanile and portico.
Cosmatesque *baldacchino*; apse fresco, *Madonna enthroned
with Saints*, attrib. to P. Cavallini (late 13th cent.); small
marble altar of period of Gregory VII (11th cent.).

S. GIOVANNI DECOLLATO** Built end 15th
cent. Rich decoration (1580–90); cloister; oratory;
Mannerist paintings by F. Zucchi, Pomerancio,
G. Vasari, G. B. Naldini, Jacopino del Conte,
F. Salviati, Jacopino, P. Ligorio, B. Franco etc.
Museum relating to capital punishment.

S. GIOVANNI DEI FIORENTINI** Begun for
Leo X (early 16th cent.) by J. Sansovino; continued by
A. Sangallo the Younger (1520), G. Della Porta (1583)
and C. Maderno (1620); façade by A. Galilei (1734).
Presbytery by Pietro da Cortona; high altar by
F. Borromini; Falconieri Chapel (in crypt) by
Borromini; tombs of C. Maderno and Borromini;
sculpture by P. Bernini, G. L. Bernini, A. Algardi,
Mino del Reame, F. Valle, E. A. Raggi, E. Ferrata,
D. Guidi, M. Slodtz; paintings by Passignano, S. Rosa,
G. B. Naldini; bronze crucifix by Prospero da Brescia
(16th cent.).

The Porta S. Giovanni in the early twentieth century. Above the walls the giant statues surmounting the façade of S. Giovanni in Laterano can be seen.

S. GIOVANNI IN FONTE*** Lateran baptistery erected for Constantine; rebuilt for Sixtus III (5th cent.) and Urban VIII (1637). In Chapel of St John the Baptist (461) ancient bronze doors; Chapel of SS. Rufina e Secunda, with 5th-cent. mosaics; Chapel of S. Venanzio (c. 642), with 7th-cent. mosaics; Chapel of St John the Evangelist (5th cent.), with bronze doors (1196) by Uberto and Pietro da Piacenza and 5th-cent. mosaics.

S. GIOVANNI DEI GENOVESI* Erected 1481, rebuilt 1864. On l., in the Ospizio dei Genovesi, entrance to Renaissance cloister by B. Pontelli (15th cent.).

S. GIOVANNI IN LATERANO*** The cathedral of Rome, founded by Constantine, many times destroyed and rebuilt radically by F. Borromini under Innocent X for Jubilee of 1650; façade and portico by A. Galilei (1735). Bronze doors from Roman Curia; ancient statue of Constantine; reliefs of *Life of the Baptist* by F. Valle, B. Ludovisi, G. B. Maini and P. Bracci. Interior: ceiling attrib. to P. Ligorio (1562); pavement of Cosmati type laid for Martin V (Colonna); above niches with statues of Twelve Apostles, reliefs of *Scenes from the Old and New Testaments* in stucco, designed by A. Algardi (1650); many tombs and monuments recomposed and enframed by Borromini; fresco, *Boniface VIII Proclaiming the Jubilee of 1300*, attrib. to Giotto; recumbent statue of Riccardo degli Annibaldi by A. di Cambio; Corsini Chapel by A. Galilei (1732); Gothic *baldacchino* by Giovanni di Stefano (1367); tomb of Martin V by S. Ghini (c. 1443); apse mosaics by J. Torriti and J. da Camerino (c. 1290); Colonna Chapel by G. Rainaldi (1625). In old sacristy, *Annunciation* by M. Venusti from design by Michelangelo (1555). In new sacristy, altar with *Annunciation* of Tuscan school (15th cent.). Cloister by the Vassalletti, father and son (1215–32); remains of sculpture by A. di Cambio and Deodatus (late 13th cent.); 9th-cent. well.

S. GIOVANNI IN OLEO** Oratory built by French prelate Benôit Adam (1509), attrib. to Bramante; interior transformed by F. Borromini (1658); stucco and frescoes by L. Baldi (17th cent.).

SS. GIOVANNI E PAOLO*** Ancient *titulus* built over Roman house of John and Paul, martyred 362; many times rebuilt; 12th-cent. monastery, campanile and portico; interior restored 1715. Chapel of St Paul of the Cross (19th cent.); Byzant. fresco *Christ Enthroned between Six Apostles* (1255); high altar with ancient porphyry urn containing remains of titular saints; beneath church remains of Roman house on 2 floors, Christian dwelling and oratory; Roman and mediaeval frescoes; mediaeval oratory; *confessio*; well (burial place of John and Paul).

S. GIOVANNI A PORTA LATINA** Built end 5th cent.; rebuilt 772; restored many times, the last recently. Twelfth-cent. frescoes, *Scenes from the Old and New Testaments*, and, in apse, *Symbols of the Four Evangelists* and *Twenty-four Elders of the Apocalypse*; paving in *opus sectile*.

S. GIROLAMO DEGLI ILLIRICI or **DEGLI SCHIAVONI** National church of the Yugoslavs. By M. Longhi the Elder (1588). *Deeds of St Girolamo* (A. Viviani and A. Lilio, 1588); bust of Pius XII by I. Mestrovič (1945).

S. GIUSEPPE DEI FALEGNAMI* By G. B. Montano (1598). Paintings by A. Viviani, M. T. Montagna etc.; below, the Chapel of the Crucifix (16th cent.); lower still, the Mamertine Prison or Chapel of S. Pietro in Carcere.

S. GREGORIO MAGNO** In 575 St Gregory converted his palace into a monastery with an oratory dedicated to St Andrew; the latter converted in Middle Ages into a church; steps, façade and forecourt rebuilt by G. B. Soria (1629), church by F. Ferrari (1725). Tombs of R. Peckham and E. Carne (16th cent.); monument to Bonsi brothers by L. Capponi (*c.* 1500); altar of St Gregory, with bas-reliefs by L. Capponi and predella of Umbrian school (*c.* 1500); St Gregory's room, with his episcopal chair; Salviati Chapel (Francesco da Volterra and C. Maderno, *c.* 1600); altar (A. Bregno, 1469). Adjoining, Chapels of St Andrew, St Sylvia (mother of St Gregory) and St Barbara by Flam. Ponzio (beginning 17th cent.); paintings by Domenichino, G. Reni, A. Viviani.

S. IGNAZIO DI LOYOLA*** Built (1626–50) by Fr. O. Grassi. Rich decoration; nave vault painting and dome in *trompe d'oeil* by A. Pozzo (*c.* 1685); altar (A. Pozzo) with high relief (P. Legros, 1698) and angels (B. Ludovisi); monument to Gregory XV (Grassi) with figures by Legros and S. Monnot (*c.* 1698); statues by A. Algardi, P. Bracci, C. Rusconi, F. Valle; paintings by F. Trevisani, L. Garzi; altar and room of S. Luigi Gonzaga.

S. ILDEFONSO E TOMMASO DA VILLANOVA Baroque. *Nativity*, high relief by F. Grassia (17th cent.).

S. ISIDORO* National church of the Irish. Arch. A. Casoni (1622); stairway and portico by D. Castelli;

Boniface VIII Proclaiming the Jubilee of 1300, attrib. to Giotto, in S. Giovanni in Laterano

façade by C. F. Bizzaccheri (1705). Chapel by G. L. Bernini; portraits by P. Bernini; paintings by C. Maratta and A. Sacchi; two cloisters; in Aula Maxima frescoes by Fra Emanuele da Como.

S. IVO ALLA SAPIENZA*** By F. Borromini (1642–60). Painting by Pietro da Cortona.

S. LORENZO IN DAMASO* Erected for Pope Damasus (380); rebuilt by Bramante (*c.* 1500) within Palazzo Cancelleria; restored by G. Valadier and V. Vespignani (19th cent.). Rich decoration; crucifix (14th cent.); Renaissance tomb of L. Scarampi, attrib. to P. Taccone (15th cent.); tomb of A. Caro by G. A. Dosio (16th cent.); statue by S. Maderno (17th cent.); paintings by C. Giaquinto, S. Conca, F. Zuccari.

S. Lorenzo fuori le Mura in the early twentieth century.

S. LORENZO FUORI LE MURA*** Formed by joining two churches: S. Lorenzo, erected for Constantine (330) on martyr's grave, and the Chiesa della Virgine, erected for Sixtus III (*c.* 432); Vassallettus built a portico and modified the edifice (1220); restored by V. Vespignani (1864). Sarcophagi (5th? and 7th cents); *Lives of St Lawrence and St Stephen* (12th–13th-cent. fresco); monument to A. De Gasperi by G. Manzù; Cosmati *ambones*, paschal candelabrum, *baldacchino* (1148), paving, episcopal throne and screen; tomb of Card. Fieschi (13th cent.); Crypt of the Confession; Chapel of St Cyriaca, with tombs designed by Pietro da Cortona, busts by F. Duquesnoy (*c.* 1629); mosaics (6th cent.); Funeral Chapel of Pius IX, with mosaics by L. Seitz; Romanesque cloister (12th cent.); campanile (12th cent.).

S. LORENZO IN LUCINA** Erected 4th or 5th cent. on site of house of the matron Lucina; rebuilt for Paschal II (*c.* 1100), who added portico and campanile; restored by C. Fanzago (*c.* 1650). Romanesque lions; St Lawrence's gridiron; Chateaubriand's monument to N. Poussin (bust, P. Lemoyne, 1829; relief, L. Desprez, 1830); chapel by G. L. Bernini, with busts of Fonseca family (1668); high altar by C. Rainaldi (1675), with G. Reni's *Cross*; Paschal II's episcopal throne; paintings by S. Vouet, C. Saraceni.

S. LORENZO IN MIRANDA Built in 2nd-cent. Temple of Antoninus and Faustina; rebuilt by O. Torriani (1602).

S. LORENZO IN PANISPERNA Erected on trad. spot of St Lawrence's martyrdom (258); several times rebuilt, lastly (1575) by Francesco da Volterra(?); *Martyrdom of St Lawrence* by P. Cati (*c.* 1600).

SS. LUCA E MARTINA*** Lower church erected (6th cent.) on Roman ruins, dedicated to S. Martina; seat of Academy of St Luke; upper church by Pietro da Cortona (1634). Stuccos of cupola by F. Valle (*c.* 1750); recumbent figure of S. Martina by N. Menchini (17th cent.); painting by S. Conca (1680). Lower church: monuments to G. B. Soria and Pietro da Cortona; *Pietà* by A. Algardi; in crypt, altar by Pietro da Cortona; terracotta group by Algardi.

S. LUIGI DEI FRANCESI*** National church of the French. Founded 1518 by Card. Giulio de' Medici (later Clement VII), arch. unknown; Late Renaissance façade attrib. to G. Della Porta. Façade statues by P. Lestache (1758); rich decoration; stuccos by A. Dérizet (1756); nave ceiling fresco by C.-J. Natoire (1756); *Scenes from the Life of St Cecilia* by Domenichino (1616); *St Cecilia*, copy of Raphael's painting by G. Reni; Caravaggio's *St Matthew* paintings (1597–1602); monuments to Mme de Montmorin (erected by Chateaubriand) and Claude Lorrain (P. Lemoyne, 1836).

MADDALENA, LA* Erected early 15th cent.; rebuilt by C. Fontana and others; Rococo façade by G. Sardi (1735). Baroque-Rococo decoration – particularly organ and sacristy; paintings by S. Conca, L. Giordano, Baciccia etc.

MADONNA DEI MONTI, LA** By G. Della Porta (1580). Rich decoration in stucco and fresco by C. Casolini and others (*c.* 1620); *Madonna and Child with Saints* (14th cent.); tomb of St Joseph Labre.

SS. MARCELLINO E PIETRO Fourth-cent. foundation; rebuilt by B. Theodoli (1751).

S. MARCELLO AL CORSO* Early 4th-cent. foundation; arch. J. Sansovino (1519); façade by C. Fontana (1682). Angels and bas-relief by E. A. Raggi; *Madonna with Child* (unknown 15th-cent. artist); paintings by Pierino del Vaga, Daniele da Volterra, P. Tibaldi, G. B. Ricci, F. Salviati, A. van Dyck(?), F. and T. Zuccari; sculpture by A. and J. Sansovino, B. Cametti, L. Stoldo, A. Algardi etc.

Eighteenth-century engraving of S. Marco.

S. MARCO** Founded 336; many times rebuilt, especially by Card. P. Barbo (1455). In Renaissance portico tombstone of Vannozza Cattanei; rich decoration by F. Barigioni (18th cent.); paintings by Palma the Younger, Melozzo da Forlì; sculpture by Isaia da Pisa, Mino da Fiesole, G. Dalmata, A. Canova; mosaics (*c.* 830).

S. MARIA DEGLI ANGELI** Built in *tepidarium* of Baths of Diocletian by Michelangelo (1564); altered by Vanvitelli (1749). Tomb of Salvator Rosa, with bust by B. Fioriti; *St Bruno* by J. A. Houdon; paintings by school of Daniele da Volterra, F. Trevisani,

G. Muziano, P. Batoni, Domenichino, C. Maratta etc.

S. MARIA DELL' ANIMA** National church of the Germans. Erected *c.* 1500; façade by G. Sangallo. *Holy Family and Saints* (Giulio Romano, 1522); monument to Adrian VI (arch. B. Peruzzi; figures by Michelangelo Senese and N. P. Tribolo); *St Anna, Madonna and Child* (wood carving of 15th-cent. German school); monument to F. van den Eyden by F. Duquesnoy (17th cent.); *Pietà* by Lorenzetto and Nanni di Baccio Bigio (1532).

S. MARIA ANTIQUA*** Built in Roman building of Imperial period; restored and decorated 8th cent.; in 13th cent. another church erected in building abandoned after an earthquake (847); this demolished and original church restored (1902). Important 8th-cent. frescoes; pagan and Christian sarcophagi; Roman remains.

S. MARIA IN AQUIRO By Francesco da Volterra (1590); restored 1856. Painting by C. Saraceni.

S. MARIA D'ARACOELI*** Existing 7th cent.; in 10th cent. Benedictine abbey, passing in 1250 to Franciscans. Cosmatesque paving (13th cent.); rich ceiling commemorating victory of Lepanto (1571); monument to Card. d'Albret by A. Bregno; tombstone of G. Crivelli by Donatello; Bufalini Chapel, with paintings by B. Pinturicchio (*c.* 1486); *ambones* by Laur. and Giac. Cosma (*c.* 1200 but reconstructed); Savelli Chapel, with fine tombs; *Madonna d'Aracoeli* (10th cent.) over high altar; Chapel of St Helena, with relics; monument to Card. M. d'Acquasparta, attrib. to Giov. di Cosma, fresco by P. Cavallini; Chapel of Holy Child (*Santo Bambino*); monument to F. Della Valle by unknown sculptor (*c.* 1500); Cesarini Chapel, with painting by B. Gozzoli (*c.* 1449); Chapel of the Crib.

S. MARIA IN CAMPITELLI** By C. Rainaldi (1663–7). *Madonna in Portico* (11th-cent. enamel); paintings by S. Conca, L. Giordano, Baciccia; baptistery with two 15th-cent. tabernacles.

S. MARIA IN CAPPELLA Consecrated 1090; restored 1875; Romanesque campanile.

S. MARIA DELLA CONCEZIONE (known as I CAPPUCCINI)** By A. Casoni (*c.* 1626). *St Michael* by G. Reni; paintings by Pietro da Cortona, Caravaggio, G. Lanfranco, A. Sacchi, Domenichino, Umbrian school (14th cent.); tombstone of A. Barberini ('here lie dust, ashes and nothing'); sacristy; ossuary in crypt chapels.

S. MARIA IN COSMEDIN*** Built 6th cent. on
Roman building; enlarged for Adrian I (8th cent.);
restored for Calixtus II (1119–24), when portico and
campanile were built. Monument to Alphanus (12th
cent.); stone disc – *Bocca della Verità*; Cosmati work of
11th–13th cents: paving, paschal candelabrum,
episcopal throne, *iconostasis*, *baldacchino* (1294, by
Deodatus, son of Cosmas the Younger); remains of
11th-cent. fresco; *Madonna and Child* (Roman school,
15th cent.); sacristy, with mosaic (706) from Old St
Peter's; crypt.

S. MARIA IN DOMNICA** Founded perhaps 7th
cent.; rebuilt for Paschal I (817–24); restored for Card.
Giovanni de' Medici (1513) and in 1820; portico by
A. Sansovino (1513). Ceiling by Pierino del Vaga from
design of Giulio Romano (1566); mosaic of Paschal I;
painting by L. Baldi (17th cent.).

S. MARIA DI LORETO* Built 1501; (arch. thought
to be A. Sangallo the Younger). In pediment *Madonna
with Child and Holy House* (A. Sansovino or J. Del
Duca, *c.* 1580); paintings by Pomerancio and Cav.
d'Arpino; sculpture: *S. Susanna* by F. Duquesnoy
(1630), two angels by S. Maderno (1628).

ABOVE S. Maria Maggiore in the early twentieth century.

OPPOSITE S. Maria sopra Minerva and, in front, Bernini's
elephant supporting an ancient Egyptian obelisk, in the early
twentieth century.

S. MARIA MAGGIORE*** Built for Sixtus III
(432–40); altered for Nicholas IV (*c.* 1290), Clement X
(*c.* 1670); façade by F. Fuga (1743–50); apse by
C. Rainaldi (1673). Mosaics: loggia, by F. Rusuti, 13th
cent.; nave and triumphal arch, 5th cent.; apse, by J.
Torriti (1295). Ceiling attrib. to Giuliano Sangallo
(*c.* 1498); Cosmati paving (1145); baptistery and sacristy
by F. Ponzio (1605), with bas-reliefs by Mino del
Reame (*c.* 1474); Sistine Chapel by D. Fontana (1585),
with Oratory of the Crib by A. di Cambio (*c.* 1289),
tombs of St Pius V and Sixtus V by C. Fontana,
paintings by P. Brill; tomb of Card. C. Rodriguez by
Giov. di Cosma (14th cent.); tomb of G. L. Bernini;
bas-relief by Mino del Reame; *baldacchino* by F. Fuga;
Pius IX by I. Iacometti (*c.* 1880); Pauline Chapel by
F. Ponzio (1611), with his tombs of Paul V and
Clement VIII; venerated *Madonna* (9th cent.); frescoes
by G. Reni and G. Lanfranco; Sforza Chapel by
G. Della Porta (1564), perhaps from design of
Michelangelo; tomb of F. and E. de Levis, attrib. to
G. Dalmata (*c.* 1489).

S. MARIA AD MARTYRES
(PANTHEON)*** Built (27 BC) for Agrippa;
rebuilt (AD 118–25) for Hadrian; consecrated by
Boniface IV (609). Tomb of Raphael; *Madonna del Sasso*
by Lorenzetto (*c.* 1520).

S. MARIA SOPRA MINERVA*** Built 8th cent.
on Temple of Minerva Calcidica; rebuilt 1280; altered
16th–18th cents; restored to Gothic form 19th cent.
Tomb of Diotisalvi Nerone (unknown 15th-cent.
artist); monument to Virginia Pucci Ridolfi (unknown
16th-cent. artist); Chapel of the Annunciation by
C. Maderno, with *Annunciation* by Antoniazzo Romano
(*c.* 1460); Aldobrandini Chapel, with monument to
S. Aldobrandini by G. Della Porta; tomb of Bishop G.
de Coca by A. Bregno, with *Christ between Two Angels*
by Melozzo da Forlì (15th cent.); Carafa Chapel, with
paintings by F. Lippi (1488–92); tomb of Bishop
Durand (d. 1296) by Giov. di Cosma; tomb of Card.
D. Capranica (d. 1458) by follower of A. Bregno; high
altar, with sepulchre of St Catherine of Siena, statue of
saint by Isaia da Pisa (1430); monuments to the Medici
Leo X and Clement VII, designed by A. Sangallo the
Younger (*c.* 1540); *Redeemer with his Cross* by
Michelangelo (*c.* 1520); tomb of Fra Angelico
(d. 1455); room where St Catherine of Siena died, with

painting by Antoniazzo Romano and others;
monument to Maria Raggi by G. L. Bernini (1643);
monument to G. B. Vigevano by Bernini (1617); the
Redeemer, painting attrib. to B. Pinturicchio: tomb of
F. Tornabuoni (d. 1480) by Mino da Fiesole;
monument to Card. Tebaldi by A. Bregno and
G. Dalmata (1466); cloister (16th cent.).

S. MARIA DEI MIRACOLI Begun by C. Rainaldi,
completed by G. L. Bernini with assistance of
C. Fontana (1662–75). Sculpture by E. A. Raggi.

S. MARIA DI MONSERRATO* National church
of the Spaniards. Arch. A. Sangallo the Younger
(1518); façade by Francesco da Volterra (1st storey).
S. Diego by Ann. Carracci; monument to Calixtus III
and Alexander VI (Borgia); sculpture by J. Sansovino,
L. Capponi, T. Boscoli, G. L. Bernini etc.

S. MARIA DI MONTESANTO Begun by
C. Rainaldi; completed by G. L. Bernini, with
assistance of C. Fontana (1675–9). *Virgin of Montesanto*
(end 15th cent.); paintings by C. Maratta, Baciccia etc.

S. MARIA NOVA: see S. FRANCESCA
ROMANA.

Detail of the *Assumption* (1488–92) by Filippo Lippi in S. Maria sopra Minerva.

S. MARIA DELL' ORTO**

By Guidetto Guidetti (1566); façade, attrib. to Vignola, completed by Francesco da Volterra. Rich decoration (mainly of 17th and early 18th cents); paintings by T. and F. Zuccari, C. Giaquinto, G. Baglioni etc; high altar by G. Della Porta (1598); holy water stoup (15th cent.); chapels with memorials of city guilds.

S. MARIA DELLA PACE***

Attrib. to B. Pontelli (c. 1482); octagon to cupola attrib. to Bramante; façade and portico by Pietro da Cortona (1656). *Sibyls* by Raphael (1514); *Madonna della Pace* (15th cent.); paintings by T. Viti, B. Peruzzi, C. Maratta, Sermoneta etc.; sculpture by C. Fancelli, E. Ferrata, S. Mosca, V. De Rossi, S. Maderno, Pas. da Caravaggio(?); high altar by C. Maderno (1611); Cesi Chapel by A. Sangallo the Younger (1550); 15th-cent. wooden crucifix; cloister by Bramante.

S. MARIA DEL POPOLO***

Earlier church rebuilt for Sixtus IV (1472–7), attrib. to B. Pontelli and A. Bregno; apse enlarged by Bramante; part of façade and interior decoration by G. L. Bernini (1655–60). Della Rovere Chapel, with paintings by B. Pinturicchio (c. 1485), tombs by A. Bregno (*Madonna* by Mino da Fiesole) and F. Sangallo(?). Third chapel on r.: tomb of Card. Foscari (d. 1463), by Vecchietta; paintings by school of Pinturicchio. R. transept, with altar by Bernini; sacristy, with altar by A. Bregno and 14th-cent. Sienese *Madonna*; over high altar, *Madonna del Popolo* (13th cent.?); monuments to Card. G. B. della Rovere and Card. A. Sforza by A. Sansovino (early 16th cent.); frescoes by Pinturicchio and stained glass by G. de Marcillat; Cerasi Chapel, with paintings by Caravaggio and Ann. Carracci; 15th-cent. crucifix; Mellini Chapel, with Renaissance monument for Card. P. Mellini, monument to G. Mellini and busts by A. Algardi (c. 1630); Chigi Chapel, designed, with mosaics, by Raphael (1516), frescoes by F. Salviati (16th cent.), *Birth of the Virgin* by S. del Piombo (16th cent.); bas-reliefs and *Jonah and the Whale* (1520) by Lorenzetto; *Habbakuk* and *Daniel* by Bernini; *Elijah* by Lorenzetto; tombs of the Chigi; Odescalchi monument by A. Pozzi (1771); monument to G. B. Gisleni by himself (1670).

S. MARIA DEL PRIORATO*

Church of the Sovereign Order of the Knights of Malta. Arch. G. B. Piranesi (1765). Two tombs (of Bishop Spinelli and the Grand Master R. Caracciolo) in Roman sarcophagi; monument to B. Carafa (d. 1405) by Paolo Romano; high altar, designed by Piranesi, stucco by T. Righi.

S. MARIA DELLA SCALA*

Arch. Francesco da Volterra (1592); façade by O. Mascherino. High altar and *baldacchino* by C. Rainaldi (1650); chapel designed by A. Algardi; reliefs by F. Valle and M. Slodtz; paintings by L. de la Haye, C. Saraceni etc.

S. MARIA DEI SETTE DOLORI*

By F. Borromini (c. 1650).

S. MARIA IN TRASPONTINA

By G. S. Peruzzi (1566), O. Mascherino, F. Paparelli. Paintings by Cav. d'Arpino, Pomerancio; altar and *baldacchino* by C. Fontana; ancient *Virgin* from the Holy Land; *Pietà* (terracotta, 15th cent.).

S. MARIA IN TRASTEVERE***

Founded by Pope Calixtus I (217–22); rebuilt for Innocent II (1130–43); restored 1702 (when C. Fontana added portico) and 1870; campanile (12th cent.). On façade

12th-cent. mosaics (restored by P. Cavallini?); Cosmatesque paving (1148, relaid 19th cent.); ceiling, with painting of the *Assumption*, by Domenichino (1617); apse mosaics: *Christ and the Virgin Mary* (mid-12th cent.) and, below, *Scenes from the Life of the Virgin* by P. Cavallini (*c.* 1290); *fons olei*; Cosmati paschal candelabrum and episcopal throne; wooden crucifix (early 15th cent.); tabernacle by Mino del Reame (15th cent.); monument to Card. F. Armellini, with sculpture by M. Senese (1524); Winter Choir (chapel) by Domenichino, with *Madonna della Strada Cupa* (16th cent.); Altemps tombs (16th cent.); monument to Card. P. Stefaneschi (d. 1417) by Paolo Romano; altar with Gothic tabernacle; tomb of Card. P. d'Alençon (d. 1397); Altemps Chapel by M. Longhi the Elder (1584); sacristy, with Roman mosaics; in adjoining room, *Madonna and Child* (Umbrian school, early 16th cent.).

S. MARIA IN TRIVIO Oratory traditionally founded by Belisarius (6th cent.); rebuilt by J. Del Duca (1575). Paintings by A. Gherardi; Belisarius' inscription.

S. MARIA IN VALLICELLA or CHIESA NUOVA** Begun 1575 on site of earlier church; continued by M. Longhi the Elder (*c.* 1583); façade by F. Rughesi (1605). Painting of nave ceiling, cupola and apse by Pietro da Cortona (1647–56); rich decoration of gilding and stucco by C. Fancelli and E. Ferrata;

The Glory of the Trinity by Pietro da Cortona in the cupola of S. Maria in Vallicella.

organ (18th cent.); paintings by P. P. Rubens (1606–8); Spada Chapel by C. Rainaldi, with *Madonna* by C. Maratta (1675); Chapel of St Philip Neri, with his tomb; sculpture by A. Algardi, F. Vacca, Vasoldo; paintings by G. Reni, F. Barocci, Guercino, L. Baldi, S. Pulzoni; rooms of St Philip Neri; sacristy by P. Marucelli (1629), with ceiling by Pietro da Cortona (1634) and painting by Guercino.

S. MARIA IN VIA Erected before 955; many times rebuilt; arch. Francesco da Volterra (16th cent.), on design of G. Della Porta; façade C. Rainaldi (1590). *Madonna del Pozzo* (*c.* 1256).

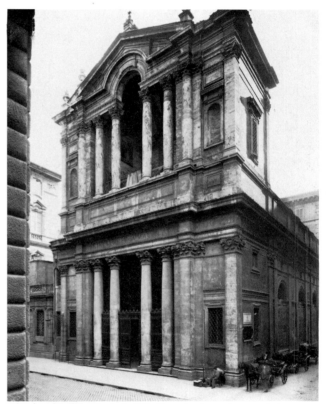

The façade of S. Maria in Via Lata in the early twentieth century.

S. MARIA IN VIA LATA* Ancient deaconate; rebuilt 11th and 15th cents; enlarged by C. Fancelli (17th cent.); façade by Pietro da Cortona (1658). Rich decoration; remains of Cosmatesque paving; on high altar (G. L. Bernini?) 13th-cent. *Virgin*; Bonaparte tombs; crypt (Roman, and remains of early church).

S. MARIA DELLA VITTORIA*** Arch. C. Maderno (1608); façade by G. B. Soria (1626). Rich Baroque decoration; paintings by Domenichino, Guercino, G. Reni etc.; *Ecstasy of St Teresa* by G. L. Bernini (1645); figures of Cornaro family by Bernini and pupils.

SS. MARTINA E LUCA: see SS. LUCA E
MARTINA.

S. MARTINO AI MONTI** Built near Pope
Silvester's (314–35) oratory in Titulus Equitii for Pope
Symmachus (c. 500); rebuilt for Sergius II (c. 845);
radically restored by Pietro da Cortona (1647–57).
Ceiling gift of Card. C. Borromeo (1560); stucco by
P. P. Naldini (c. 1655); murals by G. Poussin and
F. Gagliardi (*Old St Peter's* and pre-Borrominian
S. Giovanni in Laterano); crypt by Pietro da Cortona;
Roman remains of *titulus* etc., mosaic (6th cent.),
frescoes (9th cent.).

SS. NEREO ED ACHILLEO** Known from 337;
rebuilt for Leo III (c. 800) and in 15th cent.; restored
by Card. Baronius (1597). Byzant. mosaics (c. 800);
Cosmatesque choir, altar triptych, episcopal throne
(attrib. to school of Vassallettus, with later additions);
Renaissance *baldacchino* and paschal candelabrum (15th
cent.); pulpit, with Roman porphyry base.

Eighteenth-century engraving of S. Nicola in Carcere.

S. NICOLA IN CARCERE* Built in Roman
ruins; known in 11th cent.; rebuilt by G. Della Porta
(1599); restored 1865; mediaeval campanile, two bells
of 1286. Interior built of ancient materials; paintings by
Antoniazzo Romano, Guercino; crypt, with Roman
remains.

S. NICOLA DA TOLENTINO Erected 1599;
rebuilt by G. M. Baratta (1654–70). High altar by
A. Algardi; stucco and sculpture by Algardi, E. Ferrata
and E. A. Raggi; paintings by Baciccia, Pietro da
Cortona, C. Ferri etc.

SS. NOME DI MARIA By A. Dérizet (1736). Rich
decoration; venerated *Virgin* (possibly 18th cent.).

NOSTRA SIGNORA DEL SACRO CUORE:
see S. GIACOMO DEGLI SPAGNUOLI.

S. ONOFRIO Founded 1419. Portico, with paintings
by C. Ridolfi, Domenichino, G. Baglione(?), and
tombstone of Blessed N. da Forca Palena (15th cent.).
Interior: paintings by Antoniazzo Romano, Ag.
Carracci, B. Peruzzi (and assistants?), Domenichino,
F. Trevisani; Tasso Museum; lunette attrib. to
G. A. Boltraffio; cloister (15th cent.).

S. PANCRAZIO Founded 5th cent.; rebuilt 17th
cent.; restored 19th cent.; ceiling; stucco-work;
S. Teresa by Palma the Younger; Museum of
S. Pancrazio; catacombs.

S. PANTALEO Founded 1216; rebuilt by G. A. De
Rossi (1681); façade by G. Valadier (1806). Rich
decoration (17th cent.); paintings by F. Gherardi,
S. Ricci etc.

PANTHEON: see S. MARIA AD MARTYRES.

S. PAOLO FUORI LE MURA*** Founded by
Constantine over Apostle's grave; rebuilt by
Valentinian, Arcadius and Theodosius (386); destroyed
by fire (1823) and rebuilt; consecrated 1854; *quadriportico*
by G. Calderini (1892–1928). Ceiling of Pius IX;
triumphal arch of Galla Placidia with 5th-cent. mosaics
(restored) and, on reverse, mosaics by P. Cavallini;
baldacchino by A. di Cambio (1285); tomb of St Paul;
apse mosaics (c. 1220); mosaics outside apse by
P. Cavallini (*Madonna with Child* etc.); crucifix attrib. to
Tino di Camaino (14th cent.); paschal candelabrum by
N. di Angelo and P. Vassallettus (1180); *St Paul*,
attrib. to Antoniazzo Romano (15th cent.); Sala
Gregoriana, with mosaics (13th cent.), frescoes (15th
cent.); Chapel of Relics; art gallery; cloister by the
Vassalletti (c. 1205–c. 1214), with pagan and Christian
sculpture.

S. PAOLO ALLA REGOLA Trad. site of house
inhabited by St Paul; rebuilt by G. B. Bergonzoni (end
17th cent.); façade by G. Cioli and G. Sardi (early
18th cent.). *Madonna della Grazia* (15th-cent. icon).

S. PAOLO ALLE TRE FONTANE Fifth-cent.
church on site of martyrdom of Apostle; rebuilt by
G. Della Porta (1599). Roman mosaic paving.

S. PIETRO IN CARCERE: see S. GIUSEPPE
DEI FALEGNAMI.

S. PIETRO IN MONTORIO*** Erected before
9th cent.; rebuilt c. 1481 (attrib. to B. Pontelli) and
mid-19th cent.; façade by Meo del Caprina or follower
of A. Bregno. Del Monte Chapel by G. Vasari, Daniele

da Volterra, G. L. Bernini; paintings by S. del Piombo, N. Pomerancio, B. Peruzzi, M. Cerruti, D. van Baburen, G. Vasari, Daniele da Volterra, G. de' Vecchi etc.; sculpture by B. Ammannati, F. Baratta, A. Bolgi, N. Sale, follower of A. Bregno; body of Beatrice Cenci below altar steps. In adjoining monastery, Tempietto of S. Pietro in Montorio by Bramante (1502).

S. PIETRO IN VATICANO (or BASILICA OF ST PETER'S): see Chapter 9.

Eighteenth-century engraving of S. Pietro in Vincoli.

S. PIETRO IN VINCOLI (BASILICA EUDOSSIANA)*** Consecrated 439; restored for Adrian I (8th cent.); rebuilt for Card. G. della Rovere (Julius II) c. 1475; restored by F. Fontana (early 18th cent.). Roman remains under portico (this last by Meo del Caprina?); paintings by unknown Renaissance artist, G. B. Parodi, P. F. Mola, Guercino, Domenichino, G. Coppi; sculpture, bas-reliefs, mosaics etc; tomb of Julius II with *Moses* by Michelangelo; monument to Pollaiuolo brothers by L. Capponi; doors of gilded bronze by Caradosso (1477); chains of St Peter; palaeo-Christian sarcophagus; tomb of Nicolò da Cusa by A. Bregno.

S. PRASSEDE*** Recorded 5th cent. (Titulus Praxedis); rebuilt for Paschal I (822); many times restored. Cosmatesque paving (remade); porphyry well-cover; mosaics of triumphal and tribune arches and apse of Paschal I; palaeo-Christian urns containing bodies of S. Prassede and S. Pudenziana; Cosmati altar frontal (13th cent.); Chapel of S. Zeno, with Byzant. mosaics (9th cent.); tomb of Bishop B. Santoni (bust possibly first work of G. L. Bernini, c. 1610; tomb of Card. Alano by A. Bregno (15th cent.); tomb of Card. Anchero (d. 1286) attrib. to A. di Cambio; Olgiati Chapel by M. Longhi the Elder, with seat and table of St Charles Borromeo; trad. stone bed of S. Prassede; frescoes (9th cent.?).

S. PRISCA** Built before 5th cent. on trad. site of Roman house of Aquila and Priscilla; burnt by Robert Guiscard (1084); several times restored; façade by C. Lambardi (1660). Baptismal font (Roman adapted in 13th cent.); paintings by unknown 15th-cent. artist, A. Fontebuoni, Passignano (c. 1600), G. Odazzi; museum; remains of Roman house; crypt (9th cent.), with relics of S. Prisca; *Mithraeum* (2nd–3rd cents) with contemp. frescoes.

S. PUDENZIANA*** Erected (end 4th to beginning 5th cents) on trad. site of house of Senator Pudens, father of S. Pudenziana; rebuilt for Adrian I (772–95); many times restored, in 1589 by Francesco da Volterra; campanile (c. 1200); façade (1870), with 11th-cent. frieze. Remains of 2nd-cent. Roman baths; apse mosaics (end 4th cent.); Oratorio Mariano, with 11th-cent. frescoes; Caetani Chapel by Francesco da Volterra and C. Maderno (1601), with Caetani monuments; sculpture by G. B. Della Porta (1594), Valsoldo (17th cent.), P. P. Olivieri (c. 1599); tomb of Card. Luciano Bonaparte (1895).

SS. QUATTRO CORONATI** Built 4th cent.; enlarged 7th and 9th cents; burnt by Robert Guiscard (1084); rebuilt for Paschal II (c. 1110); restored 1914 and recently. Cosmatesque pavement; *matronea*; Renaissance tabernacle (15th cent.); frescoes (14th cent.); crypt, with martyrs' relics; cloister (12th cent.?), with *cantharus* (12th cent.); Chapel of St Barbara (9th cent.?), with mediaeval frescoes; in adjoining convent, Oratory of St Silvester, with series of frescoes, *Scenes from the Lives of the Emperor Constantine and Pope Silvester I* (1246), Cosmatesque paving.

S. ROCCO* Founded by Alexander VI (1499); rebuilt by G. A. De Rossi (1657); façade by G. Valadier (1834). Venerated *Madonna delle Grazie* (repainted 18th cent.); paintings by B. Peruzzi, Baciccia etc.

SS. RUFINA E SECONDA Romanesque campanile (c. 1100).

S. SABA** Erected 7th cent. on site of house-oratory of St Sylvia; rebuilt 1205; restored 1465 and 1943; portico (13th cent.) and loggia (15th cent.). Roman sarcophagus; doorway by Giac. Cosma (1205); Cosmatesque paving, recomposed fragments of screen and choir, episcopal throne; frescoes: *The Healing of the Paralytic* (7th cent.), a group of monks (9th–10th cents), *Madonna and Saints* (13th cent.), *Crucifixion* (14th cent.), *Annunciation* (1463); apse paintings (1575); Oratory of St Sylvia.

S. SABINA*** Built for Peter of Illyria (422–32) on Titulus Sabinae in Roman house; embellished by Eugenius II (824); given (1218) by Honorius III to St Dominic, when campanile and cloisters were added; several times restored; transformed by D. Fontana (1587); restored to early state 1914–19, 1936–8. Portico (15th cent.); cypress-wood doors (5th cent.); view of courtyard and St Dominic's orange-tree; 5th-cent. mosaics; frieze in nave arcading (5th cent.); tombstone of Muñoz de Zamora (d. 1300); restored Cosmatesque choir, *ambones*, episcopal throne; apse frescoes by T. Zuccari (1560); monument to Card. A. di Poggio (d. 1484) by follower of A. Bregno; monastery, with cloister and chapter house (13th cent.); rooms of St Thomas Aquinas.

S. SALVATORE IN LAURO** Founded 12th cent.; rebuilt *c.* 1450; destroyed by fire 1591; rebuilt by O. Mascherino (1594); completed 18th cent. by L. R. Sassi and N. Salvi; façade by C. Guglielmetti (1862). *Nativity of Jesus*, early altar-piece by Pietro da Cortona; Renaissance cloister; small Renaissance courtyard; refectory, with fresco by F. Salviati (1550); monument to Eugenius IV (*c.* 1450, from Old St Peter's), attrib. to Isaia da Pisa; monument to Maddalena Orsini (15th cent.).

S. SEBASTIANO** Erected first half 5th cent. on trad. site where bodies of St Peter and St Paul were hidden; rebuilt by F. Ponzio (1609); completed by G. Vasanzio. Ceiling, with arms of Card. Scip. Borghese; Chapel of the Relics; Chapel of St Sebastian, with statue of saint by A. Giorgetti (17th cent.); inscription of Pope Damasus (4th cent.); catacomb.

S. SEBASTIANO AL PALATINO or ALLA POLVERIERA Founded 10th cent.; restored by L. Arrigucci (1630). Tenth-cent. frescoes; epitaphs (977).

S. SILVESTRO IN CAPITE* National church of the English. Erected for Stephen II (752–7) on ruins of Temple of the Sun; rebuilt by D. De Rossi (1690). Romanesque campanile (1210); courtyard, with ancient fragments; altar and *baldacchino* by C. Rainaldi (17th cent.); paintings, largely Baroque.

S. SILVESTRO AL QUIRINALE* Known from 1030; rebuilt 16th cent.; now well above lowered street-level; façade 1877. Rich 16th-cent. decoration; pavement with Medici device, coming from the *Logge* of Raphael; *Madonna nursing Child* (13th-cent. Roman school); paintings by Domenichino, P. da Caravaggio,

Maturino; stucco by A. Algardi; hanging garden, where Michelangelo conversed with Vitt. Colonna.

S. SISTO VECCHIO Founded before 5th cent.; first Roman house of Dominicans (early 13th cent.); church and monastery restored by Fil. Raguzzini (1724); remains of more ancient church in cloister; Romanesque campanile (early 13th cent.).

S. SPIRITO IN SASSIA* Erected on site of earlier church by Ine, King of Wessex (689–726); rebuilt by A. Sangallo the Younger (*c.* 1540); façade by O. Mascherino; campanile (15th cent.). Rich decorations; paintings, mostly Mannerist.

S. STANISLAO DEI POLACCHI National church of the Poles. Founded 1580 beside hospice for Polish pilgrims; incorporated with the façade of a Baroque *palazzo* by F. Ferrari (1729–35).

S. STEFANO ROTONDO** One of the oldest round churches in Italy; consecrated by Pope Simplicius (*c.* 470); reduced by Nicholas V (1453); portico of Innocent II (12th cent.). In process of restoration. Ancient episcopal throne; Chapel of SS. Primo and Feliciano (7th-cent. mosaic); paintings (much faded) of martyrs by Pomerancio and others (*c.* 1600).

S. SUSANNA** National church of the North Americans. Erected for Leo III (795); rebuilt for Sixtus IV (1475); reduced (1595); completed with façade by C. Maderno (1603). Rich decoration; paintings by B. Croce; sculpture by Valsoldo (17th cent.) and F. Vacca(?); crypt, with remains of house of Gabirius, St Susanna's father.

S. TEODORO* Existing end 6th cent.; many times restored. Semicircular courtyard (C. Fontana, 1705); late 6th-cent. mosaics.

S. TOMMASO DI CANTERBURY From 8th cent.; rebuilt 1575 and 1869 (by G. Camporese the Younger, L. Poletti and V. Vespignani). Tombs of English prelates.

S. TOMMASO IN FORMIS Former chapel to the Hospital of the Trinitarians (destroyed). Nearby, 13th-cent. doorway by Jacobus and his son Cosmatus.

TRINITÀ DEI MONTI** Begun by Louis XII (1502); much rebuilt and restored. Stairway by Daniele Fontana (1587); *Assumption* and *Deposition* by Daniele da Volterra; paintings by Pierino del Vaga,

The beautiful façade (1603) of S. Susanna by Carlo Maderno in the early twentieth century. On the right is the façade (1626) of the neighbouring S. Maria della Vittoria by G. B. Soria.

G. B. Naldini, Nebbia, P. Nogari, T. and F. Zuccari etc.; cloister, with frescoes (*Life of S. Francesco di Paola*) by various artists; refectory, with paintings by A. Pozzo.

TRINITÀ DEGLI SCOZZESI: see S. TOMMASO DI CANTERBURY.

TRINITÀ DEGLI SPAGNUOLI By E. Rodriguez dos Santos (1741). Eighteenth-cent. decoration; painting by C. Giaquinto.

SS. VINCENZO ED ANASTASIO Built for Card. Mazarin by M. Longhi the Younger (1646–50). Formerly parochial church for nearby papal Palazzo del Quirinale; relics of popes from Sixtus V (1590) to Leo XIII (1903).

S. VITALE Founded 402 (now much below street-level); basilican form reduced for Sixtus IV (1475); restored 1859. Paintings, many by Mannerist artists (early 17th cent.).

SS. VITO E MODESTO* Founded 4th cent.(?); restored many times, lastly in 1900. Renaissance doorway (1477); *Madonna with Child and Saints* by Antoniazzo Romano (1483); stone on which martyrs suffered; at high altar *putti* by C. Rusconi (late 17th cent.).

Popes from 1417

Popes and dates of pontificates	Family name
Martin V 1417–31	Colonna
Eugenius IV 1431–47	Condulmero
Nicholas V 1447–55	Parentucelli
Calixtus III 1455–8	Borgia
Pius II 1458–64	Piccolomini
Paul II 1464–71	Barbo
Sixtus IV 1471–84	della Rovere
Innocent VIII 1484–92	Cibo
Alexander VI 1492–1503	Borgia
Pius III 1503	Todeschini-Piccolomini
Julius II 1503–13	della Rovere
Leo X 1513–21	Medici
Adrian VI 1522–3	Florensz
Clement VII 1523–34	Medici
Paul III 1534–49	Farnese
Julius III 1550–5	Ciocchi del Monte
Marcellus II 1555	Cervini
Paul IV 1555–9	Carafa
Pius IV 1559–65	Medici
Pius V 1566–72	Ghislieri
Gregory XIII 1572–85	Boncompagni
Sixtus V 1585–90	Peretti
Urban VII 1590	Castagna
Gregory XIV 1590–1	Sfondrati
Innocent IX 1591	Facchinetti
Clement VIII 1592–1605	Aldobrandini
Leo XI 1605	Medici
Paul V 1605–21	Borghese
Gregory XV 1621–3	Ludovisi
Urban VIII 1623–44	Barberini
Innocent X 1644–55	Pamphilj
Alexander VII 1655–67	Chigi
Clement IX 1667–9	Rospigliosi
Clement X 1670–6	Altieri
Innocent XI 1676–89	Odescalchi
Alexander VIII 1689–91	Ottoboni
Innocent XII 1691–1700	Pignatelli
Clement XI 1700–21	Albani
Innocent XIII 1721–4	Conti
Benedict XIII 1724–30	Orsini
Clement XII 1730–40	Corsini
Benedict XIV 1740–58	Lambertini
Clement XIII 1758–69	Rezzonico
Clement XIV 1769–74	Ganganelli
Pius VI 1775–99	Braschi
Pius VII 1800–23	Chiaramonti
Leo XII 1823–9	Sermattei della Genga
Pius VIII 1829–30	Castiglioni
Gregory XVI 1831–46	Cappellari
Pius IX 1846–78	Mastai-Ferretti
Leo XIII 1878–1903	Pecci
Pius X 1903–14	Sarto
Benedict XV 1914–22	Della Chiesa
Pius XI 1922–39	Ratti
Pius XII 1939–58	Pacelli
John XXIII 1958–63	Roncalli
Paul VI 1963–78	Montini
John Paul I 1978	Luciani
John Paul II 1978–	Wojtyla

Architects engaged on the New St Peter's

	Dates when working on St Peter's
Leon Battista Alberti (1404–72)	1452–5
Bernardo Rossellino (1409–64)	1452–5
Donato Bramante (1444–1514)	1506–14
Raphael Sanzio (1483–1520)	1514–20
Fra' Giocondo (1433–1515)	1514–15
Giuliano Sangallo (1473–1516)	*–1516
Baldassare Peruzzi (1481–1536)	1520–36
Antonio Sangallo the Younger (1483–1546)	1520–46
Michelangelo Buonarroti (1475–1564)	1547–64
Giacomo Vignola (1507–73)	1567–73
Pirro Ligorio (1510–83)	1567–83
Domenico Fontana (1543–1607)	*–1585
Giacomo Della Porta (1537–1602)	*–1602
Carlo Maderno (1556–1629)	*–1629
Gian Lorenzo Bernini (1598–1680)	1629–80

*date unknown

National Churches

AMERICAN: S. Susanna (*Episcopalian: St Paul's*)

ENGLISH: S. Silvestro in Capite (*Anglican: Ail Saints'*)

FRENCH: S. Luigi dei Francesi

GERMAN: S. Maria dell' Anima

IRISH: S. Isodoro

POLISH: S. Stanislao dei Polacchi

PORTUGUESE: S. Antonio dei Portoghesi

SPANISH: S. Maria di Monserrato

YUGOSLAVIAN: S. Girolamo degli Illirici (or degli Schiavoni)

Pilgrimage Churches

S. Giovanni in Laterano

S. Pietro in Vaticano (Basilica of St Peter's)

S. Paolo fuori le Mura

S. Maria Maggiore

S. Croce in Gerusalemme

S. Lorenzo fuori le Mura

S. Sebastiano

A Typical Early Christian Basilica
(S. Clemente, fourth century)

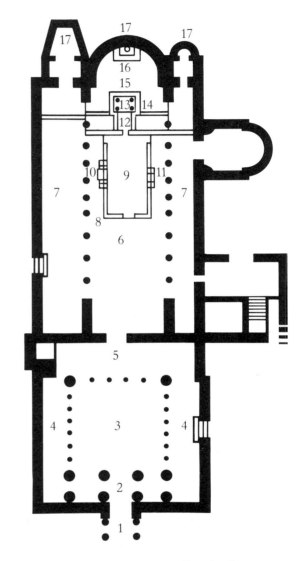

1 Porch.	10 Gospel *ambone.*
2 Portico of *atrium.*	11 Epistle *ambone.*
3 *Atrium (quadriportico).*	12 *Confessio.*
4 Colonnade of *atrium.*	13 High altar.
5 Narthex.	14 *Baldacchino (ciborio).*
6 Nave.	15 Tribune (presbytery).
7 Aisles.	16 Episcopal throne.
8 Choir screen.	17 Apses.
9 Choir (*schola cantorum*).	

Glossary

Aedicule: diminutive, from the Latin word *aedes* ('chapel'). Used to describe an architectural feature (such as a window, doorway, altar, etc.) in the shape of the façade of a small temple.

Agape (pl. *agapai*): Greek ('love-feast'). Feasts usually by burial places at which the early Christians met in remembrance of the Last Supper and where they expressed their love for one another.

Ambo (pl. *ambones*): Latin ('pulpit'). Usually there are two, one on the left side and another on the right side of a church, for the reading of the Gospel and of the Epistle respectively.

Apse: the semicircular or polygonal ending of the tribune or of a chancel or chapel.

Architrave: the lowest division of the entablature, supported by columns.

Arcosolium (pl. *arcosolia*): a table tomb, surmounted by an arched recess, in the catacombs.

Atrium: an open court in front of a church. See also *quadriportico*.

Attic: the upper portion of a building if less high than the storey, or storeys, below.

Baldacchino: the canopy, supported by four columns, above the high altar. Also called (confusingly) *ciborium* (q.v.).

Barrel vault: a round-arched ceiling.

Basilica: strictly, a Roman court of justice. A basilican church has a wide nave, ending in an apse and flanked by two (or four) aisles. The nave walls, supported by columns, are pierced by windows (clerestory, q.v.) above the roofs of the aisles. For a plan of a typical basilica see p. 281.

Breccia: fragments of stone held together with varying kinds of cement; type depends on origin of stone and type of cement. It is not a true marble although the included stone may be marble.

Calidarium: the hottest room in a Roman thermal establishment.

Campanile: the bell-tower of a church, frequently separated from the church itself; may be round, as in Ravenna, but normally square.

Cantharus: a fountain for the ritual ablution before entering a church; the forerunner of the holy water stoup.

Capital: the decorative crowning feature of a column or pilaster. See also *order*.

Cardinal: cardinal-priests take their names from their titular Roman churches. The Pope, as Bishop of Rome, is assisted by the College of Cardinals, which is constituted by the suburbicarian cardinal-bishops (of the ancient sees in the vicinity of Rome; the Bishop of Ostia is always Dean of the Sacred College); cardinal-priests and cardinal-deacons. In 1980 there were 7 cardinal-bishops, 106 cardinal-priests and 16 cardinal-deacons – that is, 129 cardinals in all.

Catacomb: the subterranean burial grounds cut in the tufa round Rome; used by the early Christians for burial, for *agapai* and services at the tombs of martyrs, and also as places of refuge during the persecutions.

Cathedra: the bishop's throne.

Cella: the inner sanctuary of a shrine or temple.

Chancel: the choir and sanctuary. See also *presbytery*.

Ciborium (or *ciborio*): (1) the tabernacle on which the Eucharist is reserved on the altar; (2) the *baldacchino* (q.v.).

Cipollino: a marble, with green veins, from Euboea.

Clerestory: the windows of the nave, above the level of the roofs of the aisles.

Coffering: sunken panels of a ceiling.

Columbarium: Latin ('dove-cote'). Chamber, with niches for burial, normally in a catacomb.

Confessio: cell, or chamber, beneath the altar, sheltering the relic of a saint.

Console: a projecting member, or bracket, usually in the form of a scroll, intended as a support.

Constantinian monogram: ☧ (*chi* and *rho*, the initial Greek letters for Christ).

Cornice: the crowning, or uppermost part, of an entablature (q.v.).

Crocket: an ornamental carving (frequently resembling curled foliage) on the sloping edge of a gable or on a pinnacle.

Crossing: that portion of a church where a transept crosses the nave.

Cupola: the circular, or oval, roofing of a drum.

Deacon: an official of the early Christian Church, usually in charge of the communal funds used for alms-giving.

Dome: the raised roofing of a church (usually over the crossing) which consists of drum and cupola.

Dosseret (or *pulvin*): a block placed above a capital supporting the arch above.

Entablature: the feature supported by columns, consisting of architrave, frieze and cornice.

Eustyle: term denoting that the space between the columns of a building is $2\frac{1}{4}$ times their diameter.

Fluting: the vertical channelling on the shaft of a column.

Half-column: a column, half of which is embedded in a wall.

Herm: squared pillar terminating in a sculpted human head.

Hypogeum: a subterranean room, often a burial place in a catacomb.

Iconoclast: Greek ('breaker of images'). One opposed to the representation and veneration of figures of God, Christ, the Virgin Mary or saints.

Iconostasis: the screen on which icons were placed.

Icthus: Greek ('fish') formed by the initial letters of 'Jesus Christ Son of God the Saviour'.

Insula: Latin ('island'). The block of buildings in a Roman town, formed by streets intersecting at right-angles.

Lunette: a semicircular panel, often decorated with painting or sculpture.

Mandorla: Italian ('almond'). An almond-shaped nimbus.

Martyrium: a shrine over a martyr's grave or over the place where he was executed.

Matronea: the upper galleries in a church, reserved for women.

Metope: the open spaces between Doric triglyphs (q.v.).

Mithraeum: temple of Mithras, the ancient Persian god of light and the sun.

Module: the measure of proportion used in the classical orders; usually taken as half the diameter of a column at the base of the shaft.

Narthex: the arcaded porch of a basilican church.

Nymphaeum: a sanctuary devoted to the nymphs in Roman private houses or gardens, usually with fountains and statues.

Opus alexandrinum: ornamental paving, with rich interweaving patterns of marble and glass based on discs of porphyry.

Opus recticulatum: walls (of a Roman building) faced with stones whose joints are placed diagonally, like a net.

Opus sectile: ornamental paving, with inlays of pieces of marble, porphyry and glass of various colours and geometrical shapes.

Orante: a figure, usually female, with arms and hands outstretched downwards, in the act of prayer or veneration.

Order: an order consists of column or pilaster (base, shaft and capital), with the entablature (q.v.) which it supports. The classical orders are six: Doric, Ionic, Corinthian, Composite, Tuscan and Roman Doric.

Pavonazzetto: natural *breccia* (q.v.) marble made of pieces of white marble set in a deep violet-coloured base, found in Asia Minor.

Pediment: the gable end of a building, which may be triangular, segmental or broken.

Pendentive: triangular curved space by which square or rectangular walls may support a circular or oval dome.

Peperino: a grey building stone of volcanic origin.

Pier: a cluster of columns and/or pilasters.

Pilaster: a rectangular variant of a column projecting slightly from a wall and with its capital composed of one of the orders (q.v.).

Plinth: a rectangular base of a column. A similar base used to support a statue, vase, etc.

Porphyry: an igneous rock with medium or large single crystals in a fine grained matrix.

Presbyter: a priest of the early Christian Church.

Presbytery (or *tribune*): the place occupied by the clergy in the apse of a church.

Pulvin: see *dosseret*.

Putto (pl. *putti*): figure of a child (usually naked).

Quadratura: illusionist architectural painting of walls and ceilings extending real architecture into imaginary space.

Quadriportico: a court, or *atrium* (q.v.), whose four sides are arcaded.

Rosso antico: porphyry (q.v.) of a red colour from southern Greece and the Red Sea.

Sacristy: room in a church where sacred vessels, vestments, etc. are kept, and where priests robe and disrobe.

Sanctuary: the part of a church occupied by the high altar.

Schola cantorum: the choir, enclosed by a screen.

Spandrel: the space formed by the curve of an arch, a vertical line taken from its springing and a horizontal line through its highest point.

String course: a moulding, or projecting course, running horizontally on a wall's surface.

Tempietto: a small temple-like structure.

Tepidarium: warm room in a Roman thermal establishment.

Tesserae: the pieces, frequently cubes, of which mosaic is composed.

Titulus (pl. *tituli*). Latin ('title'): the name given to the earliest meeting places of the Christian community: usually a room in a private house, whose owner gave his name to the 'title'. Certain ancient churches are known as 'titular', since their names are given to the cardinals who are attached to them.

Transept: the arms of a church, at right-angles to the nave.

Trabeated: constructed with beams.

Travertine: a grey building stone of calcareous origin, much used in Roman churches.

Tribune: see *presbytery*.

Triclinium: the dining-room of a Roman house.

Triglyph: block with vertical channels on the frieze of a Doric entablature.

Triumphal arch: the arch at the altar end of the nave of a church.

Tympanum: the triangular recessed face of a pediment (q.v.) or the triangular space in a door between the lintel and the arch above.

Verde antico: type of porphyry of a green colour, from the Peloponnese.

Volute (Latin *voluta*, 'scroll'): the scroll, or spiral, on Ionic, Corinthian and Composite capitals, and those frequently joining the first storey with the upper in Baroque churches.

Select Bibliography

Bamm, P., *The Kingdoms of Christ*, London 1959

Blunt, A., *Francesco Borromini*, London 1979

Burckhardt, J., *The Age of Constantine the Great*, London 1949

Deichmann, F. W., *Frühchristliche Kirchen in Rom*, Basle 1948

Demus, O., *Byzantine Art and the West*, London 1970

D'Onofrio, C., *Roma nel Seicento*, Florence 1969

Duchesne, L., *The Early History of the Christian Church*, 3 vols, London 1910

Fletcher, B., *A History of Architecture*, rev. ed., London 1975

Gaius, *Institutes*, ed. F. de Zulueta, 2 vols, Oxford 1953

Grabar, A., *The Beginnings of Christian Art*, London 1967

Gregorovius, F., *A History of Rome in the Middle Ages*, 13 vols, London 1894–1900

Hemans, C. E., *A History of Mediaeval Christianity and Sacred Art*, London 1872

Hutton, E., *The Cosmati*, London 1950

Jerome, St, *Letters*, trans. C. C. Mierow, 2 vols, London 1963

Lanciani, R., *Pagan and Christian Rome*, New York 1893
Wanderings through Ancient Roman Churches, London 1925

Larousse Encyclopedia of Renaissance and Baroque Art, ed. R. Huyghe, London 1964

Lowry, B., *Renaissance Architecture*, London 1968

Mâle, E., and D. Buxton, *The Early Churches of Rome*, London 1960

Mirabilis Urbis Romae, London and Rome 1889

Murray, P., *The Architecture of the Italian Renaissance*, London 1969

Oakeshott, W., *The Mosaics of Rome*, London 1967

Pastor, L., *History of the Popes*, 37 vols, London 1891

Pevsner, N., *An Outline of European Architecture*, Harmondsworth 1968

Pliny the Younger, *Letters*, trans. B. Radice, London 1963

Sharp, M., *A Traveller's Guide to the Churches of Rome*, London 1967

Shearman, J., *Mannerism*, Harmondsworth 1967

Stevenson, J., *The Catacombs*, London 1978

Suetonius, G., *Lives of the Caesars*, trans. R. Graves, Harmondsworth 1962

Talbot Rice, D., *Byzantine Art*, London 1962

Thynne, R., *The Churches of Rome*, London 1924

Touring Club Italiano, *Romae Dintorni*, Rome 1977

Toynbee, J., and J. Ward Perkins, *The Shrine of St Peter's and the Vatican Excavations*, London 1956

Tuker, M. A. R., and H. Malleson, *Handbook to Christian and Ecclesiastical Rome*, Pt. I, London 1897

Turcio, G., *La Basilica di S. Pietro*, Florence 1946

Ward Perkins, J. B., *Constantine and the Christian Basilica*, 'Papers of the British School at Rome', vol. xxii, London 1954

White, J., *Art and Architecture in Italy: 1250–1400*, Harmondsworth 1966

Wittkower, R., *Art and Architecture in Italy: 1600–1750*, Harmondsworth 1965

Wölfflin, H., *Renaissance et Baroque*, ed. B. Teyssèdre, Basle 1961
Renaissance and Baroque, ed. P. Murray, London 1964

Sources of Illustrations

The authors and publishers would like to thank the following institutions, agencies and individuals for supplying, and/or for permission to reproduce, the illustrations which appear on the pages listed below:

Alinari: 132, 136, 175, 267, 268, 270, 272, 273, 275, 279
Coll. Pecci Blunt: 10
Hamlyn Picture Library: 191
Instituto Nazionale per la Grafica – Gabinetto Stampe in Palazzo Farnesina: 50, 55, 64, 151, 161, 167, 184, 186 *left*, 188, 190, 192, 202, 213, 266, 271, 276, 277 (photos by Oscar Savio)
Mansell Collection: 147, 269
Museo di Roma in Palazzo Braschi: 81
Pasquale di Antonis: 154, 176, 177, 186 *right*
The Sovereign Order of the Knights of Malta and Rhodes for permission to reproduce the photographs on the following pages taken in S. Maria del Priorato by Roloff Beny: 238, 239, 240
Vatican Photographic Archives: 85, 98, 101, 134, 135, 148, 225, 246; and for permission to reproduce the photographs on the following pages taken in St Peter's by Roloff Beny: 196, 245, 248, 249, 250, 251, 252, 254, 256
Map of Rome drawn by Line and Line
Ground-plans drawn by Will Stephen

Index